THE NEW
GOLDEN TREASURY
OF
NATURAL
HISTORY

BY

B E R T H A   M O R R I S   P A R K E R

FORMERLY OF THE LABORATORY SCHOOL, UNIVERSITY OF CHICAGO
RESEARCH ASSOCIATE, FIELD MUSEUM OF NATURAL HISTORY

GOLDEN PRESS NEW YORK

Library of Congress Catalog Card Number: 68-22205

Illustrations from the Basic Science Education Series (Unitext), written by
Bertha Morris Parker and published by Harper and Row, used by permission.

CONTENTS

ILLUSTRATORS

Pauline Batchelder Adams

George Bakacs

Dorothea and Sy Barlowe

Juanita Bennett

Robert D. Bezucha

Virginia Bradendick

Matilda Breuer

Walter Buehr

Louise Fulton Bush

Arthur D. Cushman

Mrs. Lois Darling

Rachel Taft Dixon

Walter Dower

André Durenceau

E. Joseph Dreany

Olive Earle

Walter Ferguson

Rudolf Freund

Byron Gere

Marjorie Hartwell

Hans Helweg

Lowell Hess

Robert Hodgell

Wallace Hughes

Arch and Miriam Hurford

William Hutchinson

James Gordon Irving

Norman Jonsson

Matthew Kalmenoff

Robert Kissner

Enid Kotschnig

Olga Kucera

Bob Kuhn

Jack J. Kunz

Joseph Lombarero

Harry McNaught

G. I. McWilliams

René Martin

Rebecca Merrilees

Eric Mose

Arthur Mueller

Elizabeth Newhall

Raymond Perlman

Craig Pineo

Ray Pioch

Fred Poffenberger

Harold Price

Lorelle Maria Raboni

Don Ray

Allianora Rosse

Mary Royt

William De J. Rutherfoord

Rod Ruth

Arnold W. Ryan

Lloyd Sanford

Katherine Sampson

Marita and George Sandström

Sam Savitt

William Sayles

Alex Seidel

Ned Seidler

Arthur Singer

Frederick E. Seyfarth

Russ Smiley

Elmer Smith

Darrell Sweet

Valerie Swenson

James Teason

Alton S. Tobey

Ann Ophelia Todd

Dan Todd

Paul Wenck

Eloise Wilkin

Barbara Wolff

Jean Zallinger

Rudolph F. Zallinger

F O R E W O R D

IT is now fifteen years since THE GOLDEN TREASURY OF NATURAL HISTORY first made its appearance on the publishing scene. Now it is republished in a completely new, greatly expanded and updated format. The world of science moves and changes very fast these days—and authors and publishers must move with it.

The stuff the earth is made of, the seemingly countless kinds of plants and animals about us, and the life of past ages—these are subjects in which young people have a natural interest. To take advantage of that interest and build up an understanding of the world of nature is the aim of THE NEW GOLDEN TREASURY OF NATURAL HISTORY.

Young people ask many questions about their environment: How do we know that there were once dinosaurs? How can one tell a butterfly from a moth, or a toad from a frog? Is a tomato a fruit or a vegetable? Could you cross a cabbage with a rose? And so on and on. The author has used such questions as a help in selecting, from the vast amount of nature knowledge, the topics to be included in this book.

The numerous pictures will help the reader to recognize many of the rocks, plants, animals, and fossils he sees. The book is not designed as a nature guide; no section is sufficiently complete to serve that purpose. But the pictures will nevertheless help in identification and, more importantly, will illustrate many basic facts and ideas about the world of nature.

The book makes the reader's experiences with nature much more meaningful. A shiny pebble is no longer just something pretty to add to one's collection; it is a bit of one of the rock pages on which the earth has written its diary. A garden is not just a source of vegetables to eat and flowers to cut; it is also a collection of plant immigrants from many foreign lands, and of the results of experiments in plant breeding.

In science, "truth changes," because better scientific instruments and methods are constantly revealing more of nature's secrets. But one can foresee little change during the coming years in the basic ideas presented in this book—that the story of the earth is indeed one of great changes, that animals and plants are fitted in wondrous ways for living as they do, and that there are undreamed of things still to be discovered about our earth and its long yesterday.

BERTHA MORRIS PARKER

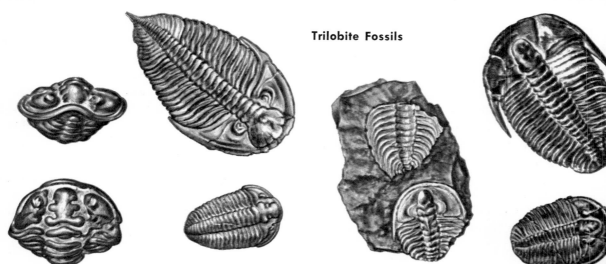

Trilobite Fossils

A Parade of Ancient Animals

Six hundred million years ago there were already a great many kinds of living things on the earth. The big picture shows a number of them. Of course, it was not painted from life, for the plants and animals pictured lived long, long before there were any people. Scientists have found out about the living things of long ago from traces of them in rocks. Such traces are called fossils.

A parade of the animals of six hundred million years ago, if there could be one, would not be exciting. For one thing, it would have to be underwater, for all the animals of that time—at least all that we know about—lived in the sea. All of them, moreover, were fairly small.

The animals that held the center of the stage in those long-ago days were the trilobites. Although few trilobites were more than 3 or 4 inches long, they were large in comparison with their neighbors, and there were huge numbers of them.

The name trilobite was given to these animals many millions of years after the last ones died. They had no name at all while they were alive because there was no one to name them. "Trilobite" means "three-lobed" —their hard covering was divided into three lengthwise lobes.

The trilobites belong in the enormous group of jointed-legged animals, or arthropods, but they were not closely related to any of the jointed-legged animals of today. They lived in the shallow water of the seashores. Feathery gills helped them swim as well as breathe. Long feelers and, as a rule, big compound eyes helped them find food. They ate other animals, probably both living and dead ones. They also ate plants. When in danger, many curled themselves up. Others simply folded in the middle and closed up like a book.

Compared with the higher animals of today, the trilobites were simple. But they had

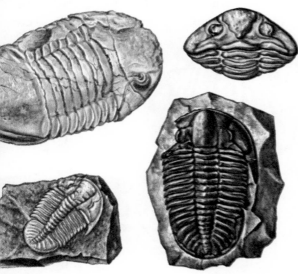

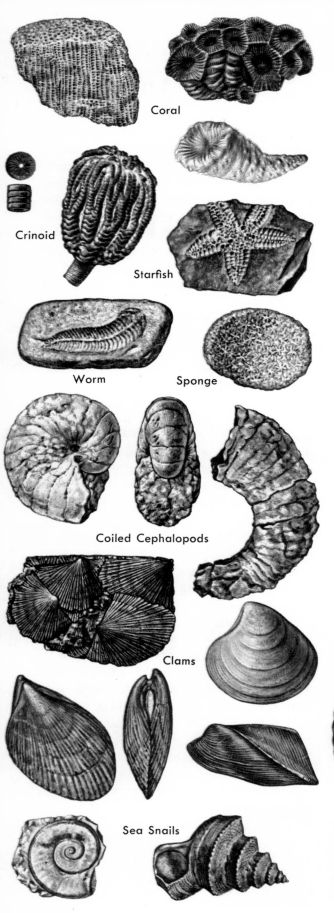

Coral

Crinoid

Starfish

Worm

Sponge

Coiled Cephalopods

Clams

Sea Snails

come a long way from the earliest animals. Animals, scientists believe, had been living and changing for many millions of years—perhaps for more than a billion—before the first trilobites appeared.

Among the neighbors of the trilobites six hundred million years ago were sponges, worms, and jellyfish. There were tiny sea snails and ancient brachiopods, or lamp shells, too. Brachiopods have shells much like clamshells, but very different bodies inside their shells. The sponges of those early times anchored themselves to rocks just as sponges do today. The worms made tracks and burrows in the mud and sand just as worms do now. The snails, jellyfish, and lamp shells were enough like those of today to be easy to recognize.

During the long reign of the trilobites, sea lilies, or crinoids, appeared and became common. So did starfish, corals, clams, and cephalopods, the group of animals that includes the squids, octopuses, and the chambered, or pearly, nautilus.

The sea lilies that lived in the days of the trilobites were not very different from the present-day crinoids. They looked more like plants than like animals, with rootlike holdfasts that anchored them to rocks, long stems, and arms that spread out like the petals of a flower. The corals walled themselves up with lime as do modern corals and left their "houses" of limestone behind when they died.

The early cephalopods, like today's nautilus, had shells. Some of the shells were

Brachiopods

coiled, like that of the nautilus. Others were long and straight. The animal's head and arms protruded from its shell.

In time the scorpion-like eurypterids, close relatives of the trilobites, appeared. The most conspicuous animal in the picture below is a eurypterid. You will recognize the trilobites, starfish, and corals in the foreground. A cephalopod is just appearing at the right, near the two snails.

For a tremendously long time—a hundred million years perhaps—the trilobites had no real rivals. Then, although trilobites continued to be very common, the cephalopods gradually overshadowed them. Many grew to be larger than any of the trilobites. Some of those with straight shells were 20 feet long. Since they were meat-eaters, the cephalopods probably devoured vast numbers of their trilobite neighbors.

Trilobites lived on for many, many millions of years after they were no longer masters of the sea. Some of the later ones developed long, and seemingly useless, projections. Approximately 230 million years ago the trilobites died out completely. We say that they became extinct.

It would be a mistake to think of the animals of the ancient seashores as living just where the seashores are today. Land and sea were not always as they are now. In long-ago times there were seashores in such inland states as Kansas and Kentucky and in many other places that today are far from the sea.

The time when the trilobites and the cephalopods were the leading animals is sometimes called "the heyday of animals without backbones," for these animals had no backbones. They had no bones of any kind. Neither did any of their neighbors pictured here. Another name for the time is the Age of Invertebrates. "Invertebrate" means "without a backbone."

Scientists divide the story of the earth into long stretches of time called eras. The Age of Invertebrates was the first part of the Paleozoic era. The word "paleozoic" means "ancient life."

The early Paleozoic was a quiet time. Not an animal in the world had a voice. There were, as you know, no land animals to make a noise by running about. Almost the only sounds were thunder and the noises of wind and waves.

Straight Cephalopod

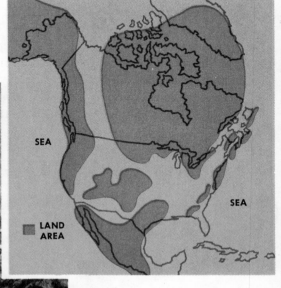

North America 450 Million Years Ago (Ordovician Period)

Animals of 400 Million Years Ago (Silurian Period)

11

Lobe-finned Fish Climbing Up on Land

The first animals with backbones to appear on the earth were fishes. They appeared in the days when the cephalopods were the terrors of the seas. The early fishes were successful. Within 50 million years or so there were so many of them that they quite overshadowed the simpler animals. The time when they were the leading animals of the earth is called, in everyday language, the Age of Fishes.

Many of the early fishes were jawless, just as the lampreys of today are. Like the lampreys, moreover, these jawless fishes had no paired fins. But they were very different from lampreys in one way—they had armor made of thick plates of bone.

Among their neighbors there were other armored fishes. Some were little; others were very large. *Pterichthys* ("wing fish") was only about 6 inches long. *Dinichthys,* on the other hand, was between 20 and 30 *feet* long. Its name means "terrible fish," and it *was* terrible. Its jagged jaws snapped shut with great force, like the jaws of a snapping turtle. Both *Dinichthys* and *Pterichthys* had paired fins. So did the other fishes in the picture with *Dinichthys.* One kind is much like the little "wing fish." The other is an early shark. Sharks were common in the Age of Fishes.

Notice the limbs of the fish climbing up on shore in the picture at the top of the page. Fishes like these are called lobefins because of their limbs, which certainly do not look much like fins. A lobefin differed in another way from most other fishes—in addition to gills it had simple lungs, which allowed it to spend some time out of water. There were other fishes with lungs—the lungfishes—living at the same time.

For all its size and fierceness and stout armor the "terrible fish" could not hold its

Pterichthys,
the "Wing Fish"

12

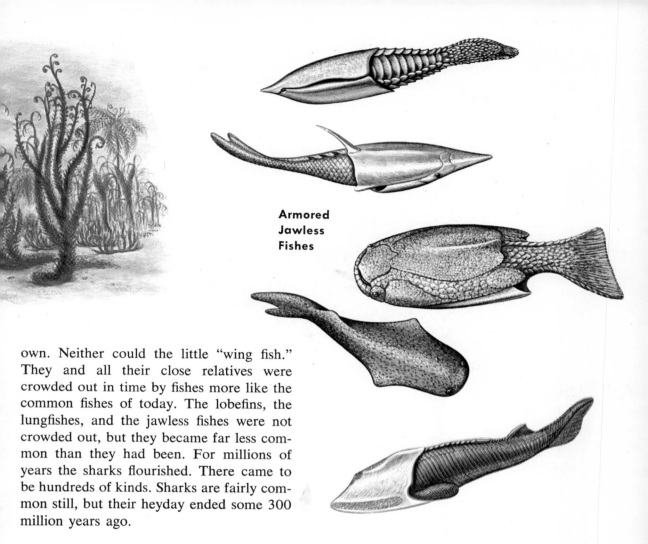

Armored Jawless Fishes

own. Neither could the little "wing fish." They and all their close relatives were crowded out in time by fishes more like the common fishes of today. The lobefins, the lungfishes, and the jawless fishes were not crowded out, but they became far less common than they had been. For millions of years the sharks flourished. There came to be hundreds of kinds. Sharks are fairly common still, but their heyday ended some 300 million years ago.

Dinichthys Pursuing a Primitive Shark

The Coal Age followed the Age of Fishes. It, too, was a part of the Paleozoic era.

At the beginning of the Coal Age much of North America was low and swampy. So were some other parts of the earth. Forests grew in the swamps. The forests were luxuriant, for the climate was mild and the air as well as the ground was very moist. The trees that died and fell into the swamp water did not rot away entirely. Instead, they formed a thick layer of rotting plant material.

In many of the swamps the water gradually grew deeper. Perhaps the land was slowly sinking. Perhaps the seas were rising and overflowing into the swamps. The change was very slow, but at last the forests were drowned. The drowned trees were added to what was left of the trees that had fallen before. Mud was washed in over the thick layer of dead trees.

Later, much of the water that covered the old swamps drained away. Again there were swamps with forests growing in them. In time these forests, too, were drowned and buried under mud and water. Time after time the same changes took place. At last in many regions there were several layers of buried forest. As millions of years went by, these layers changed to coal.

The trees that made up the Coal Age forests were not oaks and elms and pines. They were not any of the forest trees common now. Instead, they were chiefly giant club mosses, horsetails, ferns, seed ferns, and cordaites. The pictures here will give you an idea of how some of them looked.

The pictures show, too, seven kinds of Coal Age animals. Clearly an important change in the animal world had taken place, for six of the animals pictured lived all, or at least most, of their lives on land. The moment when an animal first successfully crossed the dividing line between water and land was one of the most important times in the earth's long history.

Perhaps the first animal to live on land was a scorpion. As you know, earlier there had been scorpion-like animals in the sea. Now, in the Coal Age, there were scorpions on land. There were spiders and insects, too. Scorpions, spiders, and insects of several kinds were well established on land at the beginning of the Coal Age. They were common all during that long time.

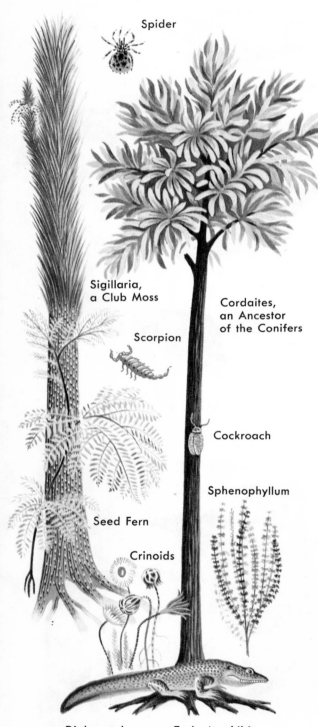

Spider

Sigillaria, a Club Moss

Cordaites, an Ancestor of the Conifers

Scorpion

Cockroach

Sphenophyllum

Seed Fern

Crinoids

Diplovertebron, an Early Amphibian

Some of the insects that lived during the Coal Age were larger than any insects of today. There were "dragonflies" measuring 2½ feet from wingtip to wingtip. There were giant cockroaches 4 inches long. Cockroaches were so common that the Coal Age is sometimes called the Age of Cockroaches.

Scorpions, spiders, and insects have no backbones. The first backboned animals to live on land were amphibians. Toads and frogs are among our common amphibians of today. Toads and frogs begin their lives in water. The tadpoles that hatch from the eggs are very much like little fish. Later they become air-breathing animals and can live on land. The first amphibians also began their lives in water but were able to live successfully on land when full grown.

Scientists believe that the amphibians descended from fishes like the lobefin pictured on page 12. The first amphibian is sometimes called "the fish that walked."

Diplovertebron was one of the earliest amphibians we know about. At a glance it does not look very different from its lobefin ancestors. Probably it did spend much time in the water. But its salamander-like legs show that it was well fitted for moving about on land. *Diplovertebron* grew to be from 1 to 3 feet long.

Late in the Coal Age there were reptiles, too. The strange-looking pelycosaur pictured below was one of them. It is easy to see why this reptile is called a sailback. There are many guesses as to what the "sail" was good for. One guess is that it helped to keep the animal's body at the right temperature.

This pelycosaur, with its big "sail" and mouthful of teeth, looks rather terrifying. But it was strictly a plant-eater.

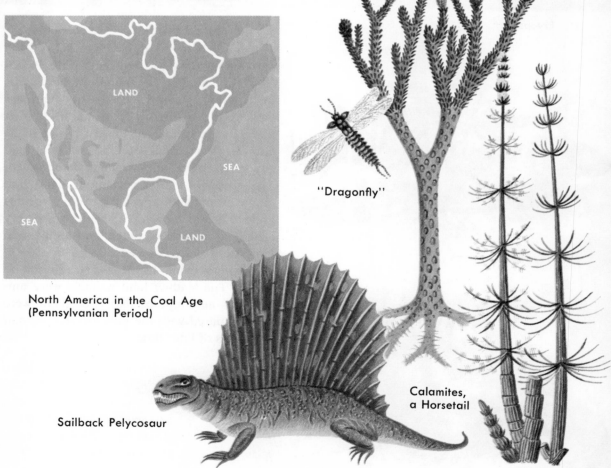

Lepidodendron, a Club Moss

"Dragonfly"

North America in the Coal Age (Pennsylvanian Period)

Calamites, a Horsetail

Sailback Pelycosaur

Eryops

Seymouria

It was about 50 million years from the end of the Coal Age to the end of the Paleozoic era. There is no common name for this long period. Scientists call it the Permian. During the Permian great changes took place in the surface of the earth and in its climate. Vast areas of land were pushed upward. Long mountain chains were formed. Many arms of the sea became dry land, and many swamps disappeared. Some regions grew to be much cooler, and some to be very arid. The number of plants and animals on land was greatly reduced.

Conifers came to be the leading land plants. The leading land animals were amphibians and reptiles. None of them were big compared with the gigantic reptiles and mammals of later times.

Limnoscelis

Eryops was a big amphibian of the period. It grew to be from 6 to 8 feet long. As you see, it looked much like a huge frog with a tail. Along with the other amphibians of its time, however, it had something which no amphibian of today has—a third eye high on its forehead.

Eryops megalocephalus is the full scientific name of this creature. The second part of the scientific name means "big-headed." Its head was truly big, and its mouth was enormous.

Eryops could walk, but not at all fast. Its legs, although stout, were so short that its body was close to the ground. It probably spent most of its time sunning itself at the edge of a swamp. It did not have to hurry to get food. "Minnows" and water plants could be scooped up easily at the water's edge. Besides, *Eryops,* with its many sharp teeth, could capture some of its smaller amphibian relatives.

Although *Eryops* had a big skull, there was not much room inside it for brains. We can be sure this big fellow, as it sunned itself, did not do any thinking about the changes that were taking place on the earth. Perhaps it let out a hoarse croak now and then, for it may, like today's toads and frogs, have had a voice. No animal before the days of the amphibians had one.

Even though some amphibians lived on, *Eryops* disappeared long ago. In the end, size did not mean success. The largest amphibian now, the giant salamander of Japan, is only about half as big.

The reptiles descended from the amphibians. *Seymouria* was an amphibian, but it was much more reptile-like than *Eryops*. In fact, from fossils it was not easy for scientists to say whether *Seymouria* was an amphibian or a reptile—it had certainly changed almost enough from its amphibian ancestors to be classed as a reptile. *Limnoscelis* was a reptile. Probably, however, it spent much of its time in the water and lived on fish just as *Seymouria* did.

At a glance it is hard to tell the difference between the sailback you met in reading

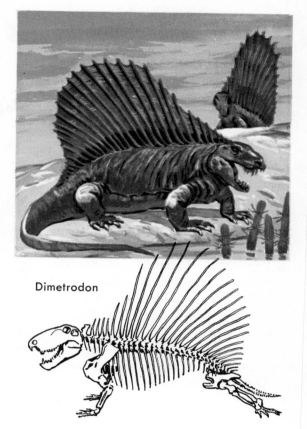

Dimetrodon

about the Coal Age and *Dimetrodon,* the sailback pictured above. The two were much the same shape. *Dimetrodon* lacked the crossbars in its sail which the other sailback had. The biggest difference between the two, however, is that *Dimetrodon* had very long, sharp teeth—it was a meat-eater. This pelycosaur was, in fact, the leading meat-eating land animal of its time. It was also by far the most common of all the reptiles in North America.

In the regions that were becoming desert, reptiles had a big advantage over amphibians. The amphibians all began their lives in water. The reptiles began theirs on land. The eggs of the amphibians were covered with a layer of jelly and were kept damp by being in water. The eggs of the reptiles had a shell around them. This shell protected them from drying out. The little reptiles that hatched from the eggs were not like little fish. They were very much like their parents. They could live on land because from the time they were hatched they had lungs to breathe with, not gills.

Compsognathus

As the long Paleozoic era ended, the Mesozoic, or "middle life," era began. This era, which lasted for some 165 million years, was the Age of Reptiles. During the long Mesozoic, reptiles flourished amazingly. They practically took over the earth.

The Age of Reptiles is sometimes called "the days of the dinosaurs," for this great group of reptiles appeared early in the era and the last ones died as the era ended.

The word "dinosaur" means "terrible reptile." It is not a good name for all the dinosaurs, for not all of them were terrible. Many were rather small animals, and some, though big, were gentle plant-eaters. But there were some dinosaurs that were truly terrible.

In all, there were thousands of different kinds—probably at least 5,000. One kind

Stegosaurus

would disappear and another kind would take its place. For most of the thousands of kinds of dinosaurs there are no common names. They have only the scientific names scientists use for them.

Plateosaurus was an early dinosaur. It was big—from the end of its nose to the tip of its tail it measured about 20 feet—but it was not terrible. It ate nothing but plants. *Plateosaurus* was rather clumsy. It must have been stupid, too. In its small head there was no room for a big brain.

The other three dinosaurs pictured came later. They all lived at about the same time, but they were not at all close relatives. As you might guess, *Compsognathus* and *Allosaurus* were much more closely related to each other than either of them was to *Stegosaurus*. All three were land animals—all dinosaurs were.

Compsognathus was small—no bigger than a rooster. This little dinosaur ran about fast on its two long hind legs, catching smaller reptiles and the mouselike early mammals to eat. Its front legs were so small that they look as if they had not grown properly.

Allosaurus was a dinosaur that really deserves to be called terrible. It was a fierce meat-eater about 35 feet long—far larger than any meat-eating animal on land today. It, too, walked on its hind legs. *Allosaurus* means "leaping reptile." This meat-eating dinosaur, it is thought, used its powerful hind legs to go leaping about after its prey.

With such a creature as *Allosaurus* on the lookout for prey, life for other land animals must have been a dangerous undertaking. It is not surprising that some of the plant-eating dinosaurs developed armor.

Stegosaurus, the "plated reptile," was one of the armored dinosaurs. It had a double row of bony plates all down its back and sharp spikes on its tail. Swinging its tail from side to side was like swinging a gigantic battle-ax.

Stegosaurus, like many other dinosaurs, was built on the pattern of big bodies—it was 20 feet long—and small brains. Its

Plateosaurus

brain was not very much larger than a man's fist—too tiny to control the muscles of the hind legs and tail. These muscles were controlled by an enlargement of the spinal cord at the base of the tail.

The enlargement of the spinal cord at the base of the creature's tail gave rise to the idea

none of what we call thinking. This armored dinosaur, moreover, was not the only dinosaur that had two "brains." Some of the others that needed an extra "brain" were the monstrous plant-eating dinosaurs you will find out about on the next two pages— the giants of the reptile world.

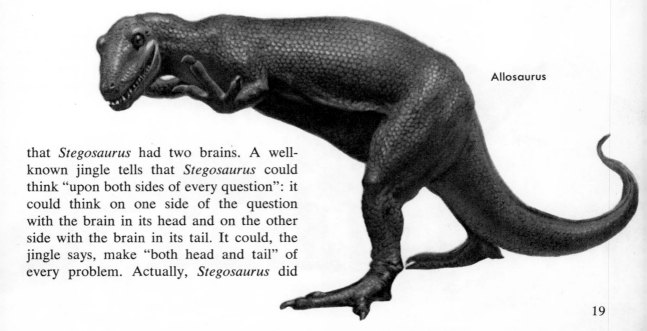

Allosaurus

that *Stegosaurus* had two brains. A well-known jingle tells that *Stegosaurus* could think "upon both sides of every question": it could think on one side of the question with the brain in its head and on the other side with the brain in its tail. It could, the jingle says, make "both head and tail" of every problem. Actually, *Stegosaurus* did

19

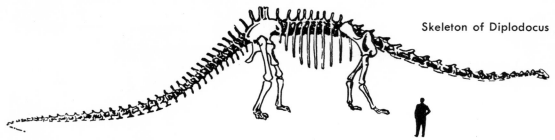

The titanic *Diplodocus* was the longest animal ever to walk on land: it measured nearly 90 feet from the end of its nose to the tip of its tail. It was as long as eight elephants standing trunk to tail. As you see, a great deal of its length was in its very long neck and very long tail.

Diplodocus ate only tender plants. It did not eat grass—there was not yet any grass in the world for it to eat. Many of the plants it ate grew in the ponds and swamps of the time. It must have taken this creature all day long to gulp in food enough for its enormous body. Probably it spent most of its life out in the ponds and swamps. Food-getting was easy there, and the water helped hold up its huge body.

The head of *Diplodocus* was small. There was not much room for brains. Indeed, its brain weighed only about a pound—not much of a brain for a body of 25 tons or so.

Diplodocus, like all the dinosaurs, came from eggs. We know that the eggs of one 9-foot dinosaur were 9 inches long. If *Diplodocus* followed the plan of an inch of egg for every foot of body, how enormous its eggs must have been!

Brachiosaurus was not quite so long as *Diplodocus,* but it was much heavier. So far as anyone knows, it was the heaviest animal that ever walked on land—it weighed 50 tons! Notice that in the picture *Brachiosaurus* is standing with only the top of its head above water. Its nostrils were in the crest on top of its head. Many of the dinosaurs had nostrils at the top of their heads. *Brachiosaurus,* you can see, had front legs longer than the hind ones. With its long front legs and its long neck, this giant of the dinosaurs, if it could walk down a city street today, could easily look into third-story windows.

Probably the best known of all dinosaurs is *Brontosaurus*. Its name means "thunder reptile." This dinosaur was not given its name because it had a voice like thunder;

Diplodocus

Brachiosaurus

no one knows what kind of sounds it may have made. The scientist who named it chose its name, it is said, because he thought that when so huge an animal walked about, the ground would shake and make a noise like thunder. The picture of its skeleton on page 45 shows that *Brontosaurus* was a giant. It was about 70 feet long and weighed over 30 tons.

There were many other dinosaurs much like these three giants. They were not armored as *Stegosaurus* was. They were all good prey for *Allosaurus* and the other big meat-eating dinosaurs of the time. They could not run away easily, for their legs were like tree trunks and their long, heavy tails were certainly not easy to pull along. Probably their habit of spending much of the time in ponds was their best protection. They had thick skins, too.

These giant dinosaurs were the biggest four-footed animals of all time. People often, however, get a wrong impression about their size. They were not the largest animals that ever lived. No dinosaur was as big as the blue whale of today.

Corythosaurus (in the foreground) and Parasaurolophus, Duckbilled Dinosaurs with Strange Crests That Probably Helped Make Underwater Feeding Possible

Trachodon,
a Very Common
Duckbilled Dinosaur

Styracosaurus

Ankylosaurus

could face up to an enemy it was well protected, but back of the great bony frill around its neck *Triceratops'* only protection was its thick skin. No doubt *Triceratops* won some battles, but often it fell prey to the giant meat-eaters.

Styracosaurus was another horned dinosaur. It, too, had to face up to an attacker if its horns were to help.

Ankylosaurus was a sort of armored tank. Its back and head were covered with plates of bone. Rings of bone covered its tail. Both its legs and its tail were protected with bony spikes. At the end of its tail there was a bony club. Except for some of the turtles, no other reptiles have ever been so well armored. This dinosaur was about 15 feet long and 5 feet high.

The other three dinosaurs are so-called duckbilled dinosaurs, a very common group. Because of their big and often strangely shaped skulls, the duckbilled dinosaurs have been called "Nature's biggest boneheads." They must have furnished many a meal for *Tyrannosaurus* and the other big meat-eating dinosaurs of their time.

Trachodon was about 30 feet long. On its toes and most of its "fingers" it had little hoofs. Its "hands," and probably its feet as well, were webbed. *Trachodon* spent much of its time in the water eating the plants growing there. Its name means "rough tooth." In its mouth this big plant-eater had close to a thousand teeth!

These dinosaurs all appeared rather late in the Age of Reptiles. Most of them were plant-eaters. Only *Tyrannosaurus* and the little turkey-like dinosaur at the far left in the picture with *Tyrannosaurus* ate meat.

Tyrannosaurus—the name means "tyrant reptile"—looked rather like its ancient relative *Allosaurus,* but it was larger. *Tyrannosaurus* grew to be almost 50 feet long and was from 18 to 20 feet tall as it walked about. It was the largest flesh-eater ever to live on land. Its jaws were so big that it could open its mouth more than a yard. Some of its sharp teeth were 6 inches long. The toes on its huge hind legs had sharp claws like an eagle's. Its "arms" were ridiculously small and weak. The heavy tail of *Tyrannosaurus* helped this giant meat-eater walk upright.

"Triceratops" means "three-horned"; this armored dinosaur had three sharp horns on its head. As a matter of fact, it had all its armor on its head and neck. As long as it

Tyrannosaurus Attacking Triceratops

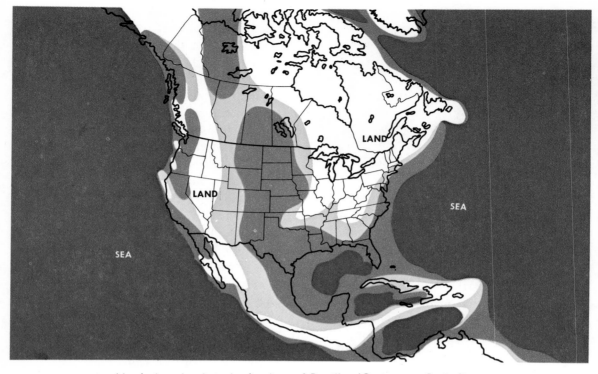

North America Late in the Age of Reptiles (Cretaceous Period)

About 65 million years ago the dinosaurs all vanished. Why they did, after being the lords of the land for 125 million years, is a mystery. With their disappearance the Age of Reptiles came to an end.

Doubtless the reason many of the giant dinosaurs died is that their bodies were too big for their brains. With smaller bodies and bigger brains they might have lived on. They were successful for a very long time because

Oviraptor, an Ostrich Dinosaur

conditions on the earth remained almost the same for millions of years. When conditions changed, the huge creatures were not suited to their changed surroundings, and they were not intelligent enough to help themselves in any way.

One of the changes that played a part in bringing about the end of the dinosaurs was the drying up of many of the ponds and swamps. There were fewer places in which water could help the giant plant-eating dinosaurs hold up their huge bodies. There were fewer water plants to serve as food for them and the other plant-eating dinosaurs. As the plant-eaters became fewer and fewer, there was less food for the flesh-eaters.

Changes in temperature were also against the dinosaurs. The dinosaurs, like today's reptiles, were cold-blooded. Their temperature was the same as the temperature of their surroundings. The climate became colder in many regions. The dinosaurs living there had no way of keeping their bodies warm. Getting cold made them sluggish and less able to fend for themselves. The eggs

Protoceratops

of the dinosaurs, moreover, probably did not hatch so well after the climate changed.

The drying up of the ponds and swamps of North America and the change in climate were caused partly by the rise of the Rocky Mountains. The Rockies are, then, partly to blame for the death of the dinosaurs.

The habit of some dinosaurs of eating the eggs of others probably played a part in bringing an end to the dinosaurs. The small ostrich-like dinosaurs that ran about on two legs could cover ground fast. Many of them are thought to have got a part of their food by stealing eggs from the nests of other dinosaurs. If so, having two free feet to serve as hands must have been a great help in digging up the eggs. Their speed was needed to escape from the bigger dinosaurs whose nests they robbed. The name of *Oviraptor,*

the two-legged dinosaur pictured, means "egg robber."

When a nest of eggs and a skeleton of the small dinosaur *Protoceratops* were found in desert land in Mongolia many years ago, the crushed skull of an ostrich-like dinosaur was found with them. Perhaps the ostrich dinosaur was trying to get the eggs when it was killed.

The rise of more advanced animals, the mammals, doubtless also played a part in the killing off of the dinosaurs. Early mammals probably ate dinosaur eggs. But many of the reptile relatives of the dinosaurs lived on. Why no dinosaurs at all survived the Mesozoic era is still puzzling.

Early Mammals Eating Dinosaur Eggs

Plesiosaurus

Ichthyosaurus

Geosaurus

During the Age of Reptiles by no means all the reptiles lived on land. There were also many in the sea. Among the reptiles in the sea were plesiosaurs, crocodiles, ichthyosaurs, turtles, and lizards.

The plesiosaurs were descendants of early land reptiles, but they certainly did not look like land animals. They were very different even from the big plant-eating dinosaurs that lived in ponds. They had stiff, rather flat bodies, and their four legs had become powerful paddles.

Some of the plesiosaurs had long necks and small heads, others short necks and long heads. *Plesiosaurus,* you can tell, was a long-necked plesiosaur. The mouth of this ancient reptile was full of sharp teeth—clearly *Plesiosaurus* was a meat-eater.

Geosaurus was a crocodile. But with its fish-fin tail and paddle-shaped limbs it was very different from its four-footed land relatives. Today's largest reptiles are crocodiles.

Some of the ancient sea crocodiles were 50 feet long—twice as long as the biggest crocodile today.

"Ichthyosaur" means "fish reptile." This name was well chosen, for the ichthyosaurs certainly looked like big fishes. Their bodies were streamlined so that they could push their way through water easily, and their tails, like that of *Geosaurus,* were fishlike. In place of legs they had paddles much the shape of fishes' fins. They swam with their tails and bodies and steered with their "fins," just as fishes do.

Ichthyosaurus and all the other ichthyosaurs had enormous eyes—bigger than those of any other animals of any time. A 25-foot ichthyosaur's eyes were as big as a man's head. If your eyes were as big in proportion to your size as an ichthyosaur's were to its size, they would be as big as baseballs. Their big eyes helped the ichthyosaurs find prey in dim light.

Flopping their way up on shore to lay their eggs must have been hard for many reptiles of the sea. It was impossible for the ichthyosaurs. But reptile eggs will not hatch in water. The ichthyosaurs solved the problem in the only possible way: they kept their eggs in the mother's body until the eggs hatched. Little ichthyosaurs were born alive. No one knows whether baby ichthyosaurs followed their mother after they were born.

The ichthyosaurs died out before the end of the Age of Reptiles. They had copied the fishes so well that it is hard to see why they did not live on. Fishes had been in the seas long before the ichthyosaurs, and the seas are still swarming with them now.

Ichthyosaurs were already scarce by the time the reptiles in these pictures appeared. These reptiles lived in the sea when *Tyrannosaurus* was "tyrant" of the land reptiles.

Like the earlier long-necked *Plesiosaurus, Trinacromerum* and *Kronosaurus* were plesiosaurs. But they belonged to the group of plesiosaurs with short necks and long heads and beaks. Apparently, long jaws were as good as long necks for catching fish. *Kronosaurus* was very large—nearly 50 feet long. Its head alone measured more than 3 yards. It was the giant of the plesiosaurs. One of the long-necked plesiosaurs of the time was almost as big. Its long, snakelike neck was twice the length of its body.

The tails of the plesiosaurs were not of much use in pushing these big reptiles along. Their limbs, however, were wonderfully built paddles. Some of their toes had over a dozen joints! The plesiosaurs rowed through the water with their paddles.

Archelon was an early sea turtle. It looked much like some of the sea turtles of today, but it was larger than any we have now. It measured up to 12 feet long and 12 feet across from flipper tip to flipper tip.

Tylosaurus belonged to the group of marine reptiles called mosasaurs. They were sea lizards, distant relatives of the big monitor land lizards now found in the Old World. *Tylosaurus* measured nearly 30 feet.

Archelon

Trinacromerum

Kronosaurus

Tylosaurus

All the mosasaurs followed the marine reptile pattern of having paddles instead of legs. Like snakes, they had scaly skins, and jaws with extra joints that let them swallow big prey. The mosasaurs were greedy fish-eaters, the so-called pirates of the Mesozoic seas.

At the close of the Age of Reptiles the plesiosaurs and mosasaurs, too, disappeared. No one knows why, since their turtle neighbors survived. But, whatever the reasons, all the great sea reptiles except the turtles went the way of the dinosaurs.

Rhamphorhynchus

Some of the descendants of the early reptiles, instead of taking to the sea, took to the air. These were the pterosaurs. "Pterosaur" means "wing reptile." The wings of the pterosaurs were made of sheets of skin, like those of bats. Each "hand" had one long "finger" to which the front edge of the wing was fastened. The wing finger of the later pterosaurs was very long. Another name for these pterosaurs is pterodactyl. "Pterodactyl" means "wing finger."

The body of a large pterodactyl was about the size of a goose or turkey, but the wings were huge. The largest had a wingspread of 27 feet, more than twice that of the wandering albatross, the largest of the present-day birds that fly, and four times that of any bat we know. The earliest flying reptiles known had wings that spread out little more than twice the length of their body.

One of the earliest of the pterosaurs had a fairy-tale-sounding name—*Rhamphorhynchus. Rhamphorhynchus* was about a foot and a half long. Its wingspread was about 4 feet. The long, thin tail of this pterosaur ended in a leaf-shaped piece of skin that served as a kind of rudder as the creature soared through the air.

Rhamphorhynchus seldom rested on the ground. Instead, it usually clung to a cliff or to the trunk or branch of a tree. Perhaps it hung head down, just as bats often do now. It could clamber around in trees easily because it had claws at the front of each wing. The skin of the wing was fastened to the fourth finger, leaving three fingers free for holding on. The "little finger" was gone.

Rhamphorhynchus had sharp teeth. Queerly enough, they pointed forward. Teeth pointing backward would, it would seem, have been much better for catching the fish this flying reptile ate, but apparently its teeth made good spears.

Pterodactylus was one of the first of the pterodactyls. It was smaller than *Rhamphorhynchus*—in many cases no bigger than a sparrow—and it did not have that flying reptile's long tail. Neither did it have so many sharp teeth. But its wings were much, much longer in proportion to its body.

Pteranodon lived much later, in the days of *Tyrannosaurus* and the duckbilled dinosaurs. With its 13-foot wings it was the giant of the flying reptiles. The long finger of each wing was 9 feet long.

Pteranodon's head was big in proportion to its body. At a glance it would seem that this reptile was an exception to the fashion among reptiles of having small brains. As a matter of fact, the brains of all the pterosaurs were rather large for reptiles. But *Pteranodon*'s brain was not so large as one would guess from the size of its skull. Most of its queer anvil-shaped head was full of air.

Scientists are not sure as to how well this giant pterodactyl could fly. Its hollow bones —for many of the bones of the pterosaurs were hollow—and its great wings fitted it perfectly for soaring through the air. But since the only way it could move its wings was by flapping them, most scientists do not believe that it could fly nearly so well as most birds.

It is certain that a bad tear in a wing would make the wing useless. It would not be at all like the loss of a feather or two from the wing of a bird. Probably many a *Pteranodon* on a fish-catching expedition tore a wing and fell into the sea, where it was soon gobbled up. It is certain, too, that if *Pteranodon,* in swooping down, had to make an

Pterodactylus

emergency landing on level ground, it would have been almost impossible for it to get into the air again.

Pteranodon had no teeth at all, even though it was a meat-eater. But it had, as you see, a very long, stout beak.

This giant flying reptile may be thought of as a last fling of the pterosaurs. Its disappearance toward the close of the Age of Reptiles was the end of these creatures of the air.

The birds of today do not look much like crocodiles. But scientists say that the birds and the crocodiles, together with the dinosaurs and the flying reptiles, descended along separate lines from the same group of early reptiles. The birds, then, although related to the flying reptiles, are not their descendants. The ancestors of the birds,

scientists believe, were instead small reptiles that ran about swiftly on their hind legs. Perhaps they lived mostly in the trees, leaping lightly from branch to branch. Gradually, it is thought, the scales of these reptiles became feathers and the front legs developed into wings. The reptiles that became birds changed in another important way, too: They became warm-blooded.

The first bird we know about is *Archaeopteryx*. *Archaeopteryx* was still so much like its reptilian ancestors that scientists could not be sure it was a bird if it were not for its feathers.

Archaeopteryx was very different from any bird of today. It had no bill, and it had jaws with teeth. No bird today has teeth.

The bony part of the tail of a bird of today is very short. The tail feathers spread

Pteranodon

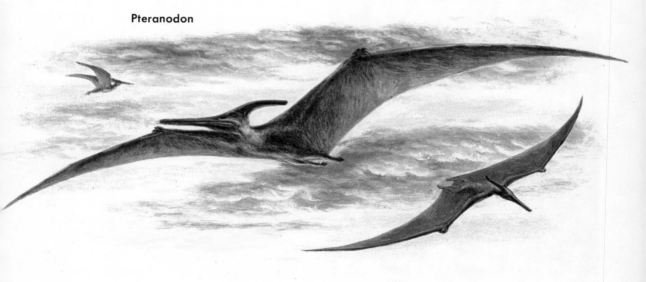

Archaeopteryx

out from this bony part like the sticks of a fan. There were many bones in the long tail of *Archaeopteryx*. Along this bony tail, feathers were arranged in pairs, one pair for every joint in the tail.

Archaeopteryx means "ancient wing." The wings of this ancient bird were not, however, true wings. Although they were feathered, they still ended in hands much

Hesperornis

like those of the meat-eating dinosaurs. Probably *Archaeopteryx* used its clawed fingers for climbing about in the trees it lived in and its outspread "wings" to glide down to the ground or from tree to tree.

The "ancient wing" was about the size of a crow. For all we know, it may have been as black as a crow. Artists have to guess at the color of prehistoric animals.

This first bird appeared well back in the days of the dinosaurs—about 150 million years ago. Many other birds, too, appeared in the Age of Reptiles. One was *Hesperornis,* the first known water bird. It appeared much later than *Archaeopteryx*.

Hesperornis was probably better fitted for diving than any bird of today. Its body, which was more than 4 feet long, was very slender, and its beak was long and sharp. It had powerful legs that made excellent oars, and big webbed feet. Like *Archaeopteryx, Hesperornis* had many teeth; it could hold fast the fish it caught.

This big diving bird could not fly. The reason is simple—it had mere traces of wings. It could not walk well, either—its feet turned out at right angles to its body, and its legs were set too far back.

Hesperornis was large, but the true feathered giants of the past were ground birds. None of these truly giant birds could fly.

Diatryma appeared soon after the end of the Age of Reptiles. It was 7 feet tall and had powerful legs and a huge beak. There were other big birds much like it. If anyone could have looked down on the earth back in those days, he might very well have thought that the birds were about to take over the earth, just as the reptiles had done many millions of years earlier. But they did not do so.

Phororhacos was much like *Diatryma*. It lived in Patagonia some 20 million years ago, long after the days of the dinosaurs. *Phororhacos* had a head as large as the head of a modern horse. Even though the bird was from 7 to 8 feet tall, its head was out of proportion. A sharp hook at the end of its beak served well to tear flesh to bits.

The largest bird of today is the ostrich. Some of the flightless giants of the past were rather like it and its relatives the cassowaries and kiwis. *Aepyornis* and the moas of New Zealand were among them.

Aepyornis is sometimes spoken of as the elephant bird of Madagascar. It was much the size of an ostrich, but it laid eggs as big as footballs. One would have been equal to several dozen hen's eggs.

The tallest birds that ever lived were moas. Some of these birds were 12 feet tall. The moas are not very ancient. When the first missionaries went to New Zealand they heard stories of birds big enough to trample men to death. Apparently man had appeared on the earth before the moas disappeared. The early inhabitants of New Zealand may have helped to bring about the end of the moas by killing them for food.

It has been suggested that the ancient flightless birds, as well as those we have

Diatryma

now, descended from primitive birds that never learned to fly. But scientists do not agree. They say that in the beginning all birds could fly, but that some lost the power to do so. Perhaps these no longer needed to fly, either to get food or to escape meat-eating enemies.

Moa

Aepyornis

Phororhacos

Borhyaena

Borophagus

Merycoidodon, an Oreodont

The first mammals were not very important-looking creatures. Back in the Age of Reptiles, no one, if he could have seen these little furry animals—most of them the size of rats and mice—would have had any idea that their descendants would one day win out over the birds and take the place of the reptiles as the lords of the earth. But they did. Scientists call the era that followed the Age of Reptiles the Cenozoic era. "Cenozoic" means "recent life." The common name for the era is Age of Mammals.

At the end of the Age of Reptiles the climate in many parts of the world had become much colder. This change worked against the cold-blooded reptiles. But it was not nearly so much of a hardship for the warm-blooded birds and for the mammals,

also warm-blooded. Their bodies stayed warm even in cold surroundings.

Their hair was a big help to the early mammals. Hair, or fur, is a very poor conductor of heat. It served well to keep the heat of their bodies from escaping. With hair to keep them warm, the mammals could be active the year round.

The early mammals, moreover, were built so that they could move very fast. They had to be quick to keep out of the way of the much bigger meat-eating dinosaurs. Besides, they, too, were meat-eaters, and being speedy gave them a great advantage.

Another great advantage the early mammals had over reptiles was the better care they took of their young. Most of the reptiles laid their eggs and then went off and left

them. The eggs and the young reptiles that hatched from them were at the mercy of meat-eating animals and the weather. The mammals, on the other hand, were live-bearing. They carried their eggs in the mother's body until the eggs developed into young animals. After they were born the babies were fed with milk from the mother. They were guarded, too, until they were able to look after themselves.

Most important of all, the mammals had bigger brains in proportion to their size than the reptiles. They were better able to hold their own in a changing world.

The scene above shows some of the mammals that grazed on the prairies of North America 20 million years ago. Most of them look much like present-day mammals.

The two animals at the left are giant "pigs." In the center foreground there is a "deer" with a strange pair of horns on its nose. A small rhinoceros is back of the deer. The horses in the background are easy to recognize. The giraffe-like animal at the far right is an early camel. Notice that it has no hump. The clumsy-looking animal near the center of the picture is a chalicothere. There are no living mammals much like it. The group it belonged to became extinct thousands of years ago.

Only one of the strange mammals pictured separately has any close relatives still living. It is *Borophagus,* an early dog. *Borhyaena* was a meat-eating pouched mammal. The oreodont ate plants. Like many other grass-eaters, it chewed a cud.

35

During the Age of Mammals—the age we are still in—mammals of thousands of kinds have developed. As one would expect, since the Age of Mammals has lasted for some 65 million years, many kinds have appeared, flourished, and then disappeared. Some of the extinct mammals were very large. It was not long, as time goes in the story of the earth, after the giant dinosaurs disappeared before there were giants among the mammals. *Baluchitherium, Uintatherium,* and *Brontops* are three that deserve a place in any parade of ancient animals.

Baluchitherium, the "Baluchistan beast," was a rhinoceros. But it was hornless and much larger than any of today's rhinoceroses. It was, in fact, the largest land mammal of all time—a tall giraffe would just have come up to its shoulders—and it was very heavy. Imagine trying to fit this big beast into a room in your house. It would need a room 30 feet long with a ceiling over 20 feet high!

Uintatherium, the "Uinta beast," gets its name from the Uinta Mountains of our West, where fossils of it are found. It lived much earlier than *Baluchitherium* and was

not nearly so enormous as that largest of all land mammals, but it was the giant of its time. *Uintatherium* specialized in horns. It had three pairs at various places on its homely face.

Brontops belonged to the group of mammals called titanotheres, or "giant beasts." It, too, specialized in horns, but it had only one pair, just back of its nose. They were, however, very large. (Its name means "thunder face.") This big mammal's skull curved downward back of its nose so that its face was the shape of a soup dish. As one would guess, the "giant beast" was not the brainiest of animals. It lived at the same time as *Baluchitherium.*

Not all the giant mammals of the past lived on land. When *Uintatherium* was the giant on land, *Zeuglodon,* an early whale, lived in the open sea. It grew to be 70 feet long, but was very slender. If *Zeuglodon* had

Baluchitherium

Uintatherium

Brontops

not disappeared long before there were any people, we would know where early sailors got their stories of enormous sea serpents.

We can trace the ancestry of many of our mammals back through millions of years. We can see what changes, in some cases very great ones, have taken place in them since they first appeared on the earth.

The horse is one with an ancestry of which we have a very complete record. The story begins with *Hyracotherium,* better known as eohippus, the "dawn horse."

Eohippus, a little animal no bigger than a fox, lived early in the Age of Mammals. Its home was in the woodlands of Europe and western North America.

The "dawn horse" had a short neck, a short face, and teeth that could chew only tender leaves. On each forefoot it had four toes—the "thumb" was gone—and on each hind foot it had three. Each toe ended in a

little hoof. Tiny bones in the feet of this little dawn horse, relics of its missing thumb and big and little toes, show that its ancestors had once been five-toed animals.

Eohippus was well fitted for living in wooded country. It could run in and out among the trees easily and hide in the shadows from its meat-eating enemies. It could reach and eat the leaves on bushes and on low branches of trees. The feet of this little horse were good for walking on soft, spongy ground.

As time went by, conditions changed in the regions where eohippus lived. The ground was not so soft as it had been. As its surroundings changed, eohippus, generation by generation, changed, too.

After many centuries it had changed so much that scientists give it a new name— *Mesohippus,* the "middle horse."

Mesohippus was about the size of an Irish setter. Its neck and its face were longer than those of eohippus and so were its legs. Its feet had also changed.

Eohippus

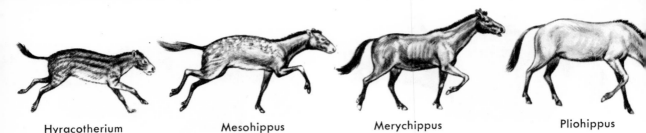

Hyracotherium   Mesohippus   Merychippus   Pliohippus

Mesohippus had three toes on each foot. The middle toe was larger than the other two, but all three reached the ground.

Conditions on the earth kept on changing. The climate became much drier in the western part of our country and in other places where *Mesohippus* lived. Much of the woodland disappeared. In its place there was grassland. If *Mesohippus* had not been able to change, too, we would never have had our horses of today.

But, generation by generation, *Mesohippus* did change. With low-branching trees scarce, its teeth changed so that instead of eating leaves it could graze on grass. It grew taller and swifter, and its neck and face grew longer. It changed so much that it is called *Merychippus,* the "cud-chewing horse." Size and speed were a help now that woods to hide in were scarce. *Merychippus* could run much faster than its ancestors because it ran on only one hoof on each foot. The two side toes dangled.

By some 10 million years ago *Merychippus* in turn had changed in so many ways that it has a new name, *Pliohippus*. The name means "more [like a] horse."

Pliohippus had only one hoof on each of its feet. Its face was long and horselike, and its teeth were even better than those of *Merychippus* for chewing grass.

From *Pliohippus* came the horses, zebras, and wild asses of today. All of them carry about with them evidence of their early ancestors' several toes. Hidden under the skin there are small splinters of bone left from the vanishing toes.

The story of the elephant is very different from the story of the horse. It has to be

African Elephant

Trilophodon

Mastodon

Equus, the Modern Horse

pieced together from a much less complete record. The story begins in Africa about 40 million years ago with a small animal that looked somewhat like a pig or a tapir. No one ever saw this animal alive. If anyone had, he would never have guessed that it would have descendants with long trunks, enormous ears, and great ivory tusks weighing more than 100 pounds apiece.

The name of this ancestor of the elephants is *Moeritherium*. Its name is taken from Lake Moeris, an ancient lake in Egypt.

Moeritherium was stocky. Its legs were thick and short and its body was long. It had two small tusks in its upper jaw—they were simply extra-large, sharp-pointed teeth— and two in its lower jaw. These tusks were useful in raking up plant food.

Generation by generation, some of the descendants of *Moeritherium* grew taller. As they did, changes took place that made it easier for them to eat from the ground. Both jaws grew longer, and so did the tusks. The nose and upper lip became longer, too. The elephant's trunk had begun.

Later descendants grew still taller. Their heads got bigger and their necks became shorter. Their jaws and tusks kept on growing longer and the snout stretched enough to make up not only for the longer legs but also for the shorter necks. They came to look like *Trilophodon*.

Then a strange thing happened. The lower jaws, after having got longer, grew shorter again until there was nothing left but a "chin." The lower tusks disappeared and the long upper ones curved upward instead of downward. With no lower jaw to rest on, the stretched-out snout was left to hang down over the chin. It was a real trunk.

The descendants of *Moeritherium* that became elephants were not the only ones with trunks. Down the long road from *Moeritherium* to the elephants there were many sidelines. *Dinotherium* was one. The mastodons were others. The mastodon pictured, as you can see, was very much like an elephant.

Indian Elephant

Dinotherium

Moeritherium

PACIFIC OCEAN

ATLANTIC OCEAN

Woolly Mammoth

Sabertooth

Mastodon

About two million years ago, the time that we call the Ice Age began. It is named for the parts of it when vast sheets of ice spread from the regions around the North Pole down over much of the northern hemisphere. By this time the elephant tribe had spread far and wide. Two of them—the mammoth and the mastodon—were common in northern lands.

The biggest mammoths grew to be 14 feet tall at the shoulder. The huge curved tusks measured 13 feet. Some mammoths were covered with coarse hair. Great herds of these woolly mammoths roamed about, often very close to the edge of the ice. Their hair protected them from the cold.

No one knows exactly when man first appeared on the earth. We do know that there were people in Europe during the last part of the Ice Age. These people lived in caves. There were woolly mammoths in Europe at the time. The cavemen drew pictures of these vanished elephants on the walls of some of their caves.

The mammoths were a great help to the cavemen. They furnished them with food.

Perhaps some of the pictures of mammoths on the walls of caves were meant to be prayers for a successful mammoth hunt.

The cavemen also drew pictures of the woolly rhinoceros. This big hairy creature, too, was found in Europe in the Ice Age.

The mastodon, like the woolly mammoth and the woolly rhinoceros, was well protected from the cold. How strange these big furry animals would look beside their almost hairless relatives of today!

The mammoth, mastodon, and woolly rhinoceros were plant-eaters. The sabertooth was an Ice Age meat-eater. Its name comes from the big cat's two enormous fangs, which were like swords, or sabers. With them it could make deep stabs into the bodies of even animals with thick hides. Mastodons were probably the chief food of this meat-eater. About the time the mastodon disappeared—first in Europe and then in America—the sabertooth, too, became extinct.

Woolly Rhinoceros

Boreostracon

limbs of trees almost without moving. Although they have four feet, these feet are not at all well fitted for walking. *Megatherium* spent its whole life on the ground. It was far too heavy to live in trees.

This "giant beast" was a harmless plant-eater. It had a thick tail and heavy hind legs. When it sat up on its haunches, as it often did, it could use its front legs with their strong claws as arms to dig out roots or to slash off branches of trees. It was so heavy that it could break down whole trees to get the leaves from them. When it sat up, it was about twice as tall as a man. It had a long, powerful tongue that it used to strip leaves off the trees.

Megatherium's sharp, curved claws were helpful in digging up roots, but they were rather a nuisance when the animal walked. They had to be doubled under in an awkward way, since they could not be pulled in as a cat's can. Perhaps they helped cause this great ground sloth to disappear.

Boreostracon was another immigrant from the south. It was one of the glyptodons, ancient mammals related to the armadillos of today. They had some hair, but they were not at all furry.

Boreostracon sometimes grew to be as big as an ox. Like all the glyptodons, it was almost completely wrapped up in armor. On its back it had a shield much like that of an armadillo. In addition to the shield on its back, *Boreostracon* had a bony plate on its head, bony rings around its tail, and

During much of the Ice Age, the climate of the part of North America that is now the United States was mild. There were long, warm periods between the times of spreading ice sheets. Many animals that had moved up from South America flourished.

One that became very common was *Megatherium*. Its name means "giant beast." *Megatherium* was a ground sloth. The sloths of today are all tree dwellers. They are queer, clumsy beasts that hang from the

Megatherium

A Tar Pool Trap

many spikes at the end of its tail. It could not roll up like an armadillo.

The picture above shows how some of the animals of the Ice Age met their death in a part of the United States not reached by the ice. Here oil welled up out of the ground and formed pools of sticky tar. After a rain, water would collect on top of the tar in these pools. Animals such as mammoths, horses, and camels would wade out into the pools to get a drink. Then they would be trapped in the sticky tar.

The cries of the trapped animals would attract the sabertooth, the giant condor, and other meat-eaters. The weapons of these big meat-eaters were of no use when they found themselves sinking into the tar, too. Many sabertooths and birds of prey were trapped. So many animals were caught in these tar pools that they are often called the "death-trap tar pools."

A number of mammals besides the mammoth furnished food for the cavemen of Europe. Among them were reindeer, musk-oxen, wild horses, and wild sheep.

The animals that furnished the cavemen with food might be thought of as friends.

The cavemen had animal enemies, too. One was the cave bear. The cavemen lived in caves during the winters to protect themselves from the cold. The cave bears sought shelter in the same caves. Many a fight must have been fought between the cavemen and the big cave bears. Of course, if a caveman won a fight with a cave bear, he had a warm bearskin for a blanket or for clothing. The caveman had to depend on wild animals for winter clothing as well as for food.

We are still in the Cenozoic era—the Age of Mammals. The Ice Age and the time since then, often called the Age of Man, form parts of it. Man, you probably know, is a mammal. Will mammals, you may very well wonder, continue to be the earth's leading animals? Or, a hundred million years or so from now, will most of the kinds of mammals of today belong in a parade of ancient animals? Will the elephants, the antelopes, and the whales, to name but a few, come to an end as the dinosaurs did? No one can tell. At the moment there is little to make us think that man himself is in danger of being crowded off the earth.

The Earth's Rock Diary

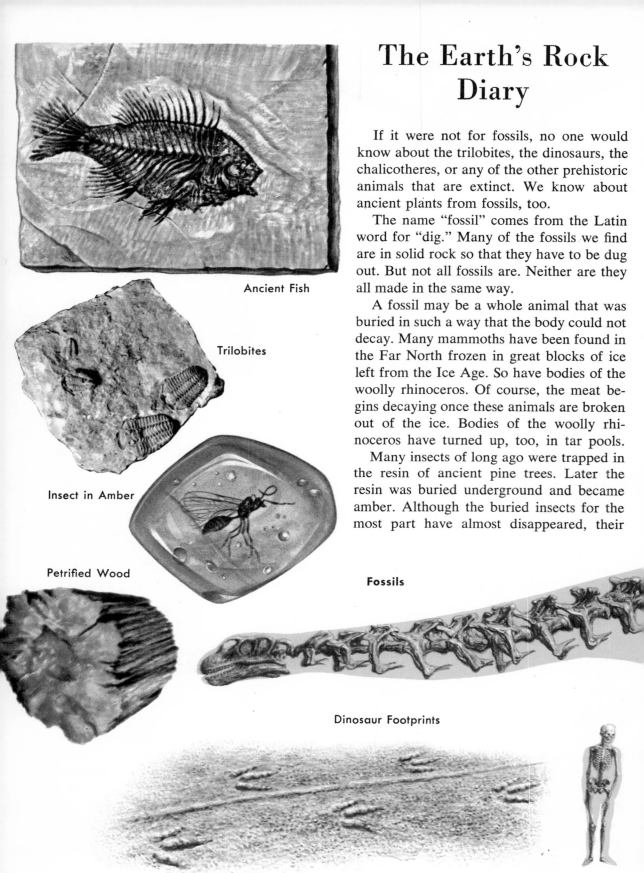

Ancient Fish

Trilobites

Insect in Amber

Petrified Wood

Fossils

Dinosaur Footprints

If it were not for fossils, no one would know about the trilobites, the dinosaurs, the chalicotheres, or any of the other prehistoric animals that are extinct. We know about ancient plants from fossils, too.

The name "fossil" comes from the Latin word for "dig." Many of the fossils we find are in solid rock so that they have to be dug out. But not all fossils are. Neither are they all made in the same way.

A fossil may be a whole animal that was buried in such a way that the body could not decay. Many mammoths have been found in the Far North frozen in great blocks of ice left from the Ice Age. So have bodies of the woolly rhinoceros. Of course, the meat begins decaying once these animals are broken out of the ice. Bodies of the woolly rhinoceros have turned up, too, in tar pools.

Many insects of long ago were trapped in the resin of ancient pine trees. Later the resin was buried underground and became amber. Although the buried insects for the most part have almost disappeared, their shapes show as sharp hollows in the amber. In many museums there are pieces of amber containing fossil insects. From them we see what the insects looked like when they were trapped millions of years ago.

Many fossils are casts. One of the pictures shows a piece of rock on which there are several trilobite casts. The story of every trilobite cast is somewhat like this: A trilobite died, and its body fell to the muddy bottom of the sea. Soon the soft parts of its body decayed. Then the hard covering served as a mold. It filled with limy mud. In time the hard covering itself decayed and the space it had taken up was filled with limy mud. Later, no one knows how much later, the limy mud hardened, just as did the mud round about, into solid rock.

The fossil fern leaf pictured is a cast, too. The leaf was pressed down in some way into mud. It decayed but left its imprint in the mud. More mud washed into the imprint. All the mud hardened into solid rock. When the rock was later split in two, there was a raised cast of the leaf on one surface and the imprint in which it was made on the other.

Fossil footprints are imprints. Those in the picture were made when a dinosaur walked across a layer of soft mud. Ordinarily

such prints would have been washed away or trampled out. But conditions were such that they were not. When the mud became solid rock the footprints remained.

The bones in the skeleton of the great dinosaur *Brontosaurus* are petrified. "Petrified" means "turned to stone." They were petrified in this way: The dinosaur died and fell into a swamp or pond. It was covered up promptly with sand or mud. The soft tissues of the body decayed rather rapidly, but the bone tissue of the skeleton was left. Then, little by little, water brought minerals that filled up all the tiny hollows in the bones and made them solid as stone. The minerals then preserved the bone itself by shutting away the air and water that would have destroyed it. The fish skeleton pictured is also petrified, but it has not been separated from the rock in which it was found.

In the petrified wood there is no wood left at all. As the trunk of an ancient tree lay covered with mud, water took away the wood, particle by particle, and replaced each one with a bit of mineral. At last the trunk was rebuilt in stone.

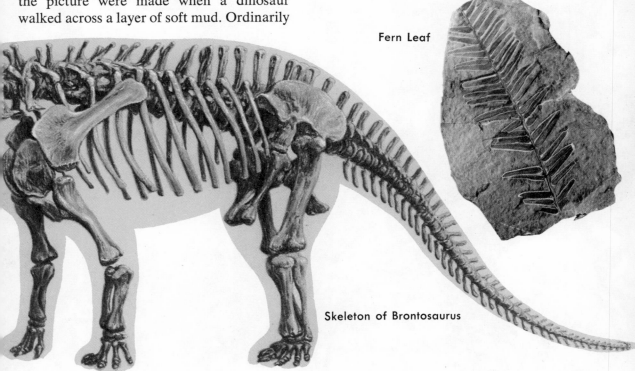

Fern Leaf

Skeleton of Brontosaurus

45

In our museums there are many skeletons built of the petrified bones of ancient animals. It takes an enormous amount of work to free the bones of a big animal from the rock in which they are found. The rock must be chipped away bit by bit. If the fossils are rather small, blocks of rock containing them may be cut out and shipped to a museum. The fossils are not freed till they reach the museum workrooms.

Large fossils may be so heavy that they are hard to ship. Just the skull of one dinosaur, when it was in a box and ready to be shipped, weighed 3,650 pounds. Imagine what a whole petrified skeleton of a *Diplodocus* would weigh! And think how hard it would be to fasten all the bones of such a dinosaur in place!

A skeleton like the one pictured below is sometimes found with the bones in almost the right position. In many cases, however, the bones are scattered about and mixed in with bones of other animals. It is not always easy to tell which ones belonged together or when all the bones of a creature have been found.

Often a fossil bone is broken. The collector may put such a bone in a plaster cast for shipping.

Some fossils are simply the hard parts of plants or animals that have been kept as they were. A fossil may be, for instance, a bone that has remained unchanged without being petrified. From peat bogs, tar pits, and bodies of quicksand have come great quantities of fossil bones.

The outside "skin" or crust of the earth is made up of rocks of many different kinds. Some of them are made from sediments, such as sand and mud, that settle to the floor of lakes and seas or from shells that fall to the bottom of the water. These rocks are often spoken of as water-made rocks. *Sedimentary rocks* is another name for them.

Other rocks are made from hot, liquid rock that comes from deep in the earth. Such rocks are called *igneous rocks*. This name is from the Latin word for fire. Sometimes igneous rocks are instead called volcanic rocks. It is easy to see why they are, since many of them are made from the hot, liquid rock that pours from the craters of volcanoes.

There are also rocks that have been much changed since they were first formed. These are the *metamorphic rocks*. "Metamorphic" means "changed."

The different layers of rock that make up the earth's crust may be thought of as pages in the earth's diary. They tell the story of the earth during the long ages before there were any people anywhere in the world who could write of living things and earth events. A deep cut in the earth's crust, like the Grand Canyon, opens up rock pages covering millions and millions of years for scientists to read.

The layers of water-made rocks are the pages that tell most of the story of life long ago. It is not surprising that they are, since mud and water play so important a part in the making of fossils.

Skeleton of the Dinosaur Hadrosaurus

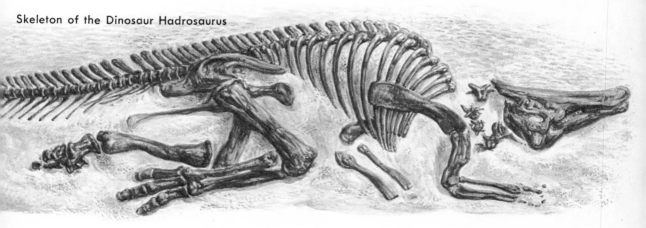

Shale

Sandstone

Limestone

Conglomerate

The rocks pictured here are all water-made, or sedimentary, rocks. There are outcrops of such rocks in many places.

Shale is made from mud. A piece of shale smells like mud when it is wet. It feels rather like soap.

Sandstone, as its name suggests, is made of grains of sand cemented together. You can feel the grains if you rub your fingers over a piece of sandstone. A layer of sandstone sometimes furnishes a clue about its formation by having ripple marks on it.

Limestone may be made of lime that settles to the bottom of a body of water from the water itself. Anyone who has seen the lime that collects on the inside of a tea-kettle knows that water may have a great deal of lime in it. Limestone may, instead, be made of the shells of water animals. Vast numbers of animals take lime from the water of lakes and seas to make shells for themselves. When they die they sink to the bottom of the water. The soft parts decay or are eaten up. Animals with shells have lived and died in such numbers that in many places thick layers of limestone have been built by their shells. A piece of limestone may be a great mass of fossil shells. Some limestones make excellent building stone.

Conglomerate is usually part sandstone, but it contains pebbles, too. One nickname for it is "puddingstone."

A pebble is a small piece of rock that has been knocked about so that it has lost its rough edges. A handful of pebbles one picks up on a beach usually includes some bits of sedimentary rock, some of igneous rock, and some of metamorphic rock. Many of them may have been carried a long way from the mass of rock they came from, perhaps by waves, perhaps by streams, perhaps by long-gone glaciers of the Ice Age.

Sometimes pebbles are so worn by their journeys that it is hard, unless they are cracked open, to tell what rock they are made of. Those pictured below are all bits of water-made rocks. One is sandstone, four are limestone, and four are shale.

A Salt Mine

Rock Salt

water is salty enough for a layer of salt to settle from it.

As you already know, coal was formed, not of sediments washed down into a lake or sea, but of buried forests. The diagrams below tell the story of how coal was made. Many plant fossils are found in coal. It is from them that we can tell what trees grew during the Coal Age.

Layers of water-made rocks tell much more about the earth's history than just what plants and animals once lived here. They tell where lakes and seas used to be. Land and sea have not remained the same through the ages. The map of North America back on page 15 shows that in the days when coal was being made great arms of the sea spread over thousands of square miles of what is now land. The map is based on layers of water-made rocks scientists have found—rocks that were made in the Coal Age.

The rock layers through which the Colorado River has cut the Grand Canyon are, except for those at the very bottom of the gorge, water-made rocks. They tell that this region was covered by water for countless centuries. Scientists can read the story of land and sea for much of the world from the rocks underlying the surface.

Those who know how to read the earth's rock diary can also read from water-made rocks about changes in climate in ages past. Rock salt, for example, is much more likely to be formed when the climate is dry and water evaporates fast from lakes and seas. Fossils found in water-made rocks help, too, to tell the stories of changes in climate. Fossils of corals and such southern plants as figs and palms found in Greenland, for instance, show that Greenland has been in times past much warmer than it is now.

Rock salt and coal are other water-made rocks. They are both so useful that we mine them in great quantities.

Since sea water contains salt, it is not surprising that in places layers of salt have been formed at the bottom of a sea. Rock salt seldom contains fossils, for although many plants and animals live in the salt water of the oceans, life becomes scarce when sea

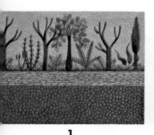

1

2

3

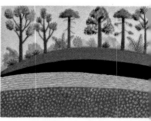

4

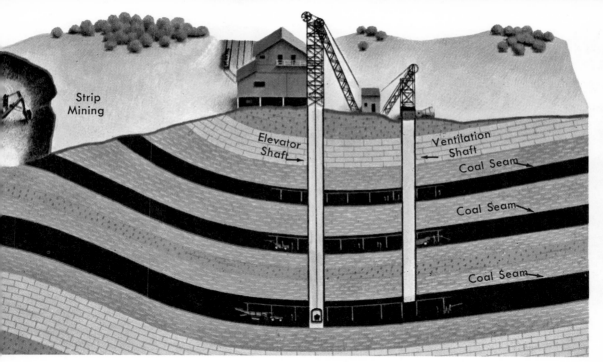

Strip Mining

Elevator Shaft →

← Ventilation Shaft

Coal Seam

Coal Seam

Coal Seam

A Shaft Mine

1. *Back in the Coal Age dense forests grew in vast swamps.*

2. *The land sank and trees were drowned.*

3. *The trees were covered with mud.*

4. *The land rose and forests grew again.*

5. *Again the land sank and once more the trees were drowned.*

6. *Again the drowned trees were covered with mud.*

7. *In time, after perhaps several ups and downs, the regions of the buried forests became dry land. Deep underground the forest layers changed to coal.*

8. *Now men dig into the ground to get the coal formed from the buried forests of millions of years ago.*

Soft Coal

Lignite

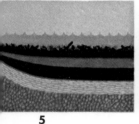

5

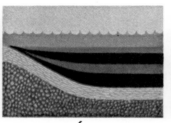

6

7

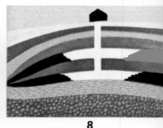

8

Basalt

All the rocks pictured on these two pages are igneous, or volcanic, rocks. Several of the specimens are basalt or granite, very common igneous rocks.

The diagrams on the next page show how a volcano can build itself into a mountain. Hot, liquid rock is squeezed up to the surface from deep in the earth. While it is underground it is called magma. When it pours out on the surface it is called lava. At times a volcano erupts so violently that lava is shot high into the air and shattered into pieces. The pieces cool and harden into cinders and bits of ash, most of which fall near the opening the lava came from. Gradually they build a cone-shaped hill around the opening. More and more lava, cinders, and ash make the hill a mountain.

Lava that pours out of a volcano may cool very quickly. It may have many spaces in it just as slag does that comes from steel mills. These spaces were filled with hot gases as the lava poured out. Two of the rocks formed in this way are pumice and scoria. Pumice is so light that it will float in water. If a volcano in or near a sea erupts, pumice may cover the water for miles around. Scoria is much coarser.

Obsidian and rhyolite are other rocks formed from lava that cools quickly. They have no spaces in them. Obsidian looks like smooth glass. In fact, it is often called volcanic glass. As a rule it is black. Rhyolite is light-colored and rather glassy.

Basalt is formed from lava that is slower to cool. It is a dull-black rock, as the pictures of it show. In some places there are layers of basalt hundreds of feet thick. A layer may break up into six-sided columns. Anyone who has driven along the Columbia River in Oregon has seen great columns of basalt. The Giant's Causeway in Ireland, pictured at the top of the page, is made of basalt columns.

Pumice

Rhyolite

Porphyry

Obsidian

Scoria

Diorite

Granite

Magma may cool when it comes near the surface and harden into solid rock underground. Granite is formed from magma that hardens beneath the surface. This common igneous rock may be mainly pink, red, or gray. It has dark crystals in it that give it a speckled look. Although formed underground, granite is often found at the surface —the rocks above it have been worn away. The Needles of the Black Hills, shown in the picture above, are granite. Granite is so hard that it has been called "the rock everlasting." It takes a high polish and is an excellent building stone.

There are a great many other igneous rocks. Some, like granite, have cooled so slowly underground that crystals large enough to be seen easily have formed in them. Among these are diorite and porphyry. Some of the crystals in porphyry are especially large. Other rocks, like pumice, obsidian, rhyolite, and basalt, are made from lava that pours out over the surface of the ground. The crystals, if there are any, in these rocks are very tiny.

From the igneous-rock pages in the earth's diary, scientists can tell that in parts of the world there were once active volcanoes where there are none today. They can tell, too, that at times in the past great cracks opened up in the earth and allowed lava to pour in floods from them.

How a Volcano
Builds Itself

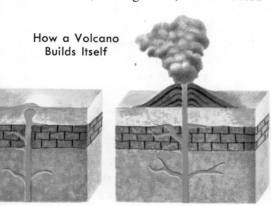

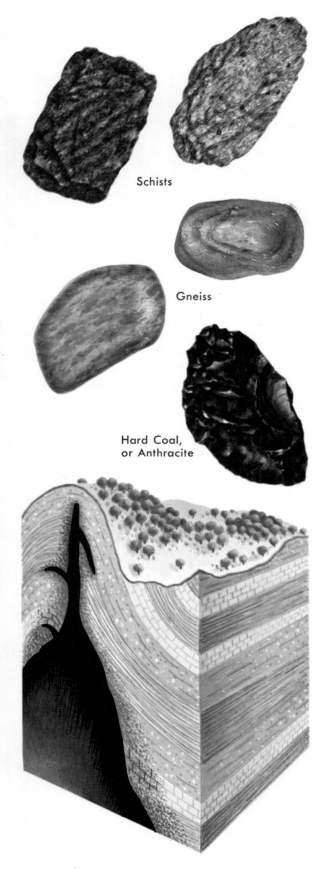

Schists

Gneiss

Hard Coal,
or Anthracite

The metamorphic rocks in the earth's crust are like pages that have been rewritten. After layers of rock have been formed, they are sometimes squeezed into great folds. They are sometimes bulged up by magma pushing from underneath. The squeezing, pushing, and heating bring about changes in the rocks.

The diagram below shows magma being forced up through layers of rock of different kinds. Around the magma there is a zone where the rocks are being changed.

Marble, slate, quartzite, and hard coal are simple metamorphic rocks. They are not very greatly changed from the rocks they came from. All marble was once limestone, all quartzite was once sandstone, all slate was once shale, and all hard coal came from soft coal.

Gneiss of the kind pictured is a simple metamorphic rock, too. It is so much like the granite it came from that it is often called banded granite. Some gneisses are more complicated.

The schists—there are many kinds—are rocks greatly changed. Just looking at them does not give much of a clue as to how they began. A schist may be formed from shale or from conglomerate or from any one of several other rocks.

Many of the metamorphic rocks are very useful. Hard coal, for instance, is a much cleaner fuel than soft coal. It is not dusty, and it produces little smoke.

Slate can be split into very thin sheets with smooth surfaces. It has long been used for blackboards and for roofing shingles. This common metamorphic rock may be red, green, blue-gray, brown, or purple.

Marble is the most beautiful of the metamorphic rocks. It can be given a high polish. The purest marble is white, but marble may be gray, green, pink, red, or black. Much marble is streaked. Many statues and fountains are made of marble.

Quartzite is an extremely durable rock. In the days of brick pavements some of the "bricks" used were blocks of quartzite instead of true bricks of baked clay.

Slate

Marble

Quartzite

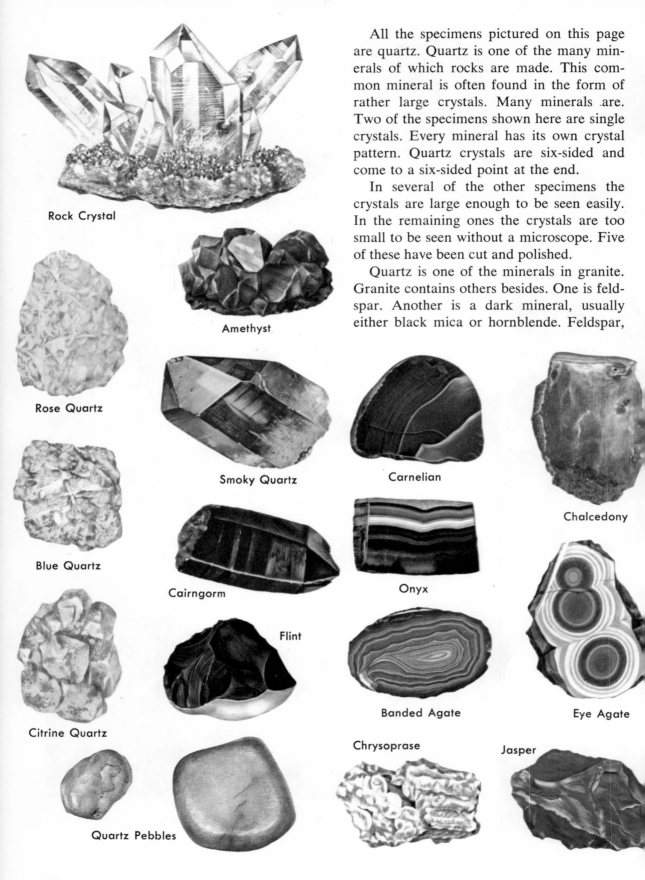

All the specimens pictured on this page are quartz. Quartz is one of the many minerals of which rocks are made. This common mineral is often found in the form of rather large crystals. Many minerals are. Two of the specimens shown here are single crystals. Every mineral has its own crystal pattern. Quartz crystals are six-sided and come to a six-sided point at the end.

In several of the other specimens the crystals are large enough to be seen easily. In the remaining ones the crystals are too small to be seen without a microscope. Five of these have been cut and polished.

Quartz is one of the minerals in granite. Granite contains others besides. One is feldspar. Another is a dark mineral, usually either black mica or hornblende. Feldspar,

Rock Crystal

Amethyst

Rose Quartz

Blue Quartz

Citrine Quartz

Smoky Quartz

Cairngorm

Flint

Quartz Pebbles

Carnelian

Onyx

Banded Agate

Chrysoprase

Chalcedony

Eye Agate

Jasper

Feldspar

Graphite

Asbestos

Apatite

Biotite, or Black Mica

Serpentine

Pyrite, or Fool's Gold

Hornblende

Muscovite, or White Mica

Fluorite

Talc

Tourmaline

Sulfur

black mica, and hornblende are pictured here along with many other rock-forming minerals. The crystals in a rock specimen are not likely to be perfect—they are too crowded together.

There are so many different minerals that it takes years of study to know them well. You can tell many of them apart by their looks. No one, for example, would confuse fool's gold and asbestos. Another way is by testing for hardness. Scientists have made a scale of hardness to help.

This is the scale, from softest to hardest:

1. Talc	6. Feldspar
2. Gypsum	7. Quartz
3. Calcite	8. Topaz
4. Fluorite	9. Corundum
5. Apatite	10. Diamond

Talc, as you see, is the softest mineral and diamond the hardest. You can scratch talc with your thumbnail. Books about minerals usually give their hardness ratings. If you have a mineral specimen you are trying to identify and you find that quartz will scratch it but that it will scratch apatite, you know that it must be one with a rating between 5 and 7. Some other ways of identifying mineral specimens can be used only in specially equipped laboratories.

The crystals of some minerals are so beautiful that we use them as jewels, or gems. Some of the varieties of quartz you have already seen are gemstones. The most popular of them is amethyst. Opal, a variety of quartz which does not form crystals, is also a popular gemstone.

Most of the other gemstones shown here are in crystal form. Some of the pictures show the crystals as they are found. Others show them after they have been cut into jewels. Emeralds, rubies, and diamonds are the most valued gems—emeralds and rubies for their color and diamonds for their brilliance. These gems are very durable. Diamond, you remember, is the hardest mineral. Emerald and ruby are almost as hard.

Jade seldom occurs as crystals. Its value as an ornament depends on its color and the skill with which it is carved.

Opal

Topaz

Zircon

Aquamarine

Spinel

Jade

Chrysoberyl

Garnet

Emerald

Ruby

Diamond

Sapphire

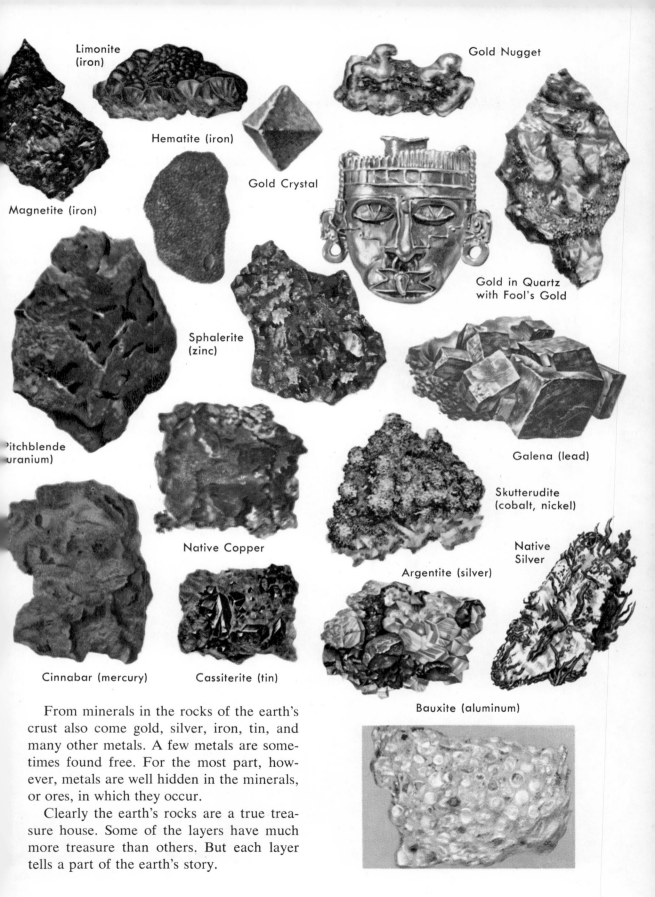

Limonite (iron)

Gold Nugget

Hematite (iron)

Gold Crystal

Magnetite (iron)

Gold in Quartz with Fool's Gold

Sphalerite (zinc)

Pitchblende (uranium)

Galena (lead)

Skutterudite (cobalt, nickel)

Native Copper

Native Silver

Argentite (silver)

Cinnabar (mercury)

Cassiterite (tin)

Bauxite (aluminum)

From minerals in the rocks of the earth's crust also come gold, silver, iron, tin, and many other metals. A few metals are sometimes found free. For the most part, however, metals are well hidden in the minerals, or ores, in which they occur.

Clearly the earth's rocks are a true treasure house. Some of the layers have much more treasure than others. But each layer tells a part of the earth's story.

Living Things

In the world today there are hundreds of thousands of kinds of living things. Many scientists classify all of them as either plants or animals. Others divide living things into three kingdoms: plants, animals, and protists. In the protist kingdom they put many small organisms not easy to classify as either animals or plants.

Living things differ greatly in size. Some, like the germs that cause typhoid, are so tiny that they cannot be seen without a powerful microscope. Others, like elephants and whales, weigh tons. Some living things have very short lives. The mayfly lives less than a day after it reaches its grown-up stage. The giant sequoia, on the other hand, is not old when it has lived for a thousand years. Living things come in almost every shape you can imagine. But in certain ways all living things are alike.

They are all built of tiny blocks, or cells, of that mysterious living material called protoplasm. Some organisms are single cells. The biggest plants and animals are made up of billions.

All living things show some organization into different parts for different purposes. An oak tree has roots, a trunk, branches,

Giant Sequoia

leaves, flowers, and seeds. A tiger has a body, head, tail, legs, eyes, ears, and a mouth, to say nothing of many organs inside its body. Even the simplest one-celled organism has different parts of its one cell that carry on different kinds of work.

All living things must have food and water. They all need oxygen, too.

Chemical changes go on in all living things. Food is used up to furnish energy. New living material is made. Old living material is worn out. Wastes are produced that must be got rid of.

All living things have the power of growth. They can all produce other living things like themselves. They all move to some extent. Even living things that stay in one place may be seen to move parts of their bodies. Barnacles, for example, after swimming freely when young, settle down for life, but their feathery legs are still very active. And though a living thing may appear to be motionless, you may be sure some movement is going on inside it.

All living things, moreover, show change in response to changes that go on around them. The leaves of a sensitive plant fold up if touched. A kitten scratches when annoyed. A sunflower turns toward the sun. Your hair stands on end and you get gooseflesh if you are cold or frightened.

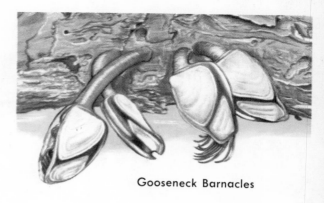

Gooseneck Barnacles

Mayfly

Sensitive Plant

The things that stand out most clearly in this picture are a toad and a toadstool. Although a toad and a toadstool are alike in many ways, you can tell easily that one is an animal and the other a plant. But it is very hard to give a definition of an animal that will fit all animals. It is even harder to give a definition of a plant that will fit all plants. There are dozens of ways in which toads and toadstools are different, but these ways would not hold for all the different plants and animals there are.

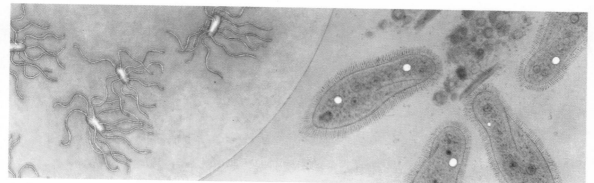

Typhoid Germs

Paramecia

One of the big differences between a toad and a toadstool is that a toad can hop about, while a toadstool must live its whole life in one place. But there are plants—some small seaweeds, for instance—that move about freely. And many animals, like the barnacle, spend most of their lives in a single spot.

A toad has eyes, ears, bones, muscles, and a brain. A toadstool has none of these things. But neither does a sponge or a coral, and they are classed as animals.

The plants we are most used to seeing have leaves. But a toadstool has no leaves. Neither does a cactus or a duckweed.

Probably you think of plants as green, and most of them are. But toadstools are not green. Neither is Indian pipe or dodder.

Most animals change faster than plants with a change in surroundings. But the leaf of a sensitive plant folds up quickly.

Most plants have cell walls made of cellulose. But not all of them do. Clearly this is not a sure way to tell a plant.

Even though it is very hard to put in words exactly what makes some living things

plants and what makes others animals, fortunately not very many of those we are used to seeing are puzzling. Most are as easy to classify as a sunflower and a bear. But the classification of some, as you know, is in dispute. The pictures on this page show a few of the puzzling organisms. They are among those often classed as protists.

Typhoid germs are bacteria, long thought of as plants. These bacteria have, as you see, hairlike projections. With these projections they can move fast in water. A typhoid germ, projections and all, is a single cell.

The paramecium is often called the slipper animalcule because of its shape and size. It belongs to the protozoa, long called animals. The paramecium is only a single cell, though it is very much larger than a typhoid germ. It is big enough to be seen in a good light without a microscope.

For part of their lives slime molds move about and act more like animals than like plants. Then they stop moving and act more like plants than like animals. No wonder some scientists call them protists.

Slime Mold

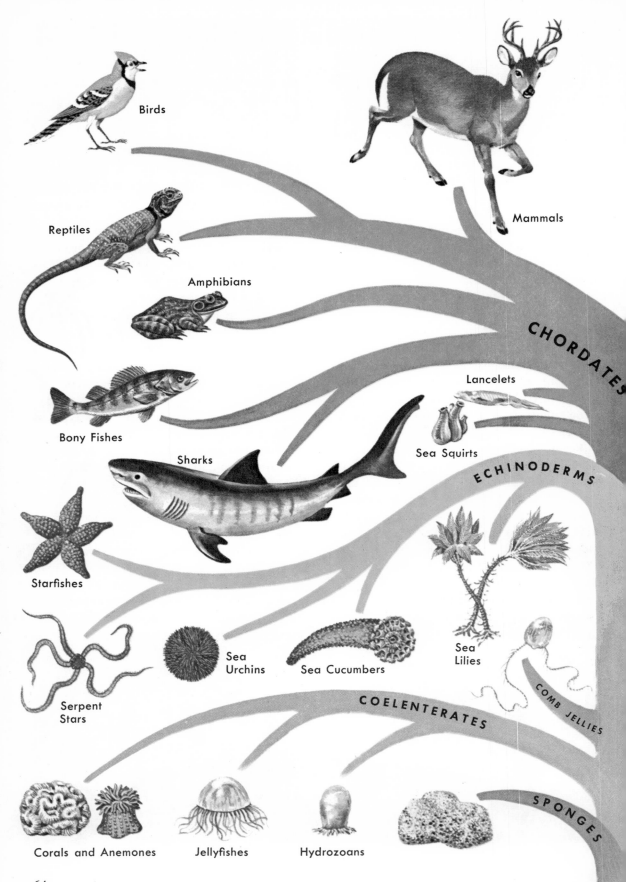

Birds

Mammals

Reptiles

Amphibians

CHORDATES

Bony Fishes

Lancelets

Sharks

Sea Squirts

ECHINODERMS

Starfishes

Sea
Urchins

Sea Cucumbers

Sea
Lilies

COMB JELLIES

Serpent
Stars

COELENTERATES

SPONGES

Corals and Anemones

Jellyfishes

Hydrozoans

The Animal Kingdom

Today about a million kinds of animals are known. There may be many more not yet discovered. Some animals are very small, and it is therefore not surprising that new ones are constantly being found.

The tree diagram gives an overview of the animal kingdom. Only the most important branches are shown. The simplest animals are near the bottom of the tree, the most advanced at the top. All the animals of today are believed to have come from one-celled organisms of long ago.

Notice that the lowest branch is marked PROTOZOA. The protozoa, you remember, are among the organisms put in the protist kingdom by some scientists.

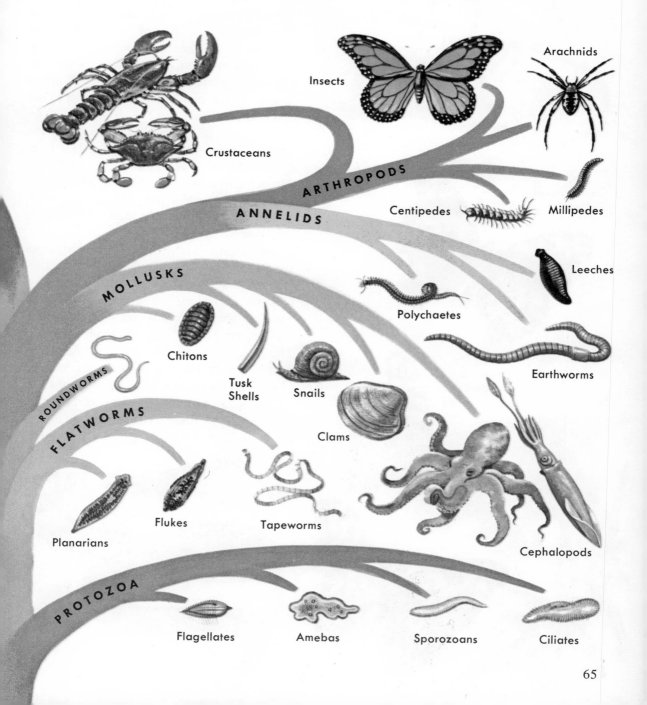

Insects

Arachnids

Crustaceans

ARTHROPODS

ANNELIDS

Centipedes

Millipedes

MOLLUSKS

Leeches

Polychaetes

Chitons

ROUNDWORMS

Tusk Shells

Snails

Earthworms

FLATWORMS

Clams

Planarians

Flukes

Tapeworms

Cephalopods

PROTOZOA

Flagellates

Amebas

Sporozoans

Ciliates

Banded Garden Spider

Red Admiral
Butterfly

Painted Lady
Butterfly

Scientists compared all the different animals they knew with one another in working out a way of classifying them. The chief divisions of the animal kingdom are called *phyla*. There are about 25 altogether, many made up of little-known animals. The tree shows less than half of them.

Phyla are divided into *classes*. Classes in turn are divided into *orders,* orders into *families,* families into *genera,* and genera into *species*. Each separate kind of animal is a species.

Every animal has a scientific name. The scientific name of the red admiral butterfly is *Vanessa atalanta*. The first part of the name tells its genus, the second its species. The name of the painted lady is *Vanessa cardui*. These two butterflies, you see, are in the same genus.

The *Vanessa* butterflies belong to the family of brush-footed butterflies. This family is in the order of Lepidoptera, the "scaly wings," a division of the class of insects. The insects are a part of the phylum of jointed-legged animals, or arthropods, by far the largest of all the phyla.

The animals pictured on these two pages are in seven different phyla. The spider, lobster, and shrimp, along with the butterflies, are arthropods. The earthworm is an annelid. The sea urchin and sand dollar are echinoderms, the "spiny-skinned" animals. The coral is a coelenterate, and the paper nautilus a mollusk. Comb jellies have a phylum to themselves. So do the sponges.

Although scattered among several phyla, the animals in these pictures are all invertebrates. They have, that is, no backbone.

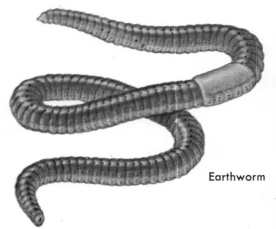

Earthworm

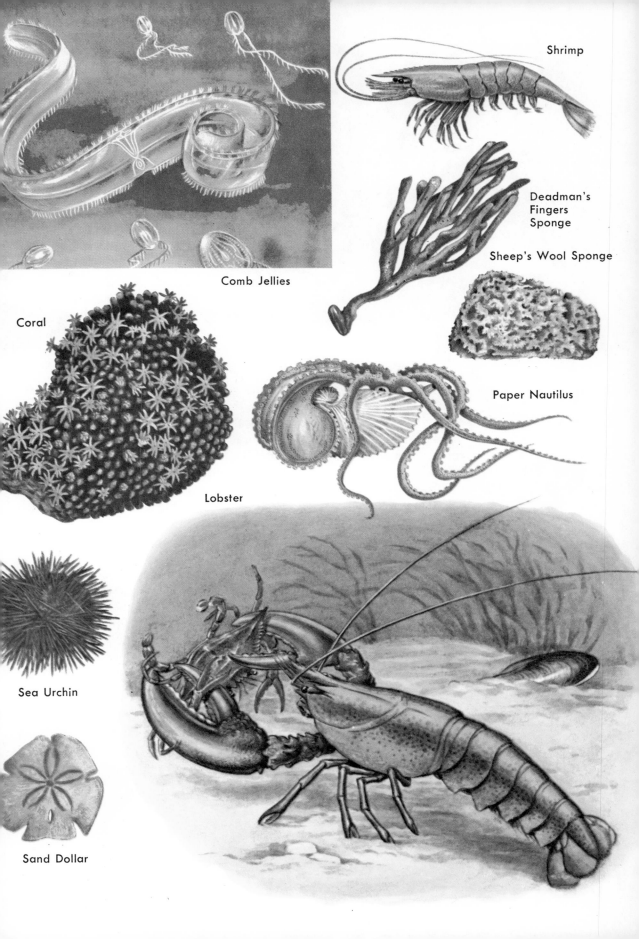

Shrimp

Deadman's
Fingers
Sponge

Sheep's Wool Sponge

Comb Jellies

Coral

Paper Nautilus

Lobster

Sea Urchin

Sand Dollar

Brook Trout

There were invertebrates, you remember, on the earth for millions and millions of years before any animals with backbones appeared. Even though they have lost the high place in the animal world they held for ages, animals without backbones are still far more common than vertebrates, the animals with backbones. In number of species the invertebrates outnumber the vertebrates about 25 to 1. The vertebrates, however, are far more conspicuous, chiefly because of their size.

The vertebrates get their name from the bones that make up the backbone. These bones are the *vertebrae*. In addition to the vertebrae, vertebrates have many other bones. All their bones together make up their skeleton, which forms a framework for their body and gives them their shape.

There are five big groups of vertebrates. The animals pictured here represent three of them—fishes, amphibians, and reptiles.

The brook trout, needless to say, is a fish. Fishes are all water animals. They have fins, not legs. Fishes breathe with gills. A few kinds have additional ways of getting oxygen. Most fishes, but not all, are covered with scales.

Green Frog

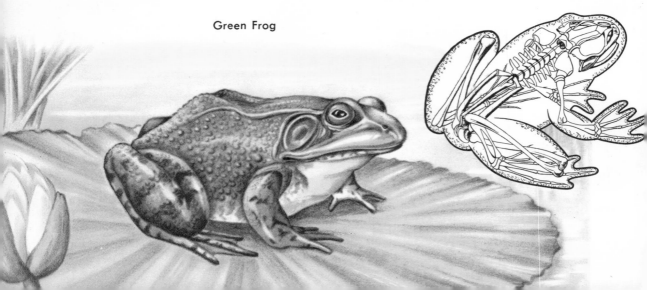

Crocodile

The green frog is an amphibian. Amphibians get their name from their life history. "Amphibian" means "living a double life." A green frog starts its life in water. It gets oxygen from the water with gills, just as a fish does. It has no legs. Later it becomes an air-breathing creature. It develops legs as well as lungs. This is the general amphibian pattern. Amphibians have no scales. Their skins are bare and, as a rule, moist.

The crocodile and the snake are reptiles. The word "reptile" comes from a Latin word which means "to creep." Reptiles have short legs, if any. The snakes have none.

No big new groups of sea reptiles have appeared to take the place of those that disappeared with the dinosaurs. Most reptiles of today are land animals. Even those that spend most of their time in the water—except for a few that are live-bearing—come up on land to lay their eggs.

Reptiles are built somewhat like adult amphibians, but they differ from amphibians in these two important ways: they breathe with lungs all their lives, and, with very few exceptions, their skins are covered with scales. Contrary to the common idea, the scales are dry, not slimy.

Fishes, amphibians, and reptiles are cold-blooded. Being cold-blooded does not mean being always cold. It means instead having to get the warmth needed from the surroundings. A cold-blooded animal may be very warm indeed if it is in the hot sun. But in freezing temperatures the animal is sure to be cold and inactive. In being cold-blooded, the fishes, amphibians, and reptiles are like insects, mollusks, worms, and all the other animals without backbones.

Gaboon Viper

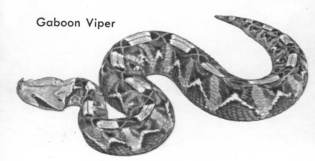

The mourning dove and the pig represent the other two groups of vertebrates. These two groups differ from the fishes, amphibians, and reptiles in being warm-blooded. Their bodies are warm inside even in cold surroundings.

The mourning dove, of course, is a bird. Birds can be told from all other animals by their feathers. A bird's body is truly warm. The normal temperature of some species is 112 degrees Fahrenheit! Birds have hearts with four rooms, or chambers.

All birds are air-breathing. They have lungs all their lives. Although the earliest birds had teeth, the birds of today, as you know, do not. Instead, they have a gizzard in which their food is ground into small bits.

The pig is a mammal. Mammals get their name from their mammary, or milk, glands. All mammals feed their young with milk.

Like the birds, the mammals have hearts with four chambers. They breathe with lungs all their lives. In this way they are like both the birds and the reptiles. They all have some fur, or hair, even though some of the biggest mammals—the elephant, hippopotamus, rhinoceros, and whale—have very little. Their hair, as well as their milk glands, serves to set the mammals apart from the other vertebrates.

One might expect that each of the five big groups of animals with backbones would be put in a separate phylum. But in spite of their differences the five are enough alike in important ways for all to be put in one. They do not even make up quite all of one phylum. The sea squirts and a few other little-known animals are grouped with the vertebrates in the phylum of chordates.

Two pictures on page 71 show sea squirts. These small animals are not much more than living sacs anchored fast in one place. They have no bones. The body of each one has two openings. Water bringing with it tiny plants and animals, which serve as food, comes in through one opening and, having picked up wastes, leaves through the other. The animal gets its name from these openings. If it is disturbed, it squirts a jet of water from each of them.

Man, of course, since he is a mammal, is a chordate. It is hard to believe that scientists put the sluggish sea squirts in the same

Mourning Dove

Duroc-Jersey Pig

phylum of animals with us. To understand why, we have to know something about a sea squirt's life history.

When a sea squirt is young, it looks much like a tadpole. It swims freely about in the water. Its body is almost transparent. The tadpole-like creature has an eye that can tell light from darkness and a nerve cord that extends backward from a small, hollow brain. Below the nerve cord there is a rod that stiffens the little animal's body. This rod is called a notochord. It is its notochord which puts the lowly sea squirt into the phylum of chordates.

In its very earliest stages every animal with a backbone has a notochord. No animal in any other phylum ever has one. Therefore, even though a sea squirt loses its notochord as it grows up and never develops a skeleton, the brief period in its life when it has a notochord earns it its place in the phylum at the top of the animal tree.

After a short period of swimming about, a sea squirt stands on its "face" and attaches itself to a solid surface. It then loses, together with its notochord, its tail, its eye, its brain, and all but a small portion of its nerve cord.

The sea vase pictured is common on both our Atlantic and our Pacific shores. Another name for it is tube sea squirt. It is only about 2 inches high.

The sea peach gets its name from its shape and its orange-red color. The color makes it

stand out from its neighbors in the cold coastal waters where it lives.

Some kinds of sea squirts never grow up and settle down. They spend their whole lives in the "tadpole" stage, moving about in the sea. One kind forms cylinder-shaped colonies several feet long. These colonies often shine vividly at night.

The lancelet, a small ribbon-shaped animal that comes to a point at each end, is another of the chordates that do not have a backbone. But it has a notochord even when it grows up. Lancelets often plunge tailfirst into the sand of a seashore with only their mouths above the surface. They never, however, follow the sea squirts' fashion of anchoring themselves in one spot for the rest of their lives.

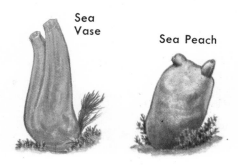

Sea Vase

Sea Peach

Portuguese
Man-of-war

Speckled
Jelly

Moon Jelly

Animals of the Seashore

The seashores of the world are the homes of thousands of kinds of animals without backbones, just as they were half a billion years ago. These animals live where the tides flow in and out and where great waves buffet the shores. Some of them move with the waves and the tides. Some bury themselves in the sand or mud when the tide goes out and wait for it to come in again. Some anchor themselves for life to rocks along the shore. A great many are protected by hard coverings. The jellyfishes are among those with no hard parts at all.

The moon jelly and the speckled jelly are much alike except that the speckled jelly has longer streamers hanging down from around its mouth, and longer feelers, or tentacles. Both its streamers and its tentacles help a jellyfish catch its food. On its tentacles there are many threads, or darts, filled with poison. When an animal comes near enough to touch a tentacle it is shot at once with poison darts. These jellyfishes swim lazily about by opening and closing their umbrellas, or else simply float.

The Portuguese man-of-war is a jellyfish, too, but it is not a single animal. Instead, it is a whole colony of animals. The separate animals are not all alike, and they do not all do the same kind of work. Some of them do the eating and digesting of food. Some serve as fishing lines and as protectors of the colony. Others are good only for feeling. Still others have the task of producing a new generation of jellyfish.

The "sail" of the Portuguese man-of-war is a bag filled with gas. It keeps the colony afloat. This "many-in-one" jellyfish got the man-of-war part of its name because it reminded people of a tiny battleship as it sailed along. Its "guns" are its darts.

Often a Portuguese man-of-war has some little fish traveling with it. These fish, called man-of-war fish, for some reason are immune to the poison of their companion.

The graceful sea fan pictured below is a horny coral. It was built by a colony of tiny, eight-tentacled animals. In the picture you do not see the animals themselves. They are hidden in the horny branches of the "fan."

Sea Fan

Sea Anemone

At night and on dark days the tiny animals of a sea fan come out of hiding and gather in food with their tentacles. Digestive canals inside the horny skeleton connect the animals of the colony.

The jellyfishes and the sea fan belong to the group of animals called coelenterates. So do the hydroids, sea anemones, and stony corals. All the animals of the group have poison darts, or threads, like those of jellyfishes, that help them get food.

The hedgehog hydroid, too, is a colony of tiny animals. The picture shows the different kinds that make up a colony. The tall ones with long tentacles do the eating and the snakelike ones the stinging. Those with "balloons" produce new animals.

Sea anemones look much like flowers. Some of them have beautiful colors. Like the Portuguese man-of-war, some sea anemones have fish companions that are not hurt by the anemone's poison threads. A grown-up sea anemone holds fast to something solid, but it is not anchored there. It can glide slowly from place to place.

The stony coral pictured lives alone, but most stony corals, like the sea fan and hedgehog hydroid, are colonies of many tiny animals. Each little animal builds a rock cup for itself out of lime from the water. It keeps

Hedgehog Hydroid
(greatly enlarged)

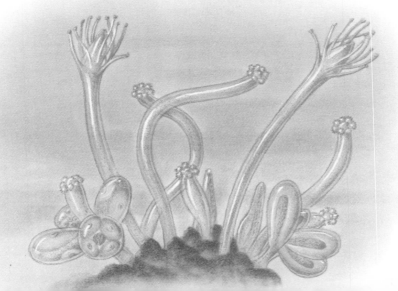

adding lime and building its cup higher. Together all the animals of a colony build a big "apartment house" of stone. Different species of coral build houses of different patterns. Often its common name comes from the kind of house a coral builds. Thus we have such names as star, brain, tree, and staghorn coral. Corals have been building rock houses in the seas for half a billion years. No wonder there are great coral reefs and even islands.

Comb jellies get their name from the rows of "combs" with which they swim. These combs are made of tiny plates joined together like the teeth of a real comb. The comb jellies used to be classed with the jellyfishes as coelenterates. Now, as you know, they are in a phylum of their own. Comb jellies are as pretty at night as in the daytime. They shine in the dark.

There are worms of many kinds along the seashores. The pictures show one, the clamworm, that swims about freely and three that stay in one place in tubes they build for themselves. Some sea worms have beautiful, bright-colored plumes. The plumes are gills with which the worms breathe and catch food. They are drawn back into the tubes in a flash at times of danger. The parchment worm almost never leaves its U-shaped shelter. This tube worm glows in the dark.

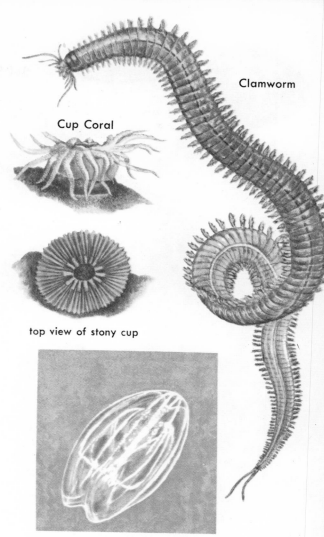

Clamworm

Cup Coral

top view of stony cup

Rainbow Comb Jelly

Fan Worm

Parchment Worm

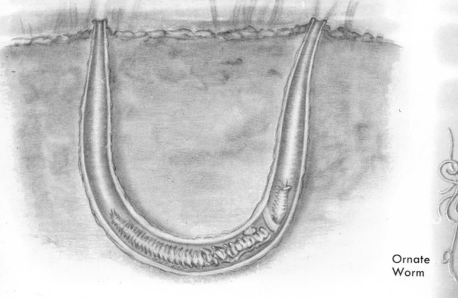

Ornate
Worm

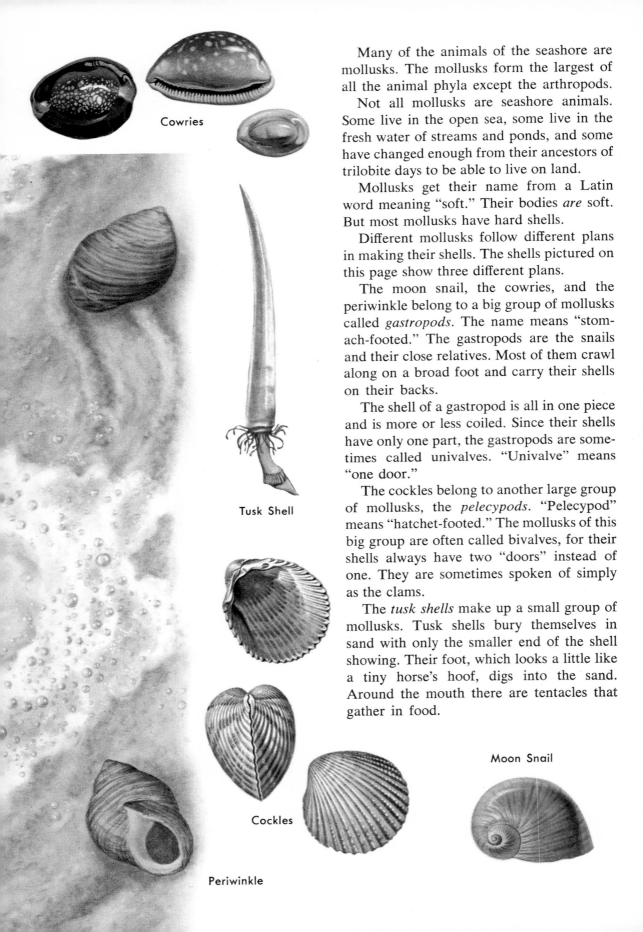

Cowries

Tusk Shell

Cockles

Periwinkle

Moon Snail

Many of the animals of the seashore are mollusks. The mollusks form the largest of all the animal phyla except the arthropods.

Not all mollusks are seashore animals. Some live in the open sea, some live in the fresh water of streams and ponds, and some have changed enough from their ancestors of trilobite days to be able to live on land.

Mollusks get their name from a Latin word meaning "soft." Their bodies *are* soft. But most mollusks have hard shells.

Different mollusks follow different plans in making their shells. The shells pictured on this page show three different plans.

The moon snail, the cowries, and the periwinkle belong to a big group of mollusks called *gastropods*. The name means "stomach-footed." The gastropods are the snails and their close relatives. Most of them crawl along on a broad foot and carry their shells on their backs.

The shell of a gastropod is all in one piece and is more or less coiled. Since their shells have only one part, the gastropods are sometimes called univalves. "Univalve" means "one door."

The cockles belong to another large group of mollusks, the *pelecypods*. "Pelecypod" means "hatchet-footed." The mollusks of this big group are often called bivalves, for their shells always have two "doors" instead of one. They are sometimes spoken of simply as the clams.

The *tusk shells* make up a small group of mollusks. Tusk shells bury themselves in sand with only the smaller end of the shell showing. Their foot, which looks a little like a tiny horse's hoof, digs into the sand. Around the mouth there are tentacles that gather in food.

Many people make collections of sea-shells. Most of them know much more about the shells than they know about the animals that make them. The shells pictured on this page are gastropod shells. Three of the pictures show living animals.

The tulip shell is a typical snail. The one in the picture is "taking a walk." Its head, eyes, and feelers show clearly. Notice the disk at the back of the foot. If there is danger, a tulip shell pulls its head and foot into its shell and closes the opening tight with this disk.

The picture does not show the tulip shell's peculiar "tongue." A gastropod's tongue, called a radula, is very long and narrow,

and on it there are many rows of tiny teeth. With its radula a gastropod can scrape little plants off stones, tear larger plants to pieces, and even drill through the hard shell of another animal in order to eat it.

If you found an abalone shell on the beach, you might think it was only half the shell of some kind of clam. The opening is very large, and the shell does not look coiled. But if you looked at it carefully you would see some whorls at one end.

With its foot an abalone can hold tight to rocks even in pounding surf. Its body is well covered by its big shell.

When an abalone is pulled away from the rock it is attached to, the edges of the foot curl up. The live red abalone pictured has just been dislodged.

The inside of an abalone's shell is beautifully colored. Partly because of their beautiful shells and partly because the abalone is good to eat, abalones are not so common as they once were.

Black Abalone

Tulip Shell

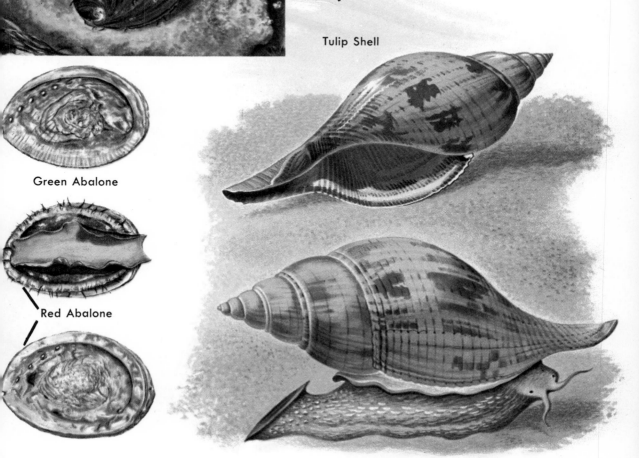

Green Abalone

Red Abalone

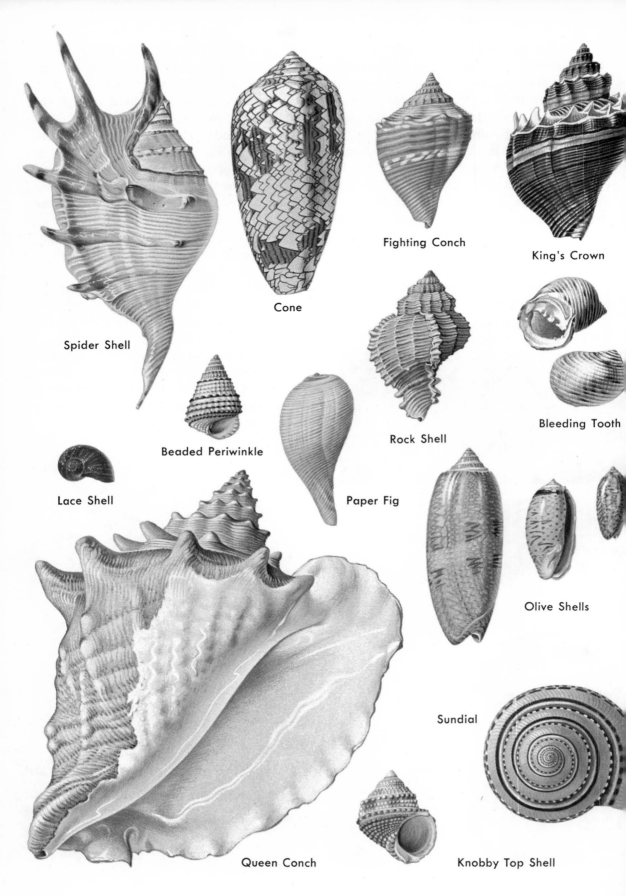

Cone

Fighting Conch

King's Crown

Spider Shell

Rock Shell

Bleeding Tooth

Beaded Periwinkle

Lace Shell

Paper Fig

Olive Shells

Sundial

Queen Conch

Knobby Top Shell

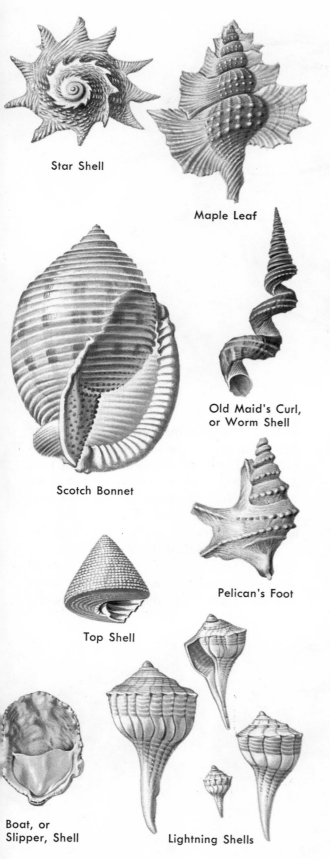

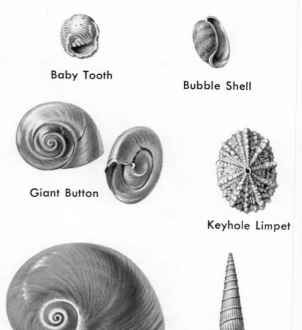

Star Shell

Maple Leaf

Baby Tooth

Bubble Shell

Giant Button

Keyhole Limpet

Scotch Bonnet

Old Maid's Curl,
or Worm Shell

Whale's Eye

Screw Shell

Top Shell

Pelican's Foot

Boat, or
Slipper, Shell

Lightning Shells

All these shells are gastropod shells. There are gastropods in fresh water and gastropods on land—there are hundreds of kinds of tree snails, for example—but all these shells are from gastropods of the sea.

Notice the names of these shells. In many cases it is easy to see how they came about. Even if the names were not given, you would be able to pick out the bleeding tooth, the star shell, and the maple leaf.

The queen conch is one of the largest gastropods. Its shell is many times as big as its picture here. Perhaps you have held a conch shell up to your ear to hear the "roar of the sea." You do hear a roar when you listen to a conch shell. But it is not caused by the sea. It is caused by the air inside the twisted shell. The roar may help you remember, however, that queen conchs are animals of the seashore.

How does a gastropod manage, you may wonder, when it gets too big for its shell? Hard shells like these will not stretch. The four lightning shells at the left tell the answer: a gastropod as it grows keeps making its shell bigger and bigger.

Hard-shell Clam,
or Quahog

Most of these pictures show live pelecy-pods, the "hatchet-footed" animals. The hard-shell clam is typical of the group. It has no head—no pelecypods do. And it has a hatchet-shaped foot it uses to burrow in the sand. You can see in the picture the clam's water tubes, or siphons, extending a little way beyond the shell. Water moves in and out of the clam's body through them.

Some clams use their foot to pull them-selves along. The series of pictures below shows a clam plowing through sand. As the clam is on edge in the sand, its foot stretches forward. The foot then swells out at the end. The end acts as an anchor. It stays in place while the foot shortens. As the foot gets shorter, the clam is pulled ahead. The foot now moves forward again, the end swells, and the clam is pulled ahead once more.

Many bivalves, after a short babyhood swimming about, settle down in one place and stay there from then on. Oysters do.

Giant, or Bear's-paw, Clam

So does the giant bear's-paw clam. A bear's-paw settles hinge down in a coral reef and the coral growing up around it builds it a made-to-measure nest.

This big clam is the largest of all bivalves. It may measure more than a yard across and weigh 500 pounds. It can clamp the two parts of its shell shut with great force. More than one underwater explorer has had an unpleasant adventure with this creature. In contrast with the giant bear's-paw, the tiny clams called basket shells are only half an inch across.

Bivalves furnish us with a great deal of food. Oysters, clams, scallops, and mussels are harvested in huge numbers. Some bivalves, especially the pearl oyster, are valuable for quite another reason. They are the source of all true pearls.

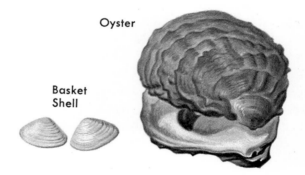

Oyster

Basket
Shell

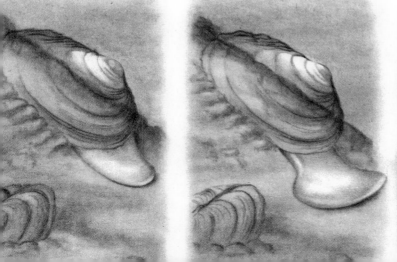

Butterfly
Shells

Scallops

Calico Clam

Kitten's Paw

Turkey Wing

Hooked Musse

Saucer Shell

Sunrise Shell

Spiny Oyster

Blue Mussel

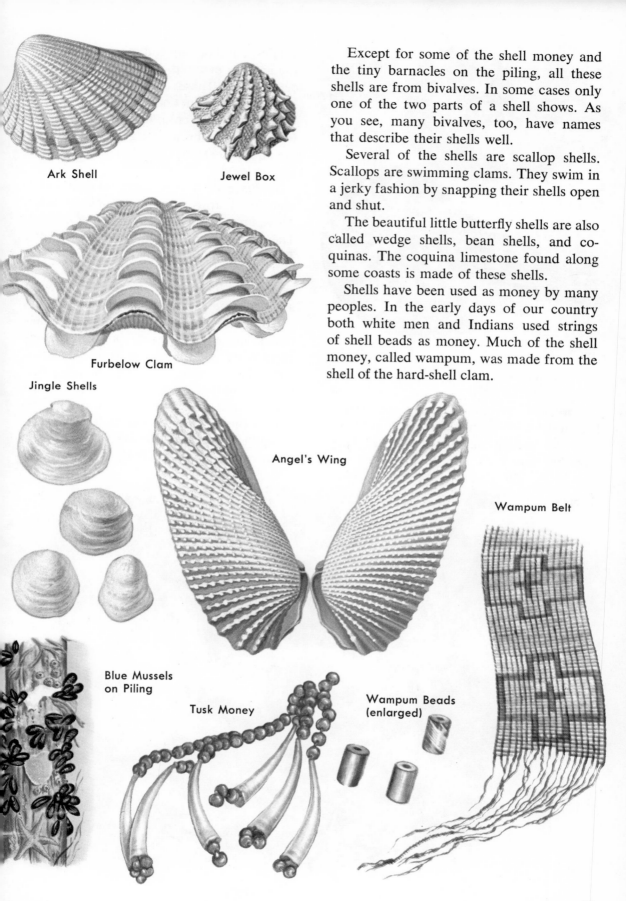

Ark Shell

Jewel Box

Furbelow Clam

Jingle Shells

Angel's Wing

Wampum Belt

Blue Mussels
on Piling

Tusk Money

Wampum Beads
(enlarged)

Except for some of the shell money and the tiny barnacles on the piling, all these shells are from bivalves. In some cases only one of the two parts of a shell shows. As you see, many bivalves, too, have names that describe their shells well.

Several of the shells are scallop shells. Scallops are swimming clams. They swim in a jerky fashion by snapping their shells open and shut.

The beautiful little butterfly shells are also called wedge shells, bean shells, and coquinas. The coquina limestone found along some coasts is made of these shells.

Shells have been used as money by many peoples. In the early days of our country both white men and Indians used strings of shell beads as money. Much of the shell money, called wampum, was made from the shell of the hard-shell clam.

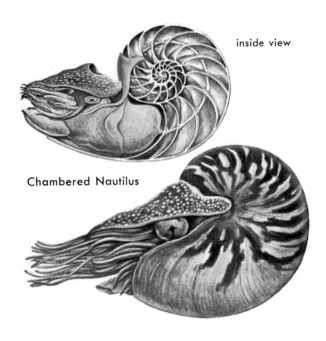

inside view

Chambered Nautilus

whales, but there are still many of them. All the animals pictured on these two pages are cephalopods. These same animals might look quite different in another picture. All of them can change color in a flash. They may be red, yellow, brown, or greenish one minute and the next be striped or white or rainbow-colored.

In place of a foot a cephalopod has a number of arms which surround its head. These arms are helpful in gathering in food. They are, as a rule, equipped with suckers. The cephalopods, like the snails, have a long, rasping tongue, or radula. On their heads they have the best eyes to be found among animals without backbones.

The beautiful shell of a chambered nautilus is made up of many rooms, or chambers. When the nautilus is young, its shell has only one room. As the animal grows larger, it adds one room after another. Finally it has a house of many rooms, but it lives in only the last room it has built.

Squids are sometimes called "sea arrows" because of their shape. With its fins a squid

The cephalopods—the "head-footed" animals—make up the third of the main groups of mollusks. At times during the earth's long history the cephalopods, as you know, were the leading animals of the sea. They have lost that high rank to the fishes and

Octopus

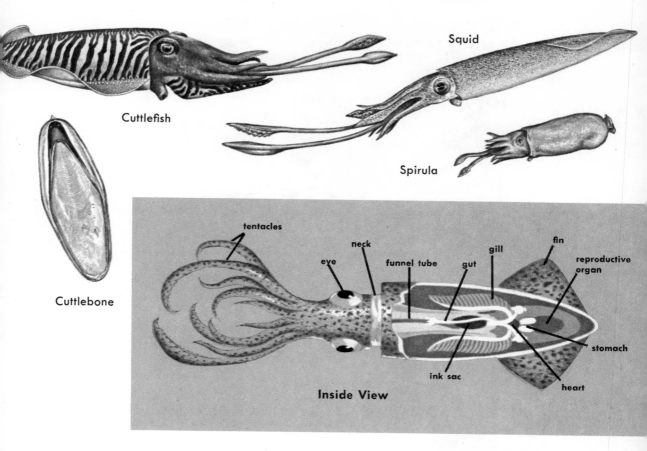

Cuttlefish

Squid

Spirula

Cuttlebone

Inside View

tentacles
neck
eye
funnel tube
gut
gill
fin
reproductive organ
stomach
ink sac
heart

can swim forward or backward, make quick changes in direction, and even hover in one place. It has a way to use jet propulsion to help itself go extra fast. Underneath its head it has a funnel tube, or siphon, that it can point backward, forward, or to either side. Squirting water out of this funnel in one direction shoots the squid in the opposite direction.

Two of a squid's arms are much longer than the other eight. When a squid is after a fish to eat, it darts forward. It catches the fish with its two long arms and pulls it back far enough for the other eight arms to hold while it eats the fish.

In escaping from an enemy, a squid usually darts backward. It has another good trick that helps it get away: it squirts out a cloud of brown ink. The ink hides the squid and gives it a chance to escape.

The squids along our seashores are less than 2 feet long. But there are giant squids nearly 50 feet long. Their bodies measure

from 15 to 18 feet and their long grasping arms stretch out for 30 feet more. Their suckers are as big as teacups.

The squids have no shells that show. Buried in their body they have only a bit of horny shell known as the "pen."

Many people who have never seen cuttlefish have bought cuttlebone for their pet birds. Cuttlebone is a limy shell remnant inside a cuttlefish.

Except for the chambered nautilus, the tiny spirula is the only living cephalopod with a shell. Like the giant squid, it is at home deep in the sea.

The well-known octopus has not even a remnant of a shell. Octopuses are sometimes called devilfish. The biggest measure 12 feet with arms spread out and are terrifying. But most are much smaller. The danger to divers from octopuses is not nearly so great as most of us imagine. They seldom attack people. But to the crabs that octopuses come across, they *are* "devil fish."

Spider Crab

Crabs, shrimps, and lobsters are closely related animals of the seashore. They are all crustaceans. The crustaceans make up one of the groups of arthropods.

Almost all the crustaceans have a horny covering, or "crust." It is quite different from the shells with which the mollusks protect themselves. The hermit crab does have a real shell, but it did not make the shell itself. A hermit crab simply borrows an empty mollusk shell. This crab is not a true crab. True crabs have short "tails," or abdomens, curled up beneath them. The hermit crab has instead a long one just as shrimps and lobsters have. But for some reason the hermit crab

Fiddler Crab

Shrimp

Blue Crab

Hermit Crab

grows no protective armor on its abdomen. It solves the problem by taking shelter in an empty snail shell of the right size.

A crustacean's suit of armor cannot stretch. The animal as it grows must shed its suit and grow a new one.

All the crustaceans pictured here have ten legs. Their two front legs end in claws, in most cases stout ones, which are helpful in catching and crushing small animals. All of them have two pairs of feelers, and eyes on stalks. They all breathe with gills. Five pairs of legs, two pairs of feelers, stalked eyes, gills, and a good suit of armor make up a common crustacean pattern.

Lobster

Barnacles are strange crustaceans. As you know, early in their lives they give up swimming about and anchor themselves in one place. A rock barnacle builds a shell around itself that holds it a prisoner for the rest of its life. It kicks food into its mouth with its feathery legs.

For the most part, barnacles are not important as food. But many of the crustaceans are. People eat lobsters, shrimps, and crabs by the millions every year.

Some of the tiniest of the crustaceans are even more important to us than those we prize as food. They form an important part of plankton, the "sea soup" that furnishes food, directly or indirectly, for most of the fishes of the sea. We depend far more on saltwater fishes for food than on lobsters and shrimps and crabs.

Surprisingly enough, small red crustaceans called krill are the chief food of some of the biggest whales. Krill are often so abundant in spots that they make the sea water look like tomato soup.

Other small crustaceans are common along the ocean's shores. Beach fleas search for food among the seaweeds. Pill bugs creep over the sand and mud, curling up into tight balls if anything disturbs them. Wharf lice scurry about in wet piling. The small crustaceans of the seashore far outnumber the larger crustaceans there.

The horseshoe, or king, crab, like the hermit crab, is not a crab. In fact, the horseshoe crab is not even a crustacean. It is, however, an arthropod just as every crustacean is. This animal is often called a living fossil, for it has existed almost unchanged for 175 million years. When young it looks much like the trilobites that were the earth's leading animals half a billion years ago.

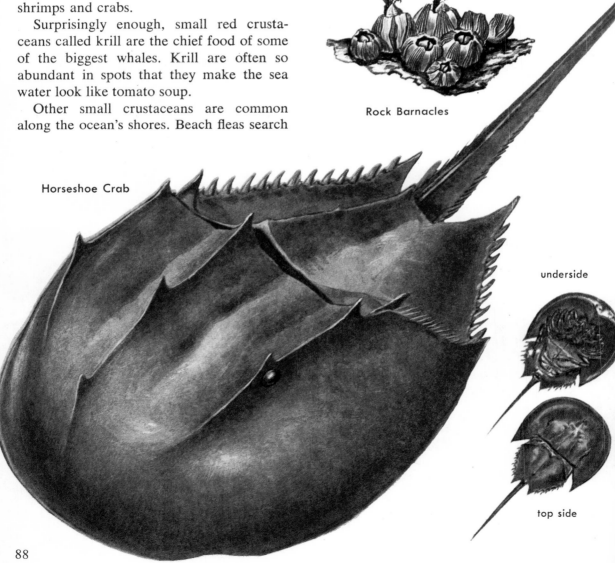

Rock Barnacles

Horseshoe Crab

underside

top side

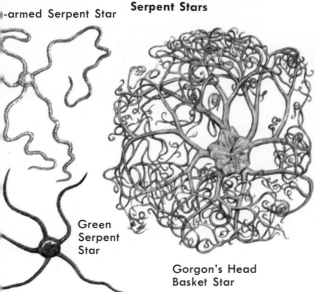

Serpent Stars

-armed Serpent Star

Green Serpent Star

Gorgon's Head Basket Star

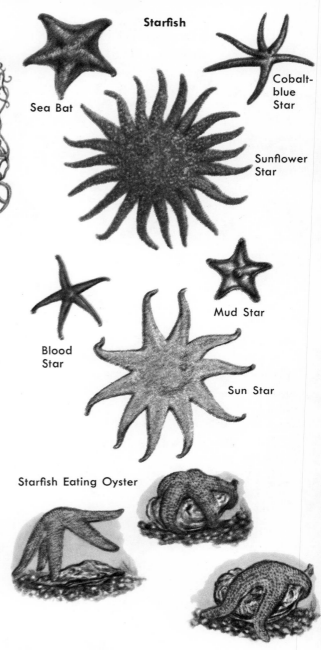

Starfish

Sea Bat

Cobalt-blue Star

Sunflower Star

Mud Star

Blood Star

Sun Star

Starfish Eating Oyster

Starfish are the best known of the spiny-skinned animals, or echinoderms. There are many kinds. As you see, they do not all have five arms as the common starfish has, and they are not all the same size or color. But they are all enough alike to be easy to recognize.

The echinoderms differ from all other animals in having inside their bodies a system of water canals connected with tube-feet which, as a rule, end in suction disks. Tube-feet are helpful in moving about and in keeping clean. In bright sunlight an echinoderm may even use its tube-feet to hold up pebbles or seaweeds as parasols.

Tube-feet also help to catch prey. A starfish, let us suppose, comes upon an oyster. With its suction disks it fastens its arms tight to both parts of the shell with its mouth where the shell will open. Using all its might the starfish makes the oyster shell open a tiny crack. A tiny crack is all the starfish needs, for it has a strange way of eating. It turns its stomach inside out and slips it into the oyster shell through the crack. Its stomach stays there till the oyster is digested.

Serpent, or brittle, stars, are enough like starfish so that you would have no trouble recognizing most of them as close relatives. The gorgon's head basket star, with its many-branched snakelike arms, is one that might be puzzling.

Common Starfish

Sand Dollar

You might not guess from their looks that the animals pictured on these two pages are also close relatives of the starfish. But they are. They are all echinoderms.

The sand dollar lives on sandy sea bottoms in rather sheltered places. It moves about on its tube-feet. If a sand dollar is turned over, it turns a somersault to get right side up again. A sand dollar's spines are short. They make the little animal look as if it were made of velvet.

Many people who have never seen a live sand dollar have seen a sand dollar's skeleton. The skeleton is made of lime. It gives the sand dollar its shape and earns for it the "dollar" in its name.

The sea urchin has a limy skeleton, too. A sea urchin's skeleton is beautifully shaped and may be a pretty color. It is the sea urchin, with its prickly spines, that gave the whole group of echinoderms their name. Some sea urchins with long, sharp spines are called hatpin urchins.

Of course, the sea cucumber is not a vegetable nor the sea lily a flower. These animals, too, were named from their shape.

Although the sea cucumber is an echinoderm, it has a tough, leathery skin rather than a spiny one. Its mouth is surrounded by branched tentacles. The animal feeds itself with its tentacles. It rubs them around in the mud and cleans them off in its mouth one by one. Tiny bits of plant and animal material in the mud are its food.

Sea Urchin

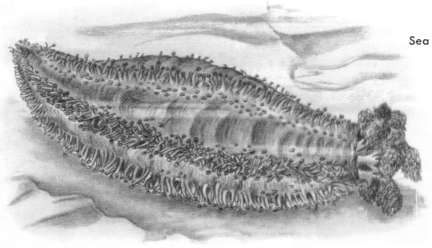

Sea Cucumber

A sea cucumber has a strange way of protecting itself from its enemies. From an opening opposite its mouth it throws out a mass of sticky pink and white threads that so entangle the attacker that it cannot move. A sea cucumber can even turn itself almost inside out and throw its breathing and reproductive organs at an enemy.

The sea cucumber cannot pull the threads or organs in again. It must get along without them until it can grow new ones. Many of the lower animals are able to grow again a body part that has been lost or injured. A lobster, for example, can grow a new claw, a starfish a new arm, and a flatworm a whole new head.

The sea lily, like its relatives back in the days of the trilobites, anchors itself to rocks and stays in one place. It must wait for food to come to it. Its tube-feet are on the branching arms of the "flower." Particles of food picked up from the water by the tube-feet are swept into the sea lily's mouth.

Except for the sea cucumbers, which move about in a flopped-over position, echinoderms have no front or back. A sea urchin, for instance, may move forward with any part of its body in front. It is built on what might be called a wheel plan rather than on a two-sided plan. All the markings on its skeleton go out from the center like the spokes of a wheel. All grown echinoderms are built on this plan. Even the sea cucumber, as you will see if you can picture it in an upright position, mouth down, is much like a stretched-out sea urchin.

Queerly enough, young echinoderms are not built on a wheel plan. They are two-sided, like all the higher animals. They are much like the young of the simplest of the chordates, the big group to which all the animals with backbones belong.

Many animals of the seashore have rather close relatives that live in the fresh water of ponds and streams. There are, for instance, freshwater crabs, clams, snails, and shrimps. But there are no freshwater echinoderms. There are no land forms, either. All echinoderms live in the sea.

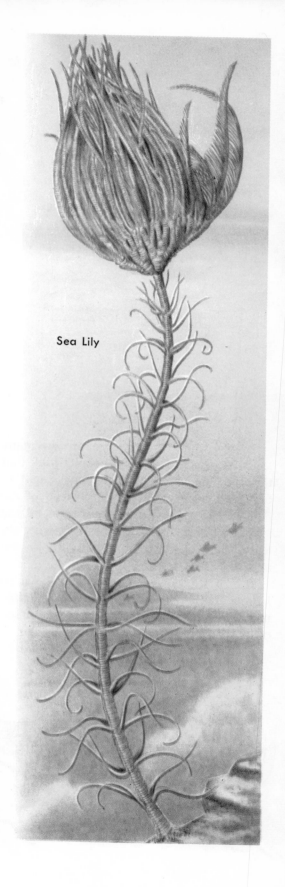

Sea Lily

Great Spangled Fritillary

Insects

In the world today there are so many kinds of insects that some people think that this time in which we are living ought to be called the Age of Insects instead of the Age of Man. Over three-fourths of all the species of animals are species of insects. At least 750,000 kinds of insects are known and the list is growing.

It is not easy to get an idea of what so large a number means. Suppose the scientific names of all the kinds of insects were printed on a strip of paper, one below another in type like this. The strip of paper would be over 2 miles long! Suppose you set out to learn about insects by studying a different one every day. To finish, you would have to live more than 2,000 years!

Suppose, as another way of trying to get an idea of what 750,000 means, you were to picture a parade of all the kinds of animals in the world, with one kind of animal going by every minute day and night. The whole parade would last for nearly two years. It would take a year and a half just for the insects to go by.

There are not only many kinds of insects; there are also many insects of a kind. A single tree may have 20 million plant lice on it. A swarm of gnats may be made up of hundreds of thousands of gnats. At times there are plagues of grasshoppers. If all the people on the earth were scattered evenly over the land, there would be about 60 people for every square mile. If the insects were scattered evenly, for every square mile there probably would be at least 25 million! Insects may outnumber people more than a million to one.

The insects form one division—of course, the largest—of the arthropods. Sometimes insects are called hexapods. "Hexapod" means "six-footed." The name is a good one, for all insects have six legs. Their common name comes from the word "incised," which means "divided." An insect's body is divided into three parts—the head, thorax, and abdomen. You can see the three parts clearly in an ant. Notice in the picture that the legs are in pairs and that they all come from the thorax.

Cricket   Katydid

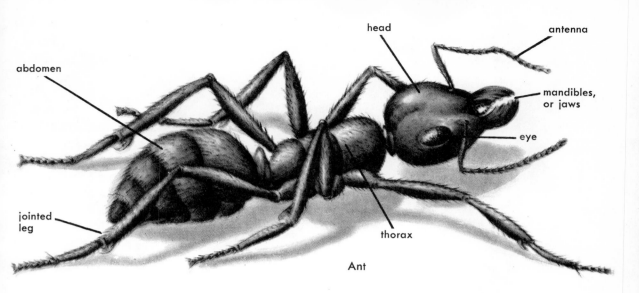

abdomen

head

antenna

mandibles, or jaws

eye

jointed leg

thorax

Ant

In addition to having three pairs of legs and three body regions, all insects are alike in having one pair of feelers, or antennas. They all have a covering of a remarkable substance called chitin. They therefore have a skeleton of a sort outside their bodies, just as many animals of the seashore do. In fact, the outside skeleton of crabs and their relatives is also made of chitin. Chitin is waterproof. It is very light, and it bends without breaking.

Most insects have compound eyes—eyes made up of many tiny eyes. Most of them, moreover, have wings. The ant pictured was chosen for showing the parts of an insect because it has no wings to hide the three

body regions. Ants, however, do have wings. In all but a few species of ants some individuals have wings, even though most do not. The ant in the picture is one of those without wings.

An insect as a rule has two pairs of wings. The butterfly's show clearly. All the winged insects in the parade below have two pairs even though, except for the flying grasshopper, only one pair shows. They hide the other pair. Some kinds of walking sticks also have two pairs of wings, but the kind in the parade has none.

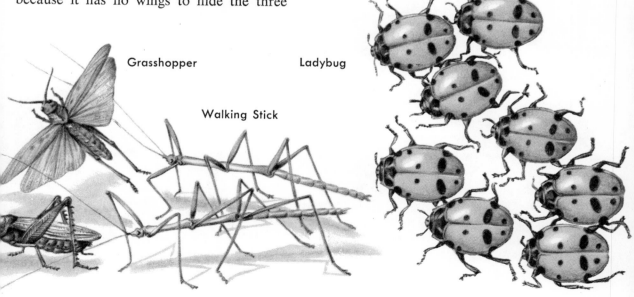

Grasshopper

Ladybug

Walking Stick

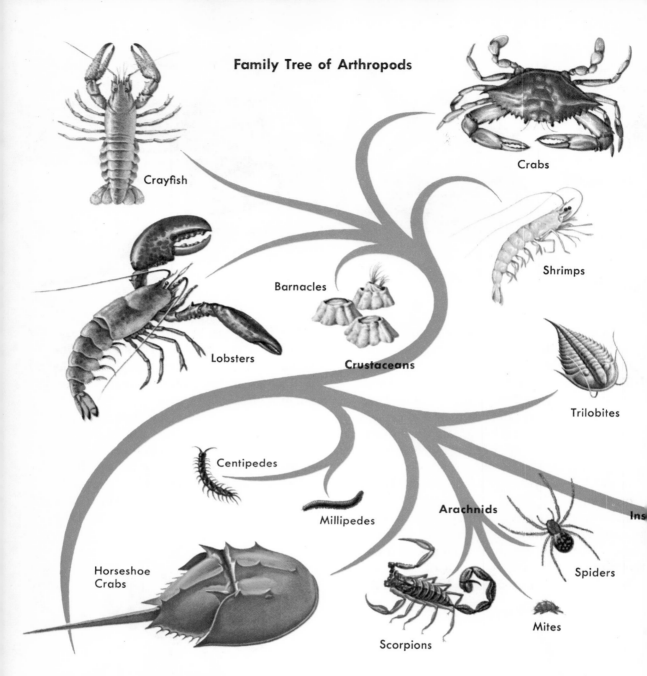

Family Tree of Arthropods

Crayfish

Crabs

Shrimps

Barnacles

Lobsters

Crustaceans

Trilobites

Centipedes

Millipedes

Arachnids

Ins

Horseshoe Crabs

Scorpions

Mites

Spiders

Insects live in more different kinds of places than do the animals of any other one group. There is almost no place on land that is not well stocked with them. The seashores and the mountains, the forests and the prairies, the hot lands near the equator and the cold lands near the poles, all have their insect populations. Insects teem in every pond and stream. They are not common in salt water, but even there, there are some. In Great Salt Lake, for example, there are huge numbers of a certain kind of fly. Almost none of the insects, however, live in or on the ocean.

The tree chart shows many of the insects' arthropod cousins as well as 14 of the more than 25 orders of insects. On one branch, you notice, are the ancient trilobites. Unlike them and many of the insects' other cousins, insects are air-breathers. Even those that breathe in water when they are babies are air-breathers as adults.

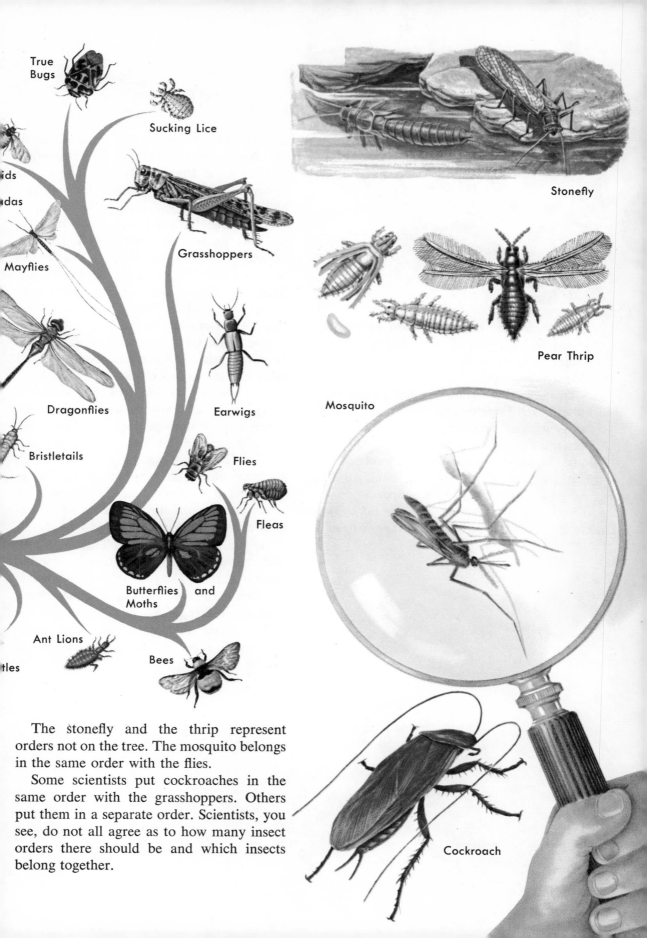

True Bugs

Sucking Lice

Grasshoppers

Mayflies

Dragonflies

Earwigs

Bristletails

Flies

Fleas

Butterflies and Moths

Ant Lions

Bees

Stonefly

Pear Thrip

Mosquito

Cockroach

The stonefly and the thrip represent orders not on the tree. The mosquito belongs in the same order with the flies.

Some scientists put cockroaches in the same order with the grasshoppers. Others put them in a separate order. Scientists, you see, do not all agree as to how many insect orders there should be and which insects belong together.

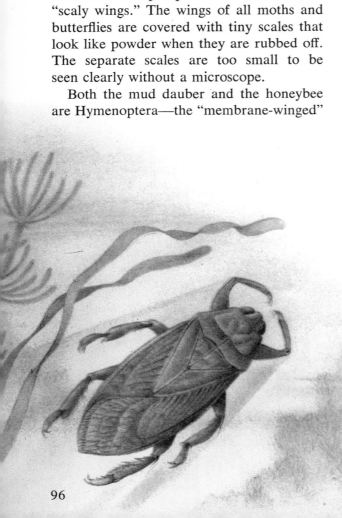

Mud Dauber

The scientific names of most orders of insects end in "ptera." This ending means "wings." Their wings are a big help in identifying insects.

The scientists' name for the moths and butterflies is Lepidoptera. The name means "scaly wings." The wings of all moths and butterflies are covered with tiny scales that look like powder when they are rubbed off. The separate scales are too small to be seen clearly without a microscope.

Both the mud dauber and the honeybee are Hymenoptera—the "membrane-winged"

insects. The giant water bug is a member of the Hemiptera, the "half wings." This order gets its name from the front wings of the insects in it. The wings are half leathery and half gauzy.

The name for the order which includes the flies, gnats, and mosquitoes is Diptera. "Diptera" means "two wings." The beetles make up the Coleoptera, or "sheath wings." There are over a dozen more orders with names that end in "ptera." The chart on page 369 lists some of them.

Every insect, to whatever order it belongs, needs oxygen and food. Insects are like all other animals in this way.

The insects have a system of tubes which carry air to all parts of their bodies. Air enters through tiny openings called *spiracles*. Some insects for at least a part of their lives have special breathing devices which fit their particular way of living. When young, for example, mosquitoes live in water and breathe through tubes which extend above the water.

As you would guess, not all the thousands and thousands of kinds of insects eat the same materials. The food of the four insects pictured here gives some idea of the variety of things insects eat.

The water bug lives on small water animals. It captures tadpoles, snails, other insects, and even small fish.

Giant
Water
Bug

Honeybee

The mud dauber, which is a kind of wasp, is a meat-eater when it is young but becomes a vegetarian later. In its babyhood it eats spiders. Mud daubers build a nest of mud. In each room of her nest a female mud dauber packs a spider or two and then lays an egg. When the young wasp comes out of the egg its spider food is ready. The adult wasps live on nectar, the sweet juice found in many flowers.

Honeybees eat honey and beebread. They make the honey from the nectar of flowers and the beebread from pollen, the yellow "dust" found in flowers, and nectar.

When young, the mourning cloak butterfly eats the leaves of elm, poplar, or willow trees. When full grown it, too, lives on nectar. Clearly, a giant water bug would starve on the food a mourning cloak eats, and the other way round.

But the story of these four insects and what they eat is only a small part of the whole story of insects and their food. The food of the hundreds of thousands of kinds of insects includes almost every variety of plant and animal material.

There is a race between people and insects for every bit of food that is raised. In a big field of sweet corn there is a great deal of food. But insects may get to the corn first and eat so much that there is little of it left for people. They may be busy eating the young green ears while people are waiting for them to ripen. Every "wormy" apple or tomato, every "buggy" bunch of broccoli, and every glass of jelly found crawling with ants after being left uncovered means a race won by insects.

Each part of a forest tree furnishes food for some kind of insect. Some insects drink the sap of the tree. Others eat the leaves, the bark, the young twigs, or the roots. After the tree has been cut down, there are other insects ready to eat both the green and the dried lumber.

In the same way, several different kinds of insects may be eating a cotton plant at the same time. There are insects that eat the young pods where the cotton is, others that suck the sap of the plant, and still others that nibble on its leaves or its roots or bore into its stalks.

Mourning
Cloak
Butterfly

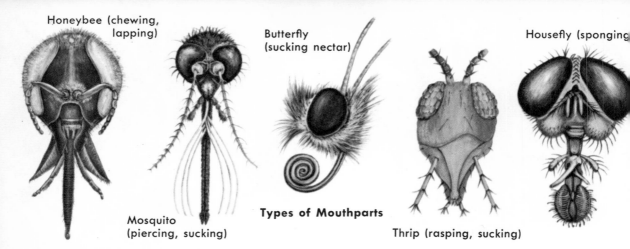

Honeybee (chewing, lapping)

Butterfly (sucking nectar)

Housefly (sponging)

Mosquito (piercing, sucking)

Types of Mouthparts

Thrip (rasping, sucking)

Fur, woolen goods, and blood—these are a few of the other things insects eat. People spend a fortune every year putting their furs and woolen clothing in cold storage so that clothes moths will not damage them. No one needs to be told that mosquitoes suck blood. Many people do not know, however, that only the adult female mosquitoes live on blood. The male mosquitoes live on plant juices. Young mosquitoes live on tiny water plants and animals. Anyone who has a dog or cat knows how carefully these pets have to be guarded against lice and fleas, which are also bloodsuckers. The ox louse is a pest on cattle. Too many on an animal do serious harm.

Some insects live part of their lives inside the bodies of other insects. An insect may, for example, lay its eggs inside the body of a caterpillar. When the eggs hatch, the young insects eat the caterpillar's body. The caterpillar, it goes without saying, dies.

Some meat-eating insects often attack dangerous prey. The picture below shows the tarantula hawk, one of the largest wasps, about to attack a tarantula, a poisonous spider much bigger than it is.

Some insects are cannibals. They eat up one another. It is not at all unusual for a female praying mantis to eat her mate. The lacewing fly lays its eggs in a special way that keeps the first lacewing flies that hatch from eating up either the remaining eggs or their brothers and sisters as they are just hatching. Each egg is put on the end of a little threadlike stalk so that it is not close to any other egg. You can see some stalked eggs on one of the leaves in the picture at the bottom of the next page.

Their mouthparts fit different insects for eating different kinds of food. The grasshopper, which eats leaves, has biting mouthparts. Its jaws grind up the plant material bitten off. The mouthparts of a grasshopper

Ox Louse

Tarantula Hawk Wasp and Tarantula

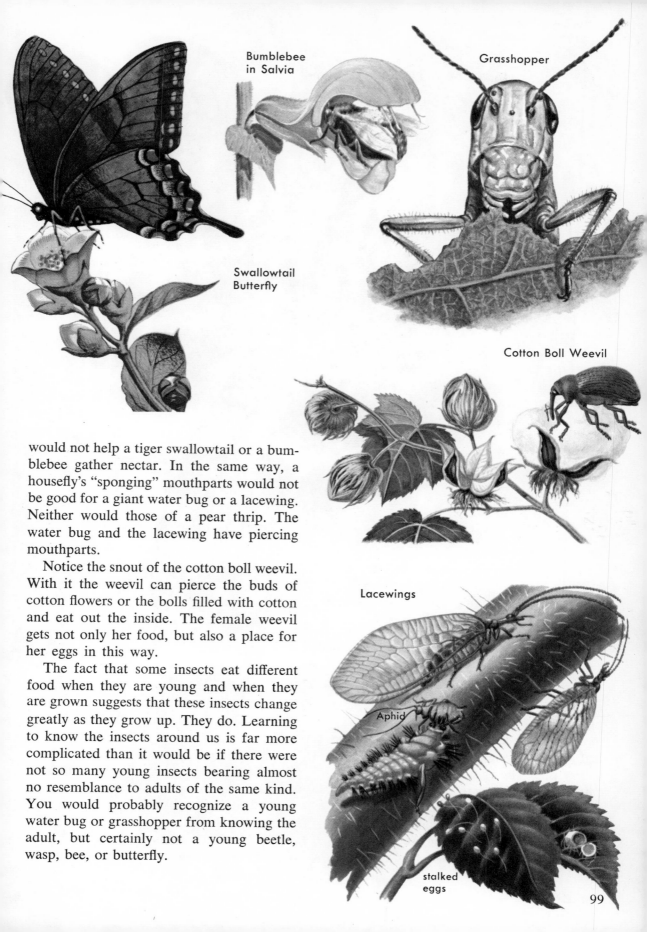

Bumblebee
in Salvia

Grasshopper

Swallowtail
Butterfly

Cotton Boll Weevil

would not help a tiger swallowtail or a bumblebee gather nectar. In the same way, a housefly's "sponging" mouthparts would not be good for a giant water bug or a lacewing. Neither would those of a pear thrip. The water bug and the lacewing have piercing mouthparts.

Notice the snout of the cotton boll weevil. With it the weevil can pierce the buds of cotton flowers or the bolls filled with cotton and eat out the inside. The female weevil gets not only her food, but also a place for her eggs in this way.

The fact that some insects eat different food when they are young and when they are grown suggests that these insects change greatly as they grow up. They do. Learning to know the insects around us is far more complicated than it would be if there were not so many young insects bearing almost no resemblance to adults of the same kind. You would probably recognize a young water bug or grasshopper from knowing the adult, but certainly not a young beetle, wasp, bee, or butterfly.

Lacewings

Aphid

stalked
eggs

99

adult

This beautiful moth, the cecropia, is one of the silk moths. The pictures on the next page help to tell its life history.

The female cecropia lays her eggs on the leaf of some plant, perhaps an apple or cherry tree. The eggs hatch into tiny black caterpillars, or *larvas*. A cecropia caterpillar does not look in the least like a full-grown moth. It shows no signs of wings or feelers. It has six short legs close to its head, but it also has several false legs on which it crawls along. Its body is clearly divided into many parts, or segments. The caterpillar's skin is studded with little bumps called tubercles.

Each caterpillar, or larva, begins at once to stuff itself with leaves. It grows fast and is soon too big for its skin. The skin has to be shed. Shedding one skin and getting another is called molting.

The black skin splits down the back, and out comes the caterpillar in a dull-orange

eggs

skin. The young insect keeps on eating and growing and is soon so big that it has to shed its orange skin.

The caterpillar's third "dress" is yellow. Some of its tubercles are bright colored. By the time it is yellow the caterpillar is more than an inch long, but it is not nearly full sized yet. It changes its skin twice more. After each of these molts, it is green with blue, red, and yellow tubercles. In the final stage, it is much bigger than in the next-to-last.

Of course, the caterpillar has to breathe while it is growing. It breathes just as adult insects do—through spiracles. Almost every segment of its body has a pair of spiracles.

A full-grown cecropia caterpillar is more than 3 inches long. After it reaches its full size, the caterpillar stops eating. It begins winding around and around its body a long thread of silk it spins from its mouth. At last the caterpillar is so well wrapped up that it cannot be seen. The larva has become a *pupa*.

The silken case the caterpillar spins is a cocoon. The caterpillar, as it makes its cocoon, fastens it firmly to a small branch or twig. At one end of the cocoon there is a weak spot, or door, through which the moth can push its way when it is ready. It is amazing that every cecropia caterpillar "knows" just how to spin its cocoon with a door. Of course, the caterpillar does not do any thinking about the matter. It inherits its way of making a cocoon, just as it inherits its legs, its spiracles, and its beautiful colors.

The pupa stage of a cecropia is often called its resting stage. But really great changes are taking place inside the silken cocoon. The caterpillar is changing into an adult moth.

A cecropia usually spends the whole winter in its cocoon. In the spring it pushes its way out. When it first emerges, its big wings are crumpled and moist. But soon the moth pumps a liquid into its wings so that they spread out. Soon, too, they dry.

By the time it comes out of its cocoon a cecropia's life is almost over. It eats nothing at all. Shortly it finds a mate. After eggs are laid, both moths die.

The life history of the cecropia can be readily told in just four words: egg, larva, pupa, adult. Many kinds of insects go through these same four stages. We say that these insects show *complete metamorphosis*. "Metamorphosis" means "change."

Life History of Cecropia Moth

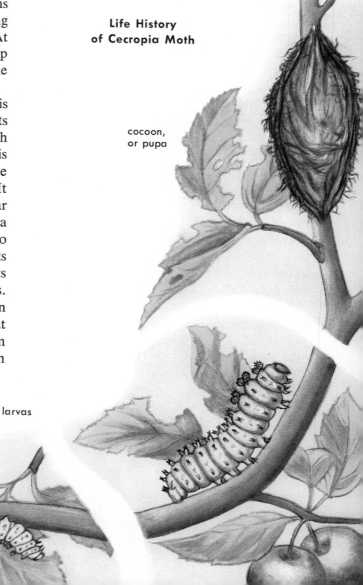

cocoon, or pupa

larvas

Grasshopper

A grasshopper has a pair of feelers, as all insects have. It has compound eyes, as most insects do. Between its compound eyes it has three simple eyes. This insect has, besides, a way of finding out what is going on around it that few insects have—it has ears. A grasshopper's ears are hidden under its wings.

Grasshoppers do not have voice boxes of any kind in their throats, but the sound grasshoppers make is well known. A grasshopper makes this sound either by rubbing its two front wings together or by rubbing a leg and a wing together.

Grasshoppers have jaws strong enough to chew even tough leaves. They eat tender leaves when they can get them, but they do not go hungry just because there are no tender leaves to be had. When a grasshopper is eating a leaf, it usually holds the leaf between its two front feet.

A grasshopper has two habits that anyone who watches grasshoppers soon learns to know. It keeps itself well groomed by cleaning itself up often. It "washes" its face with its front legs. It cleans each feeler by holding it down on the ground with one foot and then pulling it out from under the foot. It cleans its legs by rubbing them together.

Its second habit is less pleasant. At times it spits out a brown liquid often spoken of as "tobacco juice." Probably the juice helps protect this insect from birds that might relish a grasshopper dinner.

The grasshopper in the picture is a short-horned grasshopper that is often called the American locust. Its feelers are much shorter than its body. There are long-horned grasshoppers, too. The katydids are long-horned grasshoppers.

The grasshopper and dragonfly are good examples of insects that do not have four stages in their life history. They go through only three—egg, nymph, and adult.

With her egg-laying organ—an ovipositor, it is called—a female grasshopper lays a cluster of white eggs in a hole she makes in the ground or in rotten wood.

Little grasshoppers that look much like their parents hatch from the eggs. There are two big differences between these young grasshoppers, or grasshopper nymphs, and their parents. They are much smaller, and they have no wings.

As each nymph grows, it molts five or six times. When, after a few weeks, it changes its skin for the last time, it is full grown and has two pairs of strong wings. Many people are surprised to find that a grasshopper has two pairs of wings. Only one pair shows unless the grasshopper is flying. The second pair is folded up under the pair that shows.

Even as a nymph a grasshoper has hind legs that are much longer and stronger than its four other legs. These back legs are excellent for jumping.

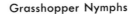

Grasshopper Nymphs

The dragonfly has several nicknames. "Devil's darning needle" and "snake doctor" are two of them. Its long, slender body explains why it might be called a darning needle. With its needle-shaped body, however, the dragonfly never pricks or stings. We can only wonder why it should have "devil" in its nickname and why it should be called a snake doctor.

This insect begins its life in the water of some pond or stream. The female lays her eggs in the water. She may simply drop them in the water. She may fasten them to some plant.

The eggs hatch into nymphs that, unlike grasshopper nymphs, do not look at all like their parents. You would probably never guess from seeing a dragonfly nymph crawling in the water that it would grow up to be one of the handsomest of insects.

The most remarkable part of a dragonfly nymph is its lower lip. This lip is long and, strange as it sounds, jointed. The young insect hides among the water plants. When something it might eat swims or floats by, out goes the creature's long lip. Then back comes the lip with the food.

The dragonfly nymph grows and molts just as the grasshopper nymph does. But it grows up rather slowly. It remains in the water for two or three years.

After the two or three years underwater, the dragonfly nymph climbs up above the surface. It sheds its skin for the last time, spreads its silvery new wings, and flies away a full-grown dragonfly. In the picture the empty discarded skin is clinging like a ghost to a water plant.

The adult dragonfly is remarkable not only for the beauty of its wings, but also for

Dragonfly

its huge eyes. Almost all insects have compound eyes, but the dragonfly has especially large ones. Each eye may be made up of as many as 30,000 tiny eyes. A dragonfly does not lose its appetite when it emerges as an adult. It darts through the air catching insects as it goes. Its front legs serve as a basket for trapping insect prey, usually flies, gnats, and mosquitoes.

Many other insects have life histories much like those of the grasshopper and the dragonfly. They show *incomplete metamorphosis*. Some of them change rather gradually to their adult form as the grasshopper does. Some seem to change suddenly as the dragonfly does. None of these insects have a stage that corresponds to the pupa of the insects with complete metamorphosis.

Dragonfly Nymphs

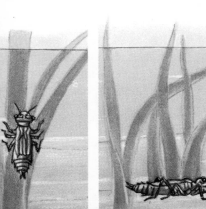

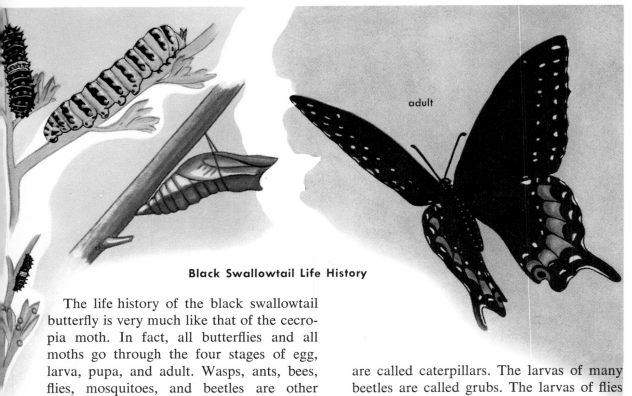

adult

Black Swallowtail Life History

The life history of the black swallowtail butterfly is very much like that of the cecropia moth. In fact, all butterflies and all moths go through the four stages of egg, larva, pupa, and adult. Wasps, ants, bees, flies, mosquitoes, and beetles are other insects with four stages in their life cycle.

We have different common names for the larvas of different kinds of insects. As you know, the larvas of moths and butterflies

Periodical Cicada Life History

are called caterpillars. The larvas of many beetles are called grubs. The larvas of flies are maggots, and those of mosquitoes are wrigglers or wigglers or wiggle-tails. Caddis-fly larvas are called caddisworms. The wormlike bodies of the two pictured are hidden in the "houses" these strange insects build for themselves out of sand, small pebbles, and bits of plants.

The larvas of some species have special common names of their own. The larva of the cankerworm moth, for example, is called a measuring worm, an inchworm, or a looper. You can see how it gets these names. The caterpillar of the Isabella tiger moth is the well-known woolly bear. It is so hairy that it deserves the name. The orange puppy is the caterpillar of the giant swallowtail. Its looks and its smell probably help protect it. The bag the caterpillar of the bagworm moth lives in, and later uses as its cocoon, is seen much more often than the moth itself. The bag, of course, gives the moth its name.

The pupa stage of an insect goes by different names, too. The pupa of a butter-fly, for instance, is often called a chrysalis. That of a moth is a cocoon. The chrysalis of a monarch butterfly is beautiful, as its picture shows. It is sometimes described as a "green house with golden nails." In contrast, the cocoon of the lovely luna moth looks like a ball of dead leaves.

After insects that show complete metamorphosis reach the final stage, they do not grow. Any fly one sees flying about is as large as it will ever be. In the same way, as soon as a moth, butterfly, beetle, bee, or wasp has wings, it has reached its full size.

The periodical cicada has a life history much like that of the dragonfly. One species takes what is for an insect a very long time to grow up. It is called the seventeen-year locust. A nymph spends 17 years underground, sucking the juice from roots. Then it crawls out of the ground, climbs up on a tree or post, and emerges from its skin as a gauzy-winged insect.

Some insects are born alive. With some flies and mayflies, for instance, the eggs hatch inside the body of the female and the larvas are born. Some generations of aphids, or plant lice, are females that instead of laying eggs give birth to aphids much like themselves. But such life histories as these are not common among insects.

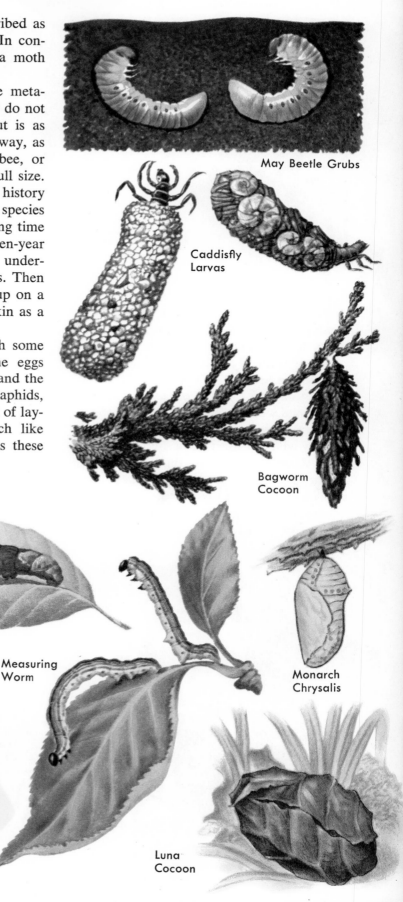

May Beetle Grubs

Caddisfly Larvas

Bagworm Cocoon

Orange Puppy

Woolly Bear

Measuring Worm

Monarch Chrysalis

Luna Cocoon

Butterfly

Moth

The scaly-winged insects—the moths and butterflies—are well known to many people. Almost everyone can call some by name.

Moths outnumber butterflies, so far as kinds are concerned, many times over. But moths as a rule fly by night and are not so likely to be seen, while butterflies flit about in the daytime. Most of us are better acquainted with butterflies than with moths.

There are several helps in telling whether a scaly-winged insect is a butterfly or a moth. Moths have rather thick bodies and big heads; butterflies as a rule have more slender bodies and smaller heads. Notice how slim the body of the cloudless sulphur, a butterfly, is in comparison with the body of the ailanthus, a moth. Moths usually rest with their wings held horizontally or in the rooflike position the widow underwing and the carpenter moth hold theirs. Butterflies, when they alight, usually fold their wings together so that they make a kind of sail above them. More helpful as a way of telling moths from butterflies are the antennas. Butterflies have clubbed antennas. The feelers of moths may look like feathers, as those of the ailanthus and the cecropia do. They may, on the other hand, be plain. Unfortunately for this moth-or-butterfly rule, there are a few moths with antennas clubbed like a butterfly's.

The skippers are all rather small butterflies. They make up a somewhat puzzling group of scaly-wings. There is even some question as to whether they should be called

male

female

Cloudless
Sulphur

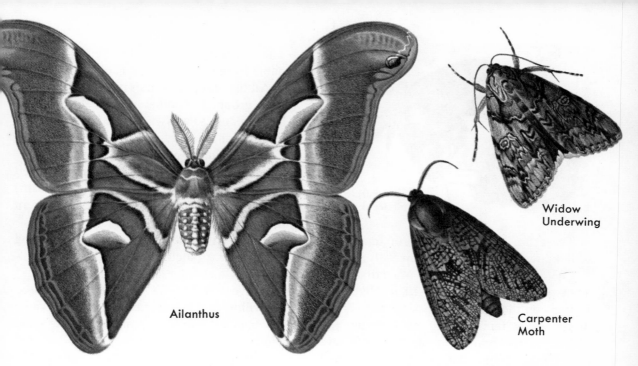

Ailanthus

Widow Underwing

Carpenter Moth

butterflies, because they are more like moths in some ways. They have, for example, rather stout bodies and big heads. Their pupas are much like moth cocoons. But skippers flit about in the daytime like butterflies, and their antennas are clubbed.

The smallest skipper has a wingspread of less than half an inch. There are moths only one-third as big. In contrast, some moths measure a foot across. And there are giant butterflies measuring almost, if not quite, as much with wings spread out.

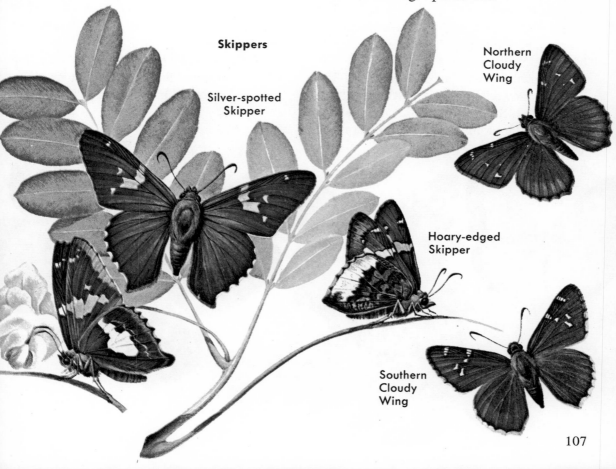

Skippers

Silver-spotted Skipper

Northern Cloudy Wing

Hoary-edged Skipper

Southern Cloudy Wing

107

Great Purple
Hairstreak

These are all butterflies. You may very well know a number of them.

There are many kinds of hairstreaks. They get their name from the hairlike projections on their hind wings. Hairstreaks are in the same family with the coppers and blues. All the butterflies of the family are rather small. One, the pigmy blue, is tied with the smallest skipper as the tiniest of all butterflies.

The orange sulphur is, of course, a close relative of the cloudless sulphur already pictured. Sulphurs are worldwide butterflies. Their name comes from their color. Dozens of these butterflies may make a yellow cloud over a puddle or a field of clover or alfalfa. The orange sulphur is often called the alfalfa butterfly.

Swallowtails are large butterflies. The giant swallowtail is the largest butterfly in the United States. It, you remember, is known as the orange puppy as a caterpillar.

The orange puppy gets the "orange" in its name from its food, not its color.

All the other butterflies pictured here were long grouped together in one big family. Now many scientists divide them among several families.

The monarch, one of our largest and best-known butterflies, is the common milkweed butterfly—its larva eats milkweed leaves. This butterfly is the one that comes from the "green house with golden nails."

Regal fritillaries are often seen flitting about over a patch of violets. The caterpillars eat violet leaves.

The caterpillars of the purples pictured eat willow and aspen leaves. You may know the banded purple by another name—the white admiral.

The question mark, named from marks on the underside of its wings, is an anglewing. The edges of its wings look as if pieces had been snipped out with scissors.

There are many species of checkerspots. Each species varies so in color and pattern that it is hard to tell one from another.

The zebra butterfly is a stray from tropical America. In the United States it is found only in the South.

The common wood nymph, as its name tells, is common. So is the food of its caterpillar. The caterpillar eats grass.

Orange Sulphur   underside   Regal Fritillary

Monarch

Banded Purple

Eastern
Tailed Blue

Spring Azure

Red-spotted
Purple

Marine Blue

Western
Pigmy Blue

Common
Wood Nymph

Checkerspot

Giant
Swallowtail

Purplish
Copper

Bronze Copper

Question
Mark

Zebra

American
Copper

Three of the moths pictured here—the io, polyphemus, and luna—are close relatives of the cecropia and ailanthus. All are silk moths, named from the silk they spin for their cocoons. Many people consider the luna the most beautiful of all insects. Another close relative is the imperial, an emperor moth. Emperors and silk moths are often put in the same family.

The great owlet and the black witch are both owlet moths. The name comes from the way the eyes of these moths shine in the dark. If the great owlet were shown here full size, there would not be room for much else, for this giant moth measures a foot across. Closely related to the owlets is the little eight-spotted forester.

You are much more likely to know the Isabella caterpillar, the woolly bear, than you are to know the adult moth. This pretty moth is one of the tiger moths, so named for their tiger colors.

The five-spotted hawkmoth, the white-lined sphinx, and the hummingbird moth are sphinx moths. The way the caterpillars of sphinx moths hold their heads when resting reminded people of the famous Egyptian sphinx. These moths are often mistaken for hummingbirds as they hover over flowers to sip nectar. Many people know all too well the caterpillar of the five-spotted hawkmoth. It is the tomato worm.

Eight-spotted Forester

Imperial

Isabella

Black Witch

Io

110

Hummingbird Moth

Five-spotted Hawkmoth

White-lined
Sphinx

Luna

Polyphemus

Great
Owlet

111

Firefly

Bombardier Beetle

Six-spotted Tiger Beetle

Mealworm Beetle

Purple Tiger Beetle

Ox Beetle

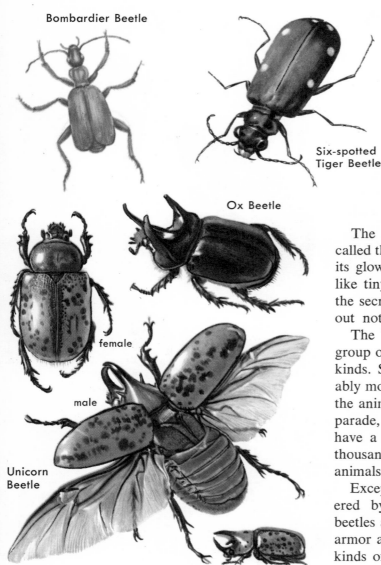

female

male

Unicorn Beetle

The firefly is a beetle. It is sometimes called the lightning bug. This insect can turn its glow on and off so that the flashes are like tiny sparks of lightning. Fireflies have the secret of cold light—that is, light without noticeable heat.

The beetles make up by far the largest group of insects. There are at least 100,000 kinds. Scientists think that there are probably more than a quarter of a million. If all the animals were to march two by two in a parade, every animal with a backbone could have a beetle partner and there would be thousands of beetles left to pair up with animals without backbones.

Except when flying, a beetle is well covered by its hard front wings. Probably beetles are successful partly because of that armor and partly because they eat so many kinds of food that they seldom go hungry.

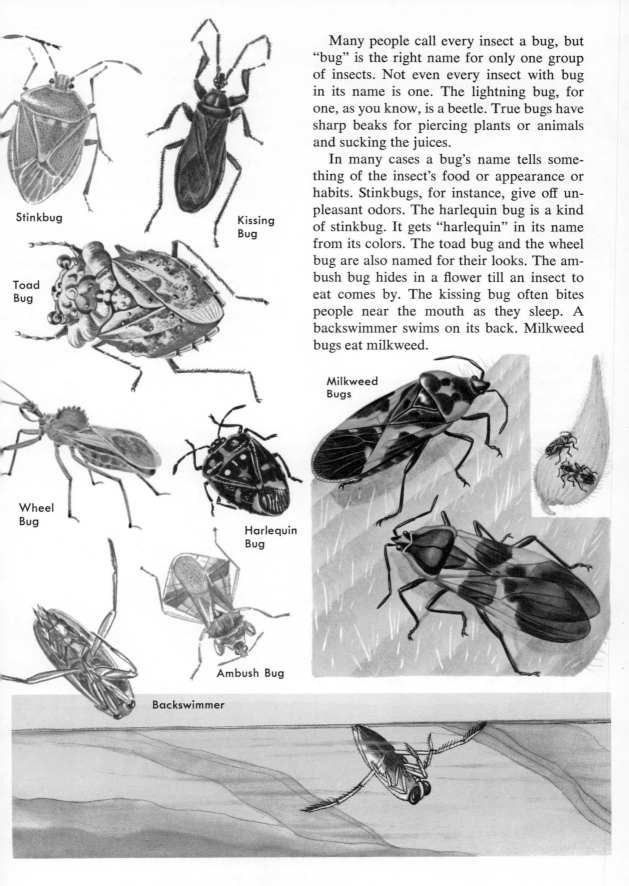

Many people call every insect a bug, but "bug" is the right name for only one group of insects. Not even every insect with bug in its name is one. The lightning bug, for one, as you know, is a beetle. True bugs have sharp beaks for piercing plants or animals and sucking the juices.

In many cases a bug's name tells something of the insect's food or appearance or habits. Stinkbugs, for instance, give off unpleasant odors. The harlequin bug is a kind of stinkbug. It gets "harlequin" in its name from its colors. The toad bug and the wheel bug are also named for their looks. The ambush bug hides in a flower till an insect to eat comes by. The kissing bug often bites people near the mouth as they sleep. A backswimmer swims on its back. Milkweed bugs eat milkweed.

Stinkbug

Kissing Bug

Toad Bug

Wheel Bug

Harlequin Bug

Ambush Bug

Backswimmer

Milkweed Bugs

113

Honeybee in
Apple Blossom

The tomato worm does a great deal of damage by eating the leaves of tomato and tobacco plants. It is one of the insects that we count as our enemies.

There are a great many harmful insects. A common term for them is insect pests. They harm us in different ways. Many of them are our enemies simply because they eat food that we want for ourselves or keep plants from producing food we need. There are crop pests, orchard pests, garden pests, and insects that eat stored food. Some insects do great harm to our shade trees and forest trees. Some ruin buildings we have built and others clothes we have made. The most dangerous of the insect pests are those that carry disease.

So many insects harm us that many people think of all insects as our enemies. To them simply saying, "It's a bug," is a legitimate excuse for killing any insect on sight. But we have good friends among the insects, too.

Many insects help by visiting flowers and carrying pollen from one flower to another. By carrying pollen they help seeds and fruits to form. Without insect pollen-carriers we would have no apples, no peaches, no clover seed—the list would be long.

The earth would lose much of its beauty if the pollen-carrying insects were to disappear. For if no seeds were formed, most flowering plants would soon die out. The beautiful yucca of our deserts—the "candle of God," it is sometimes called—would vanish if it were not for the yucca moth.

We get valuable products from some insects. Honey and silk are probably the two most important. Honey, of course, is made by honeybees. Silk comes from the cocoons spun by the larvas of the silkworm moth. Shellac, used in varnishes, is made from secretions of the lac insects. And some insects furnish useful drugs.

Some insects help us by eating insect pests. Ladybug beetles, for instance, eat plant lice. The beetles called caterpillar

Yucca Moth

Yucca

Silkworm

hunters, both as larvas and adults, search out and destroy the caterpillars of various moths harmful to trees.

There are some important insect scavengers. Tumblebugs are among them. They eat up much dead animal matter and waste.

Some insects have high food value. Ants gorged with honeydew, the sweet secretion of plant lice and scale insects, are prized in Mexico. Grasshoppers, water boatmen, termites, and stinkbugs are other insects eaten in different parts of the world. Indirectly, insects furnish us much food by serving as food for freshwater fishes we eat.

A number of insects help us fight weeds. When the prickly pear cactus was introduced into Australia, it spread rapidly and was soon a troublesome weed. As a way of fighting this weed, insects that feed on it were shipped to Australia. It was the cactus moth, sent there from Argentina, that finally brought the weed under control.

Some insects are good guinea pigs for science. One kind of fruit fly has been much used in the study of heredity.

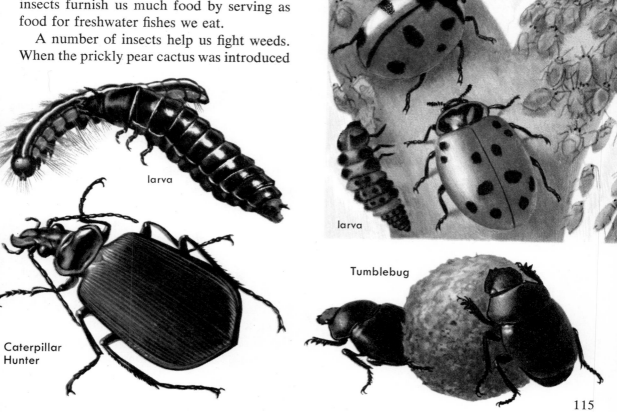

Ladybugs

larva

larva

Caterpillar Hunter

Tumblebug

115

Praying Mantis

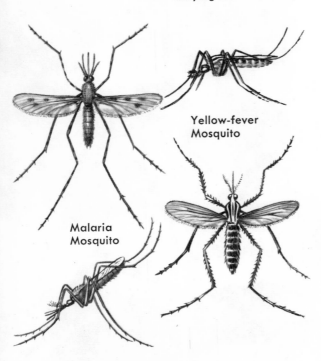

Malaria
Mosquito

Yellow-fever
Mosquito

We count the praying mantis as a good friend. It is such an enemy of harmful insects that some plant nurseries have praying mantis eggs for sale. The other insects pictured here are our enemies.

Of course, the insects that are our friends do not deserve any credit for being helpful. Neither do those that harm us deserve any blame for the damage they do. The insects are simply living their own lives. It happens that in living their lives some of them make things we want or help us in other ways. It happens that others in living their lives interfere with ours.

There were no insect pests and no insect friends before man lived on the earth. During the Coal Age, for example, there were giant cockroaches. But they were not pests, for there were no people for them to interfere with. The first honeybees were not friends, for there were no people for them to help. When we think of insects as being friends or enemies, we are being selfish. We are thinking only of ourselves and how the insects help or harm us.

But we cannot afford to be unselfish in thinking of insects. They are our greatest rivals. To hold our own against them we have to carry on a never-ending battle.

High on the list of insect enemies are mosquitoes of certain kinds. Malaria and yellow fever are two of the diseases they carry. The common housefly is not only a nuisance, but also a danger because it carries typhoid and tuberculosis germs. The tsetse fly has spread over four and a half million square miles in Africa, carrying sleeping sickness with it. Fleas and body lice both carry typhus. Fleas also carry bubonic plague, the dreaded Black Death of the Middle Ages.

The insects pictured on this page attack plants. They are all serious pests.

The cabbage butterfly, when it is a caterpillar, eats cabbage. It is one of the few black sheep among the butterflies. Most butterflies are helpful, or at least not harmful. We have a great many more enemies among the moths.

The codling moth is often called the apple worm. This insect is to blame for many of our wormy apples.

Japanese beetles are not at all particular about their food. They destroy the leaves, blossoms, and fruits of nearly 300 different kinds of plants.

The gypsy moth is one of the worst enemies of our forest and shade trees. Its caterpillars eat the leaves of the trees. Late in the 1860's, a scientist brought specimens of this moth to the United States for an experiment. Some of the moths escaped to the woods nearby. Since that time, the gypsy moth has done damage amounting to millions of dollars to the trees of New England.

Many others of our insect pests have also been brought to our country from other lands. The cabbage butterfly, boll weevil, European corn borer, and Japanese beetle are among our insect immigrants.

Cabbage Butterfly

Codling Moth

Japanese Beetle

Gypsy Moth

female

male

larva

These insects, too, attack plants. The harm some of them do comes more from plant diseases they spread than from damage they themselves do. Cucumber beetles, for example, carry a disease from vine to vine.

Like the cucumber beetle, several of these insects are named for plants they attack. Of those that are not, the chinch bug is mainly a pest of corn and sorghum, the army worm destroys alfalfa, cotton, and grains, and the tussock moth attacks our shade trees. The flat-headed borer also attacks trees. The tarnished plant bug feeds on a great variety of plants from strawberries to fruit trees and peonies.

It goes without saying that many ways of fighting insect pests have been worked out. But fighting them is not easy. One problem is to get rid of them without at the same time killing helpful insects. And we do not wish to harm the plants the pests are on or the other animals, including ourselves, that may eat the plants.

We can set traps for some kinds of insects. A band of sticky gum around a tree acts as a trap for caterpillars that try to climb the tree. It is a common way of protecting trees from the tussock moth. There are light traps that attract some night-flying insects. Trenches filled with oil have been used to trap other pests. One has to know a great deal about an insect before he can set a good trap for it. The army worm, the larva of a moth, gets its name because it moves in great armies from one field to another. An oil-filled trench is a good trap for marching army worms. It would be of no use in fighting mosquitoes.

Removing breeding places is an excellent way of fighting some insects. It makes better sense to try to keep them from multiplying than to kill them after they are at work against us. Many swamps have been drained as a way of getting rid of mosquitoes. Clearing away piles of garbage and manure takes away the chief breeding places of the common housefly.

The most widely used way of fighting insects is with chemicals. The chemicals are

Army Worm

of two kinds: stomach poisons and contact poisons. Some are both kinds in one. Some, for example, kill insects on contact when they are first sprayed on plants. Later, after they have been absorbed by the plants, they act as stomach poisons to insects that chew or bore into the plants or suck the juices.

Contact poisons may do their work by stopping up an insect's spiracles. They may eat their way through the chitin into the insect's body.

Unfortunately, insects build up resistance to chemicals used in fighting them. DDT, when it was first used, was thought to be the final answer to many of our insect problems. It is used to kill insects of many kinds. But now there are strains of these insects that are not affected by it. We have to keep on developing new insecticides.

We can use germ warfare against some caterpillar pests—the tomato worm, the cabbage worm, and the caterpillar of the gypsy moth among others. Plants the caterpillars eat are treated with a spray containing disease germs that kill the caterpillars.

A region in which there is a serious insect pest is sometimes quarantined to keep the pest from spreading. Nothing that might carry the pest can be carried or shipped from the region. The Mediterranean fruit fly was kept from spreading from Florida by quarantine. Of course, no one person can manage a quarantine. It has to be set up by a state or federal government.

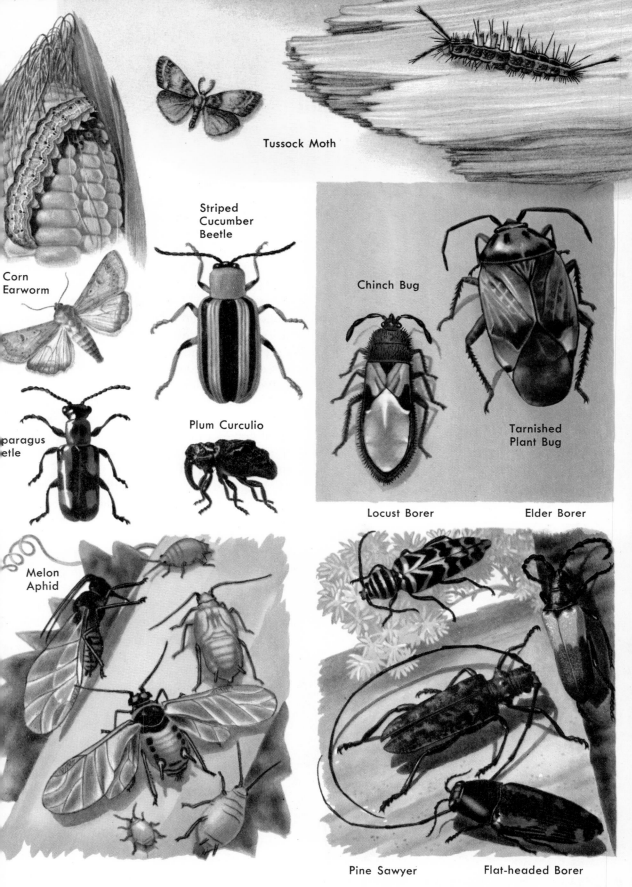

Tussock Moth

Corn Earworm

Striped Cucumber Beetle

Chinch Bug

Tarnished Plant Bug

paragus etle

Plum Curculio

Locust Borer

Elder Borer

Melon Aphid

Pine Sawyer

Flat-headed Borer

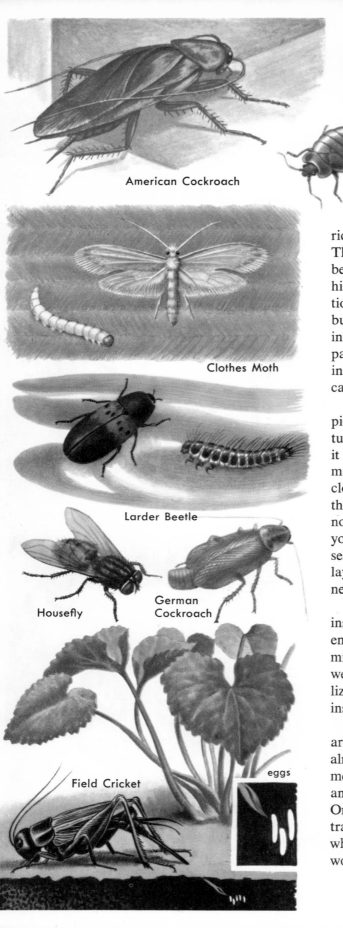

American Cockroach

Carpet Beetles

Bedbug

Clothes Moth

Larder Beetle

Housefly

German Cockroach

Field Cricket

eggs

In cities it is easy to get help in getting rid of insect pests found inside buildings. There are exterminating companies that can be called on. The owners of some buildings hire such companies to make regular inspections and get rid of any insect pests. If a building or a part of it is found to be badly infested, an exterminator may seal all or part of it up and use poison gas to kill the insects. The use of poison gas in this way is called fumigation.

It may surprise you to see the field cricket pictured here with household pests. The natural home of this insect is out of doors. But it sometimes comes into houses, where it may do harm. It may, for instance, ruin clothing and household linens. A cricket in the house, however, is not likely to go unnoticed long. Its loud, cheerful chirp tells you it is there. Field crickets, moreover, seldom settle in a house and multiply. They lay their eggs in the ground, often in gardens near houses.

One of the very best means of fighting insect pests is to encourage their natural enemies. Birds are among the natural enemies of insects. A baby bird may eat its weight in insects every day. Frogs, toads, lizards, snakes, and certain fishes are other insect-eaters of importance.

Many of an insect pest's natural enemies are other insects. Praying mantis eggs, you already know, are sold by some nurserymen. You know, too, that caterpillar hunters and ladybug beetles destroy harmful insects. One kind of ladybug brought in from Australia saved the California orange orchards when it looked as if the cottony cushion scale would ruin them.

Three other insects that fight on our side are pictured below. The tachina fly is laying eggs on a gypsy moth caterpillar. Some of these tiny flies were brought over from Europe to help fight the gypsy moth. Ichneumon wasps are other insects that destroy harmful insects by laying their eggs in the larvas. The caterpillar of the harvester butterfly eats aphids.

Developing plants and animals that can better stand the attacks of insects is another hopeful way of fighting insect pests. Changing crops often in a field—crop rotation—is still another way. But the problem of holding our own against our insect enemies is so big that every once in a while someone asks the question, "Will the insects win?"

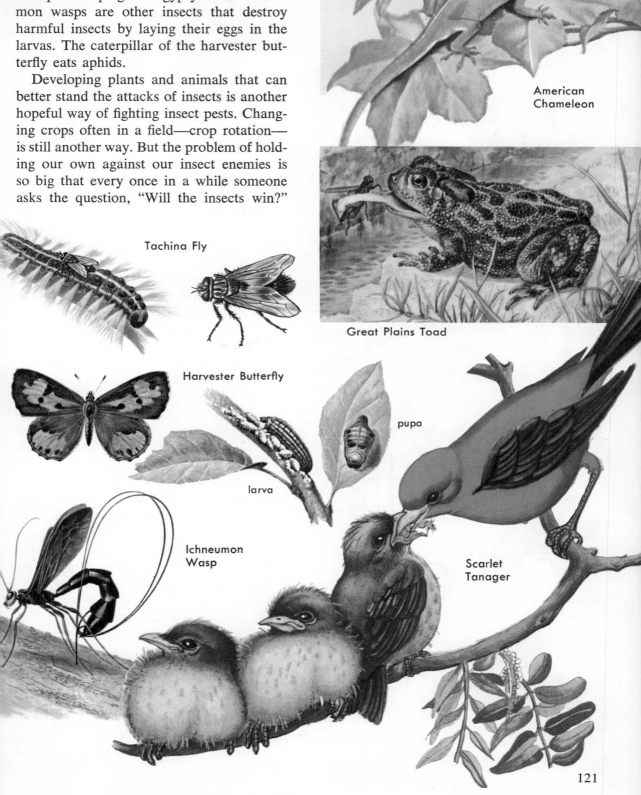

American Chameleon

Great Plains Toad

Tachina Fly

Harvester Butterfly

larva

pupa

Ichneumon Wasp

Scarlet Tanager

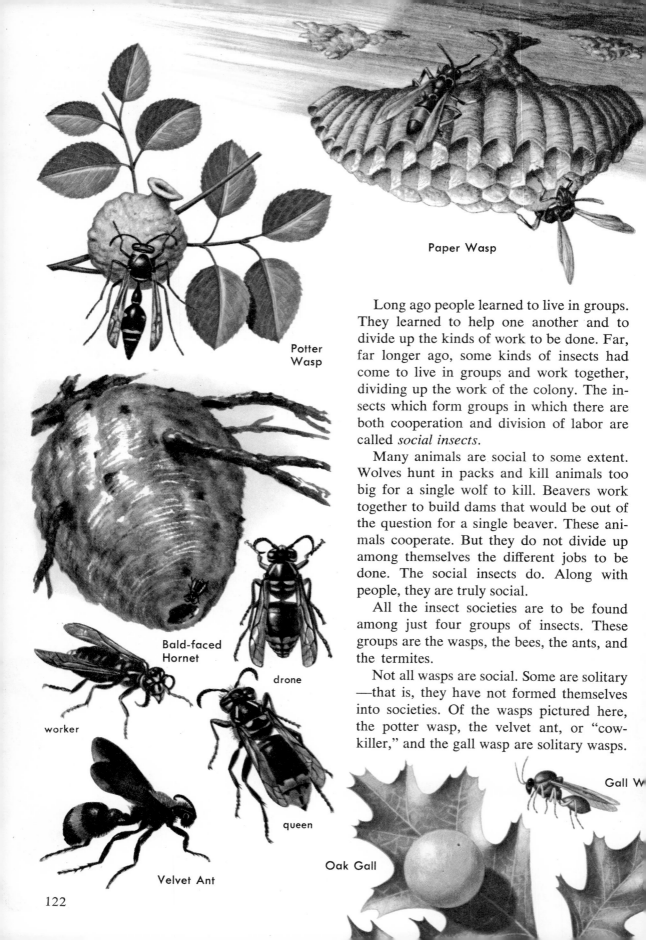

Paper Wasp

Potter Wasp

Bald-faced Hornet

worker

drone

queen

Velvet Ant

Oak Gall

Gall W

Long ago people learned to live in groups. They learned to help one another and to divide up the kinds of work to be done. Far, far longer ago, some kinds of insects had come to live in groups and work together, dividing up the work of the colony. The insects which form groups in which there are both cooperation and division of labor are called *social insects*.

Many animals are social to some extent. Wolves hunt in packs and kill animals too big for a single wolf to kill. Beavers work together to build dams that would be out of the question for a single beaver. These animals cooperate. But they do not divide up among themselves the different jobs to be done. The social insects do. Along with people, they are truly social.

All the insect societies are to be found among just four groups of insects. These groups are the wasps, the bees, the ants, and the termites.

Not all wasps are social. Some are solitary —that is, they have not formed themselves into societies. Of the wasps pictured here, the potter wasp, the velvet ant, or "cow-killer," and the gall wasp are solitary wasps.

The paper wasp and the bald-faced hornet are social.

The colonies of the paper wasp are small. A colony is made up of the queen—a female that lays eggs—a few male wasps, or drones, and a number of worker wasps. The workers are females that do not lay eggs. They find food and take care of the queen and the larvas that hatch from her eggs. The different kinds of individuals in an insect society are called *castes*. There are three castes in a society of paper wasps.

There are the same three castes in a nest of bald-faced hornets. But there are usually several thousand wasps in each nest.

Even a colony of bald-faced hornets is small beside a colony, or hive, of honeybees. In a beehive there may be 80,000 bees.

In a honeybee hive there are the same three castes as in a wasp nest—the queen, the drones, and the worker females. In a wasp colony only the queen lives through the winter. Many honeybee workers, as well as the queen, do. They live on the honey they have stored up.

The making of honey is complicated. It involves several different kinds of work—hunting for flowers, gathering nectar from them, building comb, filling it with honey made from the nectar, and capping the cells to seal the honey in. There are many housekeeping chores to be done in a hive, too. Among them are taking care of the queen bee, keeping the hive clean, ventilating it by fanning fresh air in, feeding the baby bees, and mending any cracks that appear in the hive. Worker bees also protect the hive from intruders. They have good weapons—stings. But if a worker has to sting an enemy, she is giving up her life for the group. For she cannot pull out her sting, and without it she dies.

Bumblebees are social, too, but their societies are simple. There are seldom more than 500 workers. Only queen bumblebees live through the winter. As with the wasps, some bees are solitary.

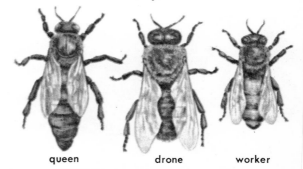

queen   drone   worker

Honeybee

Ants

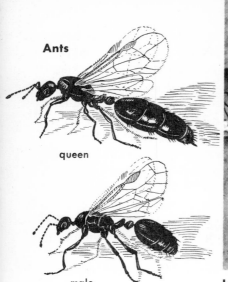

queen

male

worker

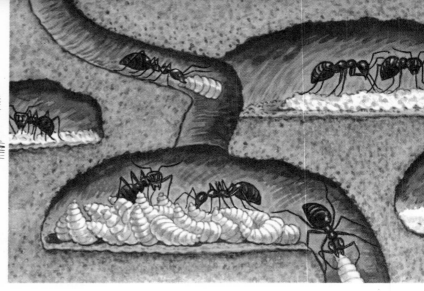

Inside an Ant Nest

egg

pupa

larva

adult

All ants are social. Some live in rather simple societies. But some ant societies are almost unbelievably complex. In many there are several castes of workers. In some there is a special caste called soldiers. As one would guess, their work is to protect the colony from attack. They have especially powerful jaws.

Among the most remarkable ant societies are those of the army ants and the leaf-cutter, or parasol, ants. Both have soldier castes and other workers of several sizes.

Army ants eat other insects. They move slowly about in large armies searching for food beneath the litter on the floor of a forest. If the trail is rough, worker ants make it smooth by filling in the hollows with their own bodies. Where there is a gap in the trail, workers hang on to one another to form a bridge over the gap. When an army stops to

Parasol Ants

124

rest, workers may even build themselves into a nest of many rooms. As soon as the army is ready to move on, the walls fall apart to become the separate workers that formed them.

Parasol ants raise underground gardens of fungus plants much like tiny mushrooms. They cut up leaves and bring them to their gardens for the fungus plants to grow on.

Some ants have domesticated animals, among them ant "cows." Ant cows are aphids. The ants take care of the aphids and protect them from enemies. The aphids in turn give off the sweet juice honeydew when the ants stroke them with their feelers. The ants eat the honeydew.

All termites, too, are social. Termite castes differ in one way from the castes of wasps, bees, and ants. All the workers among the wasps, bees, and ants are females.

There are both male and female workers among the termites.

The biggest colonies of termites make even the biggest colonies of the other social insects seem small. A single termite colony may have several million workers in it. A termite queen has been known to lay from 8,000 to 10,000 eggs in one day. It is not surprising that such an egg-laying machine has a large body.

In some ways an insect society is far ahead of a community of people. Every individual that is old enough to work has work to do: there is no unemployment. Each one knows exactly how to carry on its work without having to be taught how. There is no quarreling between members of the group. But neither is there any freedom. Our own human society, in spite of its faults, is much better for us.

Termites

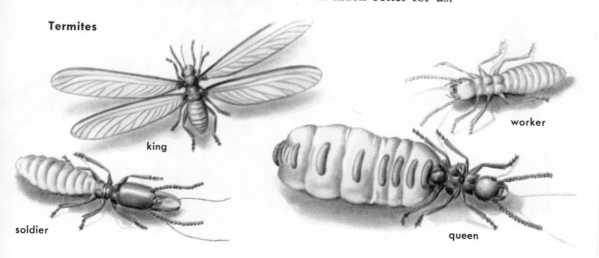

king

worker

soldier

queen

Spiders

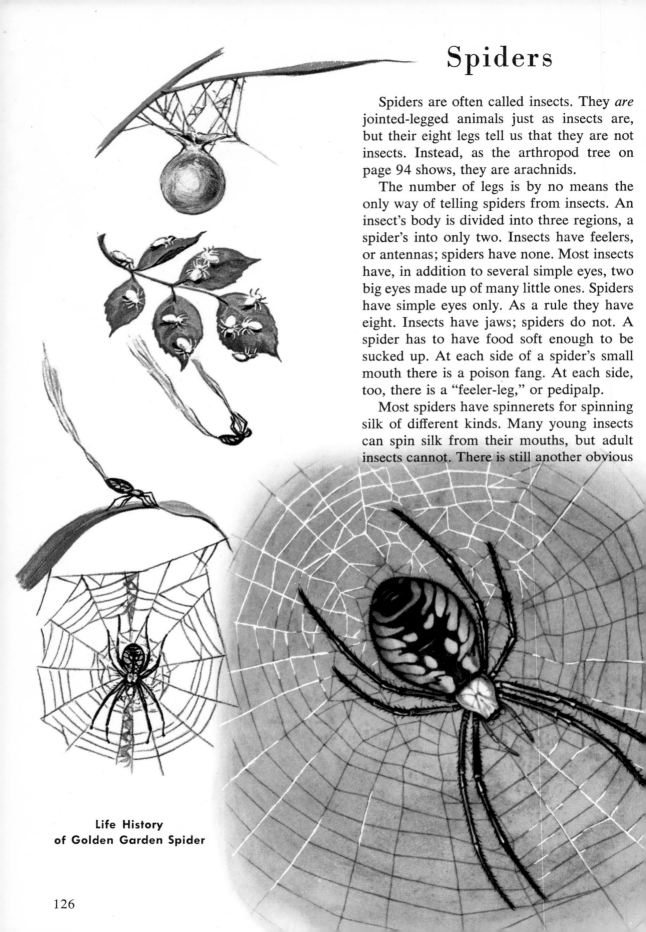

Spiders are often called insects. They *are* jointed-legged animals just as insects are, but their eight legs tell us that they are not insects. Instead, as the arthropod tree on page 94 shows, they are arachnids.

The number of legs is by no means the only way of telling spiders from insects. An insect's body is divided into three regions, a spider's into only two. Insects have feelers, or antennas; spiders have none. Most insects have, in addition to several simple eyes, two big eyes made up of many little ones. Spiders have simple eyes only. As a rule they have eight. Insects have jaws; spiders do not. A spider has to have food soft enough to be sucked up. At each side of a spider's small mouth there is a poison fang. At each side, too, there is a "feeler-leg," or pedipalp.

Most spiders have spinnerets for spinning silk of different kinds. Many young insects can spin silk from their mouths, but adult insects cannot. There is still another obvious

Life History of Golden Garden Spider

126

way in which spiders differ from insects: no spiders have wings.

Spiders hatch from eggs. A female spider may lay more than a thousand eggs at a time. In many cases she spins a silken sac for them. When little spiders, or spiderlets, hatch, they look like full-grown spiders except that they are smaller and are very pale. There is never any food stored up for the baby spiders. They may turn cannibal and eat one another.

There are thousands of kinds of spiders. They differ greatly in size. The large hairy spiders called tarantulas are many times as big as the little crab spiders. Spiders differ in color and shape, too.

Spiders are scattered far and wide over the earth. The warm lands near the equator have the most different kinds. But there are many that live where it is cold, some even in the Far North or on mountaintops. An explorer found jumping spiders on Mount Everest 22,000 feet above sea level. Some spiders are found more often in buildings than out of doors. The common house spider —the spider to blame for most of our cob-webs—is one of them.

Most spiders are land animals. But there are some water spiders. The freshwater spi-der carries air down to a silken sac under the water so that it can breathe there. For all spiders are air-breathers. They do not, how-ever, all breathe the same way. Some have air tubes inside their bodies. Some have book lungs, air sacs filled with thin flaps of skin. Many spiders have both air tubes and book lungs.

Black Widow

Wolf Spider

Trapdoor Spider

Jumping Spider

Tarantula

Crab Spider

**Construction
of an Orb Web**

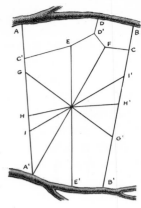

The spider begins the web by dropping thread from A on top branch to A' on bottom branch. Then it climbs back up that thread, along the branch to B, and drops down to B'. It returns along this thread and starts a new thread at C. It trails this thread as it climbs on up and across the branch and down thread A-A' to C'.

2 The spider climbs back up to the branch and drops a new thread at D. This is secured around thread C-C' and pulled tight.

3 From the thread C-C', the spider drops to the lower branch for the first radial thread, then weaves the other radial lines.

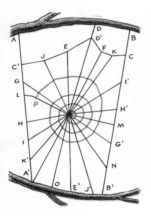
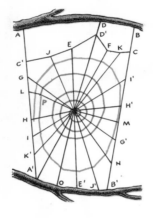
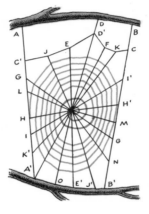
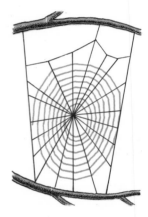

4 After completing the radial thread system, the spider begins the primary spiral (shown in red). Neither of these is sticky.

5 The viscid, or sticky, threads follow (blue), working from the outside and in toward the center of the web.

6 As the spider nears the center of the web, it cuts away the primary spiral, replacing it with the viscid thread.

7 In the finished web, the primary thread has been removed, leaving the heavy supporting framework and the spiral of sticky thread.

"Arachnid" comes from the name of a girl in a Greek myth, Arachne. The goddess Athena, the myth tells, changed Arachne to a spider and condemned her to spinning and weaving silk all her life. Actually, being able to spin and weave silk is an enormous help to spiders. Spider silk is a marvelous material. It is fine, smooth, and very strong. With it, as you know, many spiders make silk egg cases. Almost everywhere it goes, a spider pays out a fine thread of silk that serves as a "lifeline" on which it can retreat if there is danger ahead. Young spiders spin many threads that together catch the wind and act

as balloons to carry the spiders to new homes. And spiders spin webs to catch food.

Different spiders follow different patterns in building webs. Trapdoor spiders spin tube-shaped webs in holes dug in the ground, complete with trap-door lids. Many spiders build orb, or wheel-shaped, webs. Building such a web is not simple, as the chart above shows.

Spiders eat only the juices of living animals. Insects are the commonest spider food. But large spiders near water may eat tadpoles or even small fish. One big tarantula is named the bird spider because it is

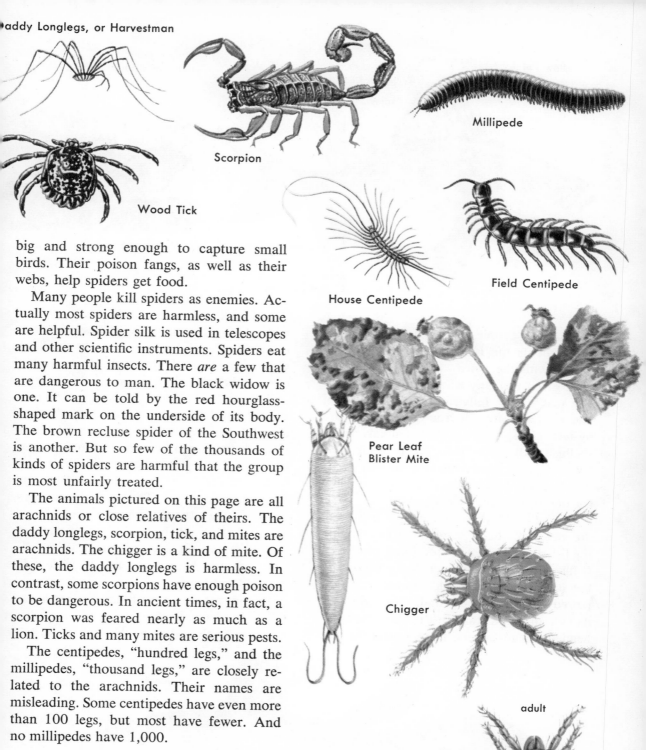

Daddy Longlegs, or Harvestman

Scorpion

Millipede

Wood Tick

House Centipede

Field Centipede

Pear Leaf Blister Mite

Chigger

big and strong enough to capture small birds. Their poison fangs, as well as their webs, help spiders get food.

Many people kill spiders as enemies. Actually most spiders are harmless, and some are helpful. Spider silk is used in telescopes and other scientific instruments. Spiders eat many harmful insects. There *are* a few that are dangerous to man. The black widow is one. It can be told by the red hourglass-shaped mark on the underside of its body. The brown recluse spider of the Southwest is another. But so few of the thousands of kinds of spiders are harmful that the group is most unfairly treated.

The animals pictured on this page are all arachnids or close relatives of theirs. The daddy longlegs, scorpion, tick, and mites are arachnids. The chigger is a kind of mite. Of these, the daddy longlegs is harmless. In contrast, some scorpions have enough poison to be dangerous. In ancient times, in fact, a scorpion was feared nearly as much as a lion. Ticks and many mites are serious pests.

The centipedes, "hundred legs," and the millipedes, "thousand legs," are closely related to the arachnids. Their names are misleading. Some centipedes have even more than 100 legs, but most have fewer. And no millipedes have 1,000.

egg

larva

nymphs

adult

Life History of Spider Mite

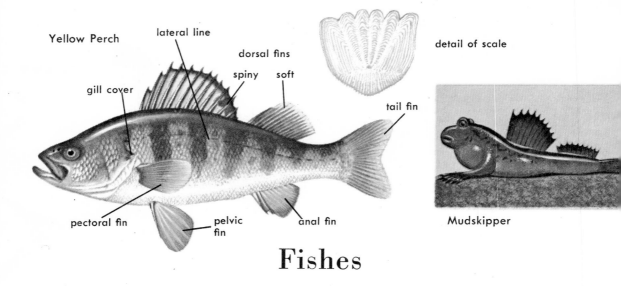

Yellow Perch — lateral line — dorsal fins (spiny, soft) — gill cover — detail of scale — tail fin — pectoral fin — pelvic fin — anal fin — Mudskipper

Fishes

To many people any animal that lives in water all its life is a fish. For this reason names with the word "fish" in them have been given to many water animals that are not really fish. Jellyfish, starfish, crayfish, and cuttlefish are not true fish. Neither are oysters, clams, and the other animals called shellfish. All these "fish" are invertebrates. Even a backboned animal with fish in its name may not be a fish. The common name for one of the whales is blackfish.

Even though there are many "fish" that are not fish, there is great variety among the fishes. The yellow perch is a typical fish. It has two pairs of fins which correspond to the legs of a four-legged animal, and unpaired fins on its back, under its body near its tail, and on its tail. Just back of the fish's head are its gill covers. They protect the gills

with which it breathes. The yellow perch has the streamlined shape we usually think of as the fish shape. It has scales that overlap one another like shingles on a roof.

The saying "as lost as a fish out of water" is sound; all fishes are water animals. But a few fishes, while they are not fitted for living on land, can take short excursions out of water. The flying fishes, for instance, can leap from the water and sail through the air for hundreds of feet. The mudskipper stays on shore when the tide moves out and skips about in the mud. It can be out of water a long time and get oxygen enough if its gills and part of its body—as a rule its underside and tail—stay wet.

In contrast with most fishes, the sea horse swims head up. It also has a tail very different from the tails of other fishes. Its tail

Coelacanth

130

Flying Fishes

can be twisted around the stem of a plant. The sea horse differs from most fishes in still another way: the male fish has a pouch on its stomach in which it carries the eggs the female lays.

Notice how very different the fins of the coelacanth are from those of the yellow perch. This fish is truly a living fossil, for it is very much like its lobefin ancestors that lived back in the Age of Fishes. Until 1938 scientists had thought that the lobefins disappeared at about the same time that the dinosaurs did. But in 1938 a living coelacanth was caught off the southeast coast of Africa. Since then others have been found.

The gar is another living fossil. It has remained almost unchanged for millions of years. Its scales, instead of overlapping, fit together like tiles on a wall.

Longnose Gar

Sea Horse

Longear Sunfish

Barndoor Skate

Cutlass Fish

Cowfish

Porcupine Fish

Chub Mackerel

Fishes differ greatly in appearance, as these pictures clearly show. The cutlass fish with its long, thin body is very different in shape from the ocean sunfish, which looks to be almost all head. The flat barndoor skate is not at all the same shape as the narrow-bodied longear sunfish.

In many cases a fish's shape gives us a clue as to where the fish lives. The skate and the stingray are bottom dwellers. The streamlined mackerel spends its life in the open sea, where it can swim fast and free. The longear sunfish lives in quiet water. There are no strong waves or currents there to tip it over. The cutlass fish's shape is a big advantage in winding in and out among rocks and seaweeds.

It is easy to see that not all these fishes are built for fast swimming. The cowfish, the porcupine fish, and the stargazer lack by a great deal the streamlining that makes for speed.

Some of these fishes have ways of protecting themselves that make it unnecessary for them to swim fast to escape enemies. The porcupine fish blows itself up so that it makes too big and prickly a mouthful for an enemy to swallow. The stargazer has electric organs on its head that give a strong electric shock to an attacker. The stingray can sting an enemy with a poison spine on the top of its whiplike tail.

Weapons, however, are not limited to the fishes that are not fast swimmers. The ocean surgeon carries a sharp "knife" on each side of its body just in front of the tail. Its knives are hinged like jackknives so that they can be "open" or hidden. The knives of some surgeonfish are immovable, but there may be several of them on each side, all very sharp. The sword of a swordfish has been known to pierce the thick wooden hulls of small boats. Its sword not only protects the fish but also helps it to get food.

A person who has fish as pets is likely to think of fish as quiet creatures. Some of them are. But some fishes are noisy. During World War II underwater devices meant to locate enemy submarines by sound picked up so many fish noises that the drone of a submarine's engines was likely to be lost. The grunts get their name from the sounds they make. They make these sounds by grinding their teeth together. The air bladder, an air-filled sac inside their bodies, acts as a sounding box.

Croakers and sea robins are other noisy fishes, but they do not make their sounds by grinding their teeth. Instead, they snap muscles attached to the air bladder. The muscles act like the strings of a guitar, and the air bladder acts like the sounding box of the guitar. Sea robins play their "guitars" so well that they are among the noisiest of fishes. Of the croakers, those called drums make the loudest clatter.

White Grunt

Bluestriped Grunt

electric organs

Northern Stargazer

Ocean Surgeon

Bluntnose Stingray

Swordfish

Ocean Sunfish

The story of the cod is a typical fish life history. A female cod lays many eggs at a time, thousands or even millions. An egg hatches into a tiny fish that still has, in a yolk sac on its underside, some food left from the supply stored in the egg. By the time this food is used up, the young cod is able to forage for itself. Without any great changes like those which moths and butterflies go through in their lives, the young cod grows to be an adult.

The cod takes no care of its eggs. Some fishes, however, do. A number of them even build nests for their eggs. Sticklebacks make their nests of water plants. The bluegill sweeps a nest in the sand at the bottom of a pond or stream. After a female stickle-

egg hatches
in 10-40 days

just hatched

larva at about 2-3 weeks

young—4-6 months old

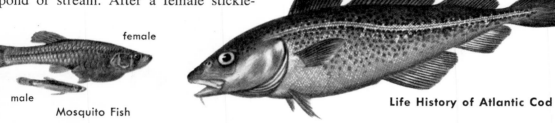

female

male

Mosquito Fish

Life History of Atlantic Cod

back or bluegill has laid eggs in the nest, the male stands guard until the eggs hatch.

Sea catfishes use their mouths as nests for their eggs. After the female lays her eggs in the water, the male picks them up in his mouth. He carries the eggs about for a month or so before they hatch and the babies for two weeks afterward. All this time he has to go without food.

The little mosquito fish protects its eggs in quite a different way. The female keeps the eggs inside her body until the young fish develop from them. We say that the

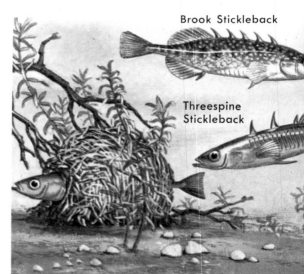

Brook Stickleback

Threespine
Stickleback

Bluegill

mosquito fish is live-bearing. There are many other live-bearing fishes.

As a rule the fishes that do not take care of their eggs produce more at a time than the fishes that do. You can see why. Little fish are such good food for larger fishes and other water animals that a baby fish has little chance of growing up.

Even grown-up fishes are in constant danger of being eaten. Every fish is fair prey to other, usually bigger, fishes and other animals. These in turn are food for still other meat-eaters. The diagram at the bottom of the page shows an important food chain in the sea. Notice that it begins with green plants. Every food chain, both on land and in the sea, begins with plants. The fishes in this chain are all meat-eaters. But some fishes eat plants.

The food habits of the five fishes at the right differ considerably from one another. The little killifish eats mosquito larvas. The clown fish lives among the poisonous tentacles of sea anemones and steals food gathered in by the tentacles. The dace eats plants and small crustaceans. The piranha—the cannibal fish—is bloodthirsty. Even a horse that wanders into a stream where piranhas are numerous may be torn to shreds in just a few minutes. A pilot fish follows sharks and ships about and eats any scraps of food it can find.

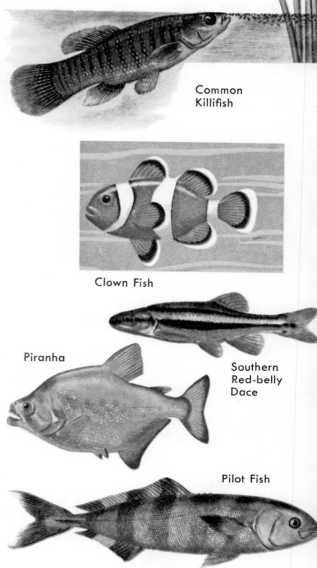

Common Killifish

Clown Fish

Piranha

Southern Red-belly Dace

Pilot Fish

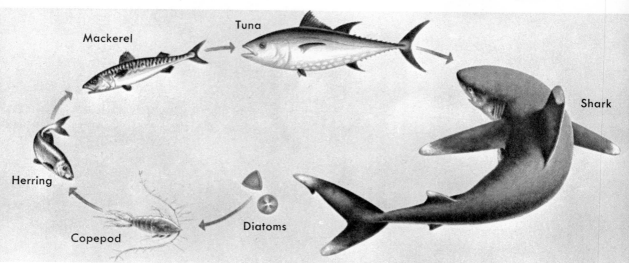

Mackerel

Tuna

Shark

Herring

Copepod

Diatoms

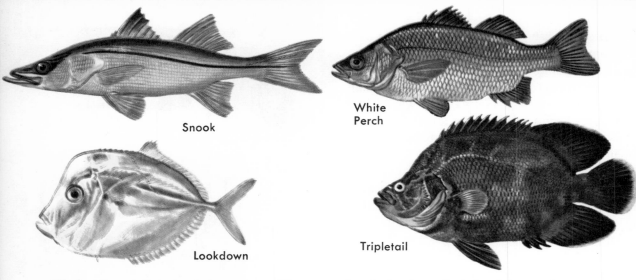

Snook

White Perch

Lookdown

Tripletail

Their sense of taste helps some fishes find food. A bullhead has taste buds scattered over its skin. The fish can taste its food even before it eats it. But this plan for tasting is not common.

Many fishes have a keen sense of smell. They find food by tracing its odor. In only a very few cases are a fish's nostrils of any use in breathing.

Some fishes have, hanging down from their "chins," sensitive whiskers, or barbels, that help them find food by tasting or by feeling. The sketches at the lower left show some of the ways barbels vary.

Many fishes have a line of special cells along their sides that let them feel movements in the water. On the four fishes pictured at the top of the page the lateral line shows clearly.

Fishes have ears with which they hear sounds in the water, but their ears do not show. A fish's ears are deep in its head.

Probably most fishes depend at least partly on seeing to find their food. Almost all of them have eyes for seeing, with one eye on each side of the head. The hammerhead shark's eyes are far out at the ends

Hammerhead Shark

Barbels

Starry Flounder

of its strange "hammer." Most fishes can see very little of the same thing with both eyes at the same time. But there are exceptions. When they are grown up, the flatfishes, of which the flounder is one, swim on their sides and have both eyes on the upper side. The eyes are always open. Only a few fishes have eyelids. The hammerhead shark is one that does.

Being able to see may lead some fishes into danger. The big goosefish, one of the anglerfishes, has a "fishing rod" on its head. A fish that sees this lure and swims to it may end up inside the goosefish.

Deep down in the sea it is very dark. The anglers living there have a "lantern" at the end of their fishing rods. Many deep-sea animals are partly luminous. Perhaps the glowing plays a part in getting food.

Goosefish

Deep-sea Fishes and Crustaceans

Yellow Perch

Bullhead

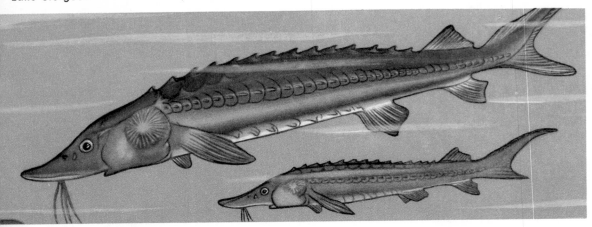

Lake Sturgeon

"He can swim like a fish" is high praise for a swimmer, for most fishes are wonderfully built for swimming. Their finned tails make good oars for pushing their streamlined bodies forward. Their other fins help them guide themselves and keep their balance. Their air bladders make it easy for most fishes to go up or down as they please. In order to sink, a fish expels some of the air from its air bladder. To rise, it forces more air in. Some sharks use their stomachs the same way. Sharks, unlike more modern fishes, have no air bladder.

Except perhaps for the eel, the fishes pictured on these two pages are easily recognized as fishes. But they can readily be told from one another. And they would never all be found in the same body of water. The yellow perch, lake sturgeon, and bullhead are freshwater fishes. The cod and

Menhaden

Eel

Atlantic Cod

menhaden are saltwater fishes. The eel lives most of its life in fresh water, but it spends part of it in salt water.

The yellow perch is so common in lakes and streams that it is sometimes called "everybody's fish." It is the one, you remember, diagrammed as a typical fish. Either the menhaden or the cod would have served just as well. But none of the other three would have. The lake sturgeon is a reminder of the fishes of ancient times. Like the gar and the coelacanth, it differs very little from its ancestors of millions of years ago. Its scales are bony plates. In contrast, the bullhead, a small catfish, has no scales at all. The eel, as you see, is rather snake-like. It has scales, but they are buried so deep that they are very hard to see.

The cod, catfish, perch, and sturgeon are well known as food fishes. Of them the cod

139

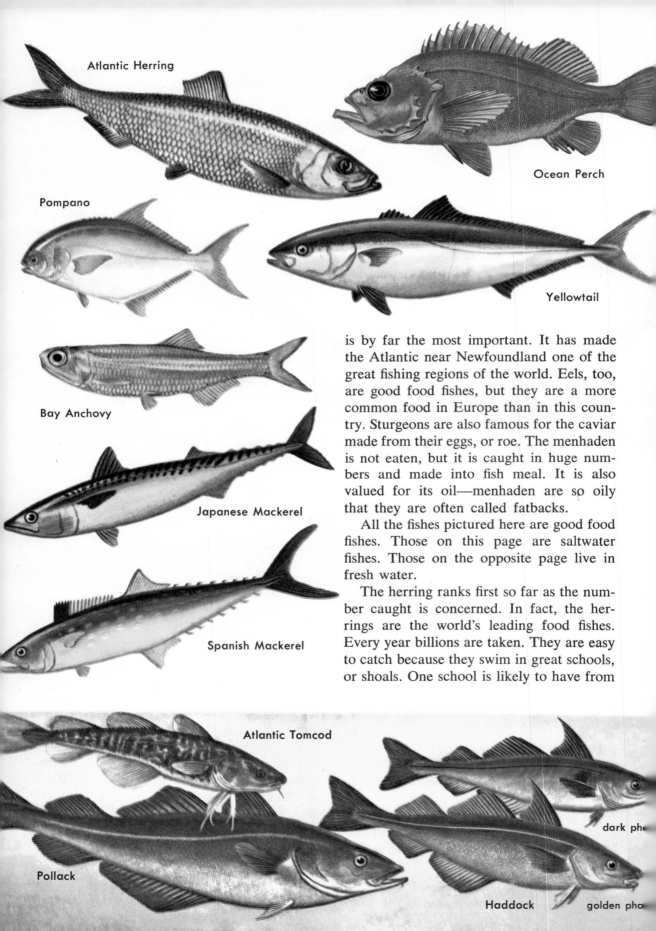

Atlantic Herring

Ocean Perch

Pompano

Yellowtail

Bay Anchovy

Japanese Mackerel

Spanish Mackerel

is by far the most important. It has made the Atlantic near Newfoundland one of the great fishing regions of the world. Eels, too, are good food fishes, but they are a more common food in Europe than in this country. Sturgeons are also famous for the caviar made from their eggs, or roe. The menhaden is not eaten, but it is caught in huge numbers and made into fish meal. It is also valued for its oil—menhaden are so oily that they are often called fatbacks.

All the fishes pictured here are good food fishes. Those on this page are saltwater fishes. Those on the opposite page live in fresh water.

The herring ranks first so far as the number caught is concerned. In fact, the herrings are the world's leading food fishes. Every year billions are taken. They are easy to catch because they swim in great schools, or shoals. One school is likely to have from

Atlantic Tomcod

Pollack

Haddock

dark pha

golden pha

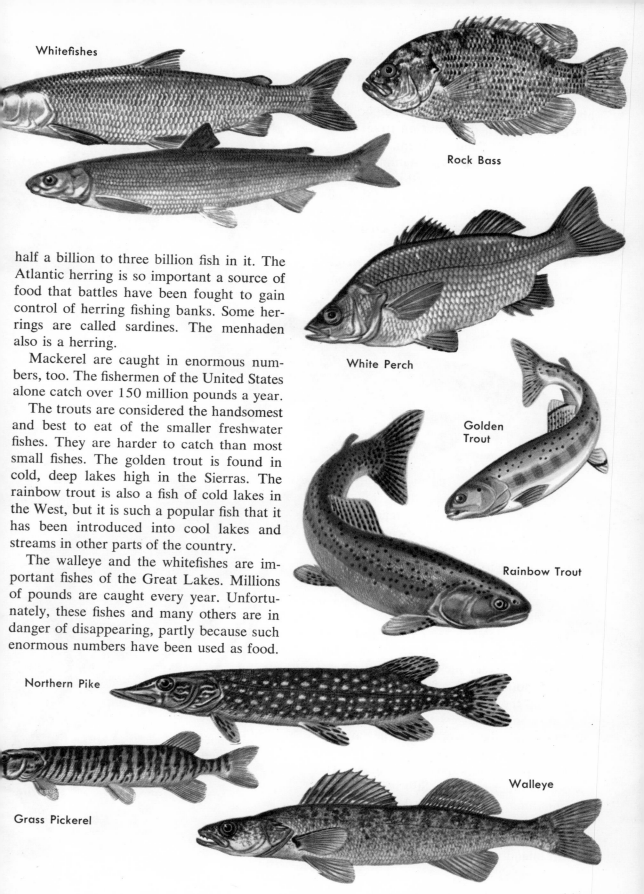

Whitefishes

Rock Bass

White Perch

Golden Trout

Rainbow Trout

half a billion to three billion fish in it. The Atlantic herring is so important a source of food that battles have been fought to gain control of herring fishing banks. Some herrings are called sardines. The menhaden also is a herring.

Mackerel are caught in enormous numbers, too. The fishermen of the United States alone catch over 150 million pounds a year.

The trouts are considered the handsomest and best to eat of the smaller freshwater fishes. They are harder to catch than most small fishes. The golden trout is found in cold, deep lakes high in the Sierras. The rainbow trout is also a fish of cold lakes in the West, but it is such a popular fish that it has been introduced into cool lakes and streams in other parts of the country.

The walleye and the whitefishes are important fishes of the Great Lakes. Millions of pounds are caught every year. Unfortunately, these fishes and many others are in danger of disappearing, partly because such enormous numbers have been used as food.

Northern Pike

Grass Pickerel

Walleye

Some fishes are called game, or sport, fish. They are fishes that fishermen think are fun to catch because they put up a fight to avoid being landed. As a rule fish swim about as fast as a man walks. When hooked, however, some of them put on tremendous bursts of speed. Some of them, moreover, show amazing strength and stamina.

These three fishes are well-known game fishes. Two of them, the tarpon and the sailfish, are saltwater fishes. The muskellunge, "muskie" for short, is found in cold lakes and streams of the Great Lakes area.

The tarpon is a large fish. Tarpon weighing from 50 to 100 pounds are fairly common, and some weigh in at more than 300

Atlantic Tarpon

Muskellunge

pounds. A hooked tarpon may reach a speed of 30 miles an hour trying to escape.

Sailfish, too, are large game fish, but they never get to be the size of the largest tarpon. Even though not so large as a tarpon, a sailfish is faster. In short bursts it can go 60 miles an hour.

The muskellunge is large for a freshwater fish. A big one may weigh 70 pounds. But a fisherman is very lucky to find one more than 25 pounds in weight.

Among the largest of the saltwater game fish are some relatives of the sailfish—the marlins and the swordfish. The average weight for a blue marlin is 300 pounds, and 800-pound ones have been caught. The swordfish reaches 1,200. Still larger are the bluefin tuna and some of the sharks. Although not in the same class with these giants of the sea, the freshwater game fish afford inland fishermen plenty of sport.

Atlantic Sailfish

The fishes pictured on this page give people a great deal of pleasure, too, but of a different kind. They are tiny tropical fish suitable for raising in aquariums. Four—the guppy, mollie, platy, and swordtail—are cousins of the little mosquito fish and, like it, are live-bearing. The other four lay eggs. One of these, the neon tetra, is a close relative of the bloodthirsty piranha.

One problem in raising live-bearing fishes is to keep the adult fish from eating the young ones. The aquarium must have plenty of plants to afford hiding places. There is a similar problem in raising some egg-laying tropical fish. The parents may eat the eggs. The betta, on the other hand, takes good care of its eggs and young. The father fish makes a nest of bubbles on the surface of the water. When the eggs are laid he carries them to the bubble nest and watches over them until after the babies hatch and use up the food of their yolk sacs.

Bettas are also called Siamese fighting fish. The males are fierce fighters. For centuries people of the Orient have bet on the outcome of battles between these fish.

Seeing that the water is warm enough during the winter months and providing the right kind of food are important in keeping tropical fish. One of the easiest to care for is the guppy. Of all these fishes, it is the most popular.

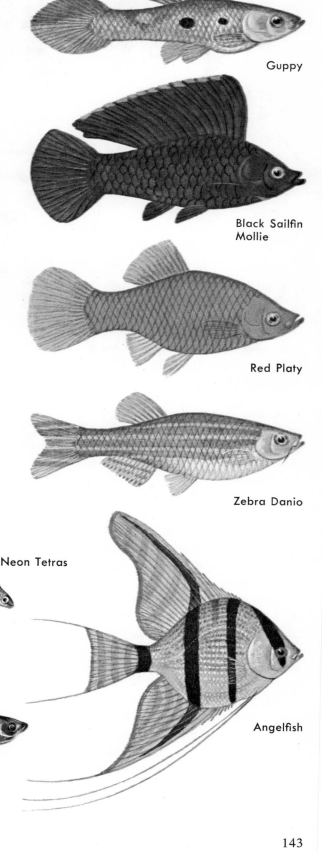

Guppy

Black Sailfin Mollie

Red Platy

Zebra Danio

Neon Tetras

Swordtail

Betta

Angelfish

143

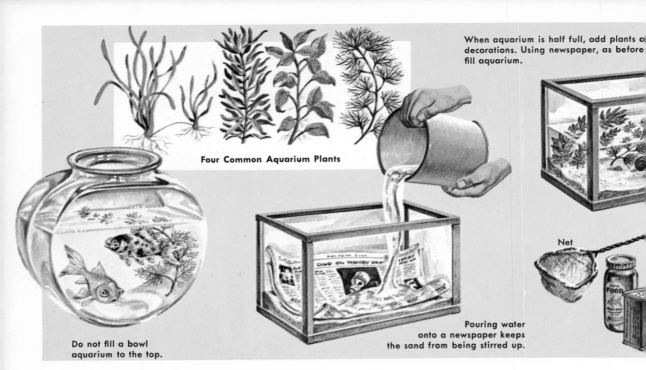

Four Common Aquarium Plants

When aquarium is half full, add plants or decorations. Using newspaper, as before, fill aquarium.

Net

Do not fill a bowl aquarium to the top.

Pouring water onto a newspaper keeps the sand from being stirred up.

The goldfish is by far the most popular of all our aquarium fishes. Goldfish may be bought in a great variety of colors. You may choose goldfish with bulging "pop eyes" and with long, flowing tails. You may have them with conspicuous scales or with scales so thin that they are nearly invisible. There are even goldfish with thick, round scales that look like pearls. Some, moreover, have eyes turned upward, and others have short bodies and "lion" or "buffalo" heads. The pictures show several of the many varieties. The story of the goldfish is a story of man's ability to change some animals, by careful selection and breeding over the years, to suit his purposes.

All the goldfish of today are descendants of the wild goldfish that lives in the streams of China and Japan. This wild goldfish is not an especially pretty fish. It is usually dull greenish-brown, and it has small fins and a rather short tail.

The Chinese found out more than 15 centuries ago that it is easy to raise goldfish in small ponds and aquariums. Many kinds of fish do not do well in captivity, but the goldfish does. The Chinese who raised goldfish noticed that not all the goldfish were alike in color. Occasionally they found a fish that had the dark pigment left out of its skin in places. In those places the skin was yellowish, or gold.

The Chinese goldfish breeders watched carefully for fish with a gold color. They chose these fish as breeding stock and took good care of them and their eggs. Some of the fish that came from the eggs had more gold color than their parents.

The breeders kept on choosing and mating the fish that were best. In time they had fish that were all gold.

By a thousand years after the Chinese began raising goldfish, the Japanese, too, were breeding them. Breeders in both countries found that they could produce not only fish that were gold all over and fish part gold, part brownish-green, but also goldfish of other colors. They could have black goldfish, silver goldfish, white goldfish, and goldfish as mottled as a tortoiseshell cat.

The breeders discovered, too, that color was not the only thing they could change. They could also change the eyes, the fins, the scales, and the shape of the body.

Now goldfish are raised in many parts of the world. Millions of goldfish of different colors and shapes are raised and sold in this country every year.

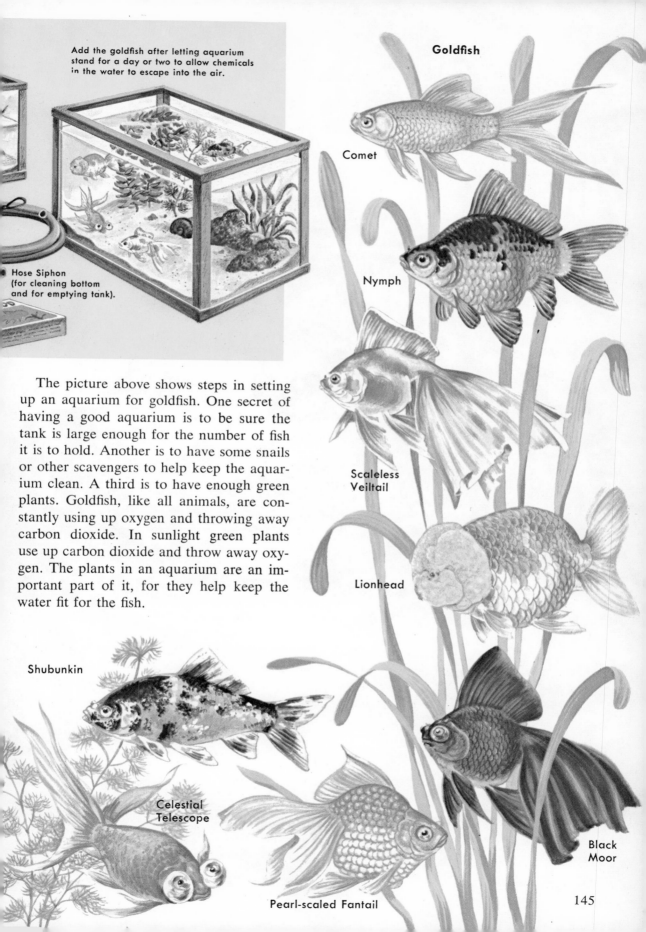

Add the goldfish after letting aquarium stand for a day or two to allow chemicals in the water to escape into the air.

Hose Siphon
(for cleaning bottom
and for emptying tank).

Goldfish

Comet

Nymph

Scaleless
Veiltail

Lionhead

The picture above shows steps in setting up an aquarium for goldfish. One secret of having a good aquarium is to be sure the tank is large enough for the number of fish it is to hold. Another is to have some snails or other scavengers to help keep the aquarium clean. A third is to have enough green plants. Goldfish, like all animals, are constantly using up oxygen and throwing away carbon dioxide. In sunlight green plants use up carbon dioxide and throw away oxygen. The plants in an aquarium are an important part of it, for they help keep the water fit for the fish.

Shubunkin

Celestial
Telescope

Pearl-scaled Fantail

Black
Moor

145

Amphibians

The frogs and toads are the best known of the amphibians. They are sometimes spoken of as the tailless amphibians since, when they are full grown, they have no tails. In addition to the frogs and toads, there are two other groups of amphibians: the caecilians and the salamanders.

Although most amphibians are able to live on land for part of their lives, almost none of them are able to stand extreme dryness. They have no protecting scales or fur or feathers. A few, by using water stored in the body, can live where there is no rain for months or even years at a time, but most amphibians must stay close to water or moist places. The part of its life an amphibian spends in water is spent in fresh water. There are no amphibians of any kind that live in the salty sea.

Like fishes, all amphibians are cold-blooded. Those that live in regions of cold winters, as many of them do, protect themselves from the cold by hibernating.

Most amphibians lay their eggs in water. With those that lay eggs out of water, the early stages, as a rule, are passed inside the egg. A very few—some caecilians and salamanders and a toad—are live-bearing.

Amphibians vary greatly in size. They range from tiny frogs less than an inch long to the 5-foot giant salamander of Japan. But even this salamander is not much of a giant compared with *Eryops* and some other large amphibians of the past.

The story of a bullfrog is a typical amphibian life history. It shows clearly how the amphibians got their name.

In early summer a female bullfrog lays her eggs in the water near the edge of a pond or a quiet stream. Each egg is surrounded by a layer of clear, tough jelly. The jelly holds the eggs together. There are so many eggs that they form a "pancake" 2 feet or more across.

As soon as they are laid, the eggs begin to develop. Each egg elongates till it is bean-shaped. One end is larger than the other. The larger end will become the head, the smaller end the tail.

In about a week the eggs hatch. A tiny tadpole wriggles out of each jelly covering. The tadpole is less than half an inch long. There is a tiny bump in the place of each eye. And beneath where its mouth will be it has a sucker which enables it to hold on to the jelly it wriggled out of. Its tail looks much like a fish's tail.

Very soon tiny fringes appear at the sides of its head. These are its gills. A tadpole is truly a water animal.

By the time it is a day old, the tadpole can swim a little. But whenever it runs into a stick or a plant it holds on with its sucker and rests for a while.

Bullfrog

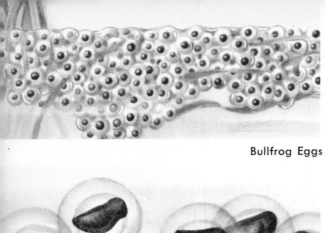

Bullfrog Eggs

Eggs (magnified)

New-hatched Tadpole

Tadpole with Hind Legs

Tadpole with All Four Legs

Young Bullfrog with Remnant of Tail

In two or three days the tadpole has eyes and a mouth. Now it can see where it is going, and it can nibble tiny plants off the stones and sticks in the water.

The tadpole's body soon bulges out so that it is much bigger in proportion to the tail. Its sucker disappears, and skin grows over its gills and hides them. To breathe, the tadpole gulps water into its mouth. The water goes past its gills and out through a little hole, the breathing pore, on the left side of the tadpole's body.

The tadpole eats a great deal—mostly tiny green water plants. Sometimes it gets scraps of food left by the bigger animals that share the pond or stream.

In time two legs begin growing out from near the base of the tadpole's tail. Later two front legs appear. The left one pushes its way out first and is soon followed by the right leg. The tadpole is now a four-legged animal. But it still has a long tail.

Other changes are going on in the tadpole. Lungs are developing. The tadpole's mouth is changing, too. It is getting wider, and a long, sticky tongue is forming inside.

While its mouth is changing, the tadpole cannot eat. It lives on its tail. Gradually the tail shrinks as the food in it is used up. Before all the food is gone the little frog takes excursions on land. With its tongue it now catches insects. It has become a meat-eater at the same time that it has become an air breather.

Finally the last stub of its tadpole tail disappears. The young bullfrog has the shape it will keep for the rest of its life. It grows fast, so fast that it has to shed its skin several times.

At last the frog is an adult. It is ready to mate and start many thousands of new bullfrogs on their way. By this time it has developed a voice, and its croaking mingles with the voices of its neighbors in the breeding pond or stream.

It may take as much as five years for a bullfrog to grow up. In cold regions the growing up is interrupted by winters spent in the mud at the bottom of a pond.

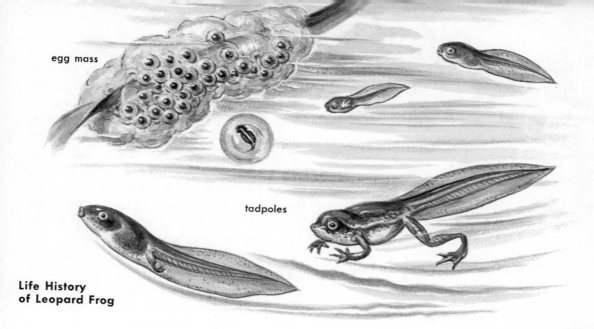

egg mass

tadpoles

Life History of Leopard Frog

A leopard frog goes through the same stages in growing up that a bullfrog goes through, but it takes less time. This frog gets its adult form the same year it hatches from the egg, and is ready for mating two years later. Most other frogs, too, pass the tadpole stage their first year. Some go through all the stages from egg to adult in only a little more than three weeks!

Another name for the leopard frog is meadow frog. It is often seen in wet, grassy places rather far from water. This slim, spotted frog is the champion long-distance jumper of its family in North America. In one jump it can travel thirteen times its body length. The world champion of this family of frogs, however, lives in Africa. It can jump over forty-five times its length.

The life of a frog is not nearly so safe as the story of it makes it seem. Actually very, very few of the eggs a female frog lays go through all the stages and become adult frogs. Tadpoles have many enemies. They furnish food for many of their neighbors in the water and along its banks.

young adult

Leopard Frog

We call all the tailless amphibians frogs or toads, but these names in many cases do not mean much. There are several groups of tailless amphibians, and in each some are commonly called toads and others frogs. Many of these animals, in fact, have both a frog and a toad name. "Frog" and "toad" have separate meanings only when they are used for the frogs and toads of two well-known families—the Ranidae, or true frogs, and the Bufonidae, or true toads. It is easy to tell these frogs and toads apart.

True frogs have soft, moist, smooth skins. True toads have tough, dry skins covered by little bumps that are often spoken of as warts. Frogs are slender; toads have broad bodies. Toads, with their short legs, are clumsy looking. Frogs are far more graceful. They are faster, too. Frogs have more conspicuous eardrums. Toads have large poison glands just back of the eyes. Frogs have small teeth in their upper jaw; toads have none. The two frogs and the toad on this page and the American toad on the next show some of these differences between frogs and toads.

The warts on toads are not like the warts people sometimes have. They are small glands. When an enemy comes near, the glands give off an irritating fluid that is highly poisonous to some animals.

The life of most toads is very much like that of a bullfrog. The stages, however, as with most frogs, last a shorter time.

Few true toads and frogs take any care of their eggs. Some of the other tailless

Wood Frog

Fowler's Toad

**Life History
of American Toad**

American Toad

amphibians, however, have strange ways of doing so. The female midwife toad lays her eggs in long strings which the male puts around his body. He hides in a hole in the ground or under a stone by day. At night he comes out of hiding and lets the eggs soak for a while in a pool of water or in dew. In a month or so, when the eggs are ready to hatch, he goes into a pond or stream. The tadpoles hatch out in the water, where they will live until they have four legs.

The Surinam toad spends most of its time in the water. As the female toad lays her eggs, the male puts them on her back. Her skin swells and covers them so that each egg is in a separate pocket. There the eggs develop into tadpoles. The tadpoles stay in the pockets till they are little four-legged toads. Then each pocket opens up and the toadlets wriggle out and swim away.

Midwife Toad

Surinam Toad

American Toad Croaking

Green Tree Frog

The croaking and trilling of toads and frogs are familiar sounds. The loudest singing comes from males with vocal sacs. When the sacs are filled with air they serve as sounding boxes for the noises made by the vocal cords. A frog or toad can sing even underwater. The little green tree frog does most of its singing in the rain. A very few frogs and toads are voiceless. The bell toad is one of them. Even if it had a voice, it would never be heard above the roar of the water in the cold mountain streams where it lives.

All frogs and toads are meat-eaters. When they are eating such a tasty morsel as an earthworm, they may use their front feet to help push it into their mouths. Their tongues are a big help in catching insects. Most have tongues fastened at the front, not at the back as ours are. A toad or frog can flip out its tongue a long way. It will strike at nothing that is not moving. It does not, therefore, eat dead animals.

When a toad or frog swallows its food it blinks. Doing so helps it to push food from its mouth into its stomach, for closing its bulging eyes means pulling them downward.

Frogs and toads have big appetites. A toad may eat 50 insect larvas at a single meal. Many of the insects and other animals toads and frogs eat are harmful to us. The marine toad, for example, eats quantities of sugar beetles. It is shipped from its home in

American Toad Eating

Three-striped Poison Frog

Fire-bellied Toad

tropical America to sugar-producing areas in many other regions to fight this pest.

The three-striped poison frog produces a poison that is used by natives on their poison arrows. Of course, its poison is a good protection. The pickerel frog also protects itself with poison. The fire-bellied toad frightens its enemies by throwing its head up so that the bright-red spots on its undersurface show. Most toads and frogs depend on hiding, jumping away, or blowing themselves up to protect themselves. Many find it easy to hide because their colors match their surroundings.

Toads and frogs differ greatly in size. The 10-inch goliath is a giant beside the inch-long greenhouse frog. The smallest frogs measure less than half an inch.

Bell Toad

Pickerel Frog

Goliath Frog

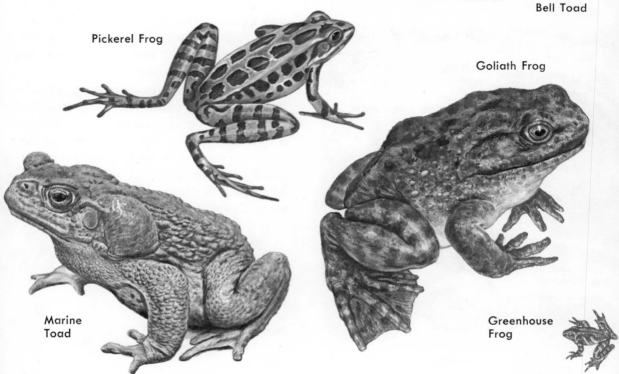

Marine Toad

Greenhouse Frog

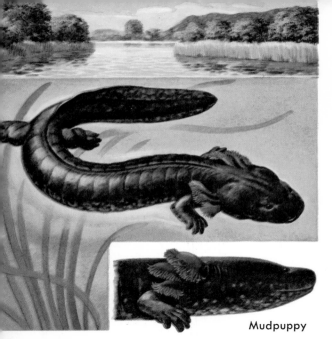

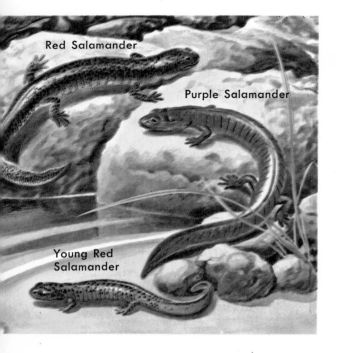

Mudpuppy

Tiger Salamander Eggs and Larva

One of these pictures shows a caecilian. The others all show salamanders.

Salamanders are fairly common. As adults they have both legs and tails. Caecilians are found chiefly in tropical regions. They look like oversized earthworms.

Even people who live in the regions where there are caecilians seldom see them. The caecilians spend their lives in underground burrows. Their eyes are small and in most cases useless. They have feelers which they can use in place of eyes to find their way about their dark homes. Most caecilians are less than a foot long, but a giant species found in Colombia may measure over 4 feet. They are all meat-eaters.

Caecilians differ from other amphibians in another way besides lack of legs. Most of them have scales buried in their skin.

Some caecilians are live-bearing. Others lay eggs, but the larvas that hatch have, as a rule, already lost their gills and are air-breathing animals. The picture shows two gilled larvas taken from eggs before the time of hatching.

The salamanders are not nearly so well known as the toads and frogs. For one thing they live in out-of-the-way places. Many live under the rubbish on forest floors. Some spend all their lives in water. A few live in trees. And some make their homes in caves. The cave-dwelling salamanders are nearly or entirely blind.

Another reason salamanders are not so well known is that they do none of the singing or croaking toads and frogs do. A few, however, can "bark" and scream. Newts can make a squeaking noise.

Most salamanders hatch from eggs laid in the water and follow the usual frog-toad plan of growing up. The mudpuppy follows a different plan. It never becomes an air-breathing animal. A mudpuppy lives underwater all its life and keeps its fringe of gills. The tiger salamander follows both plans. In some regions the larva changes into an air-

Red Salamander

Purple Salamander

Young Red Salamander

Sticky Caecilian

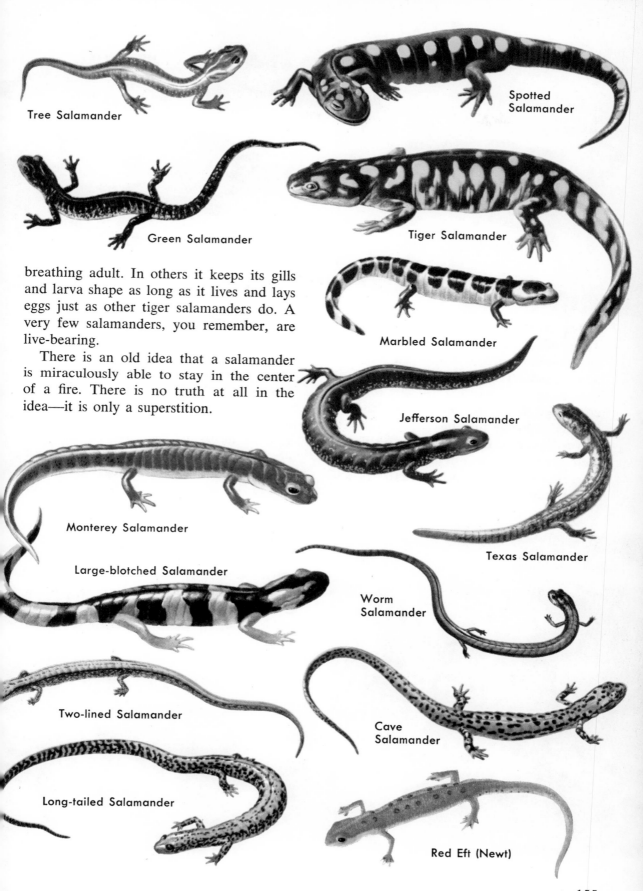

Tree Salamander

Spotted Salamander

Green Salamander

Tiger Salamander

Marbled Salamander

breathing adult. In others it keeps its gills and larva shape as long as it lives and lays eggs just as other tiger salamanders do. A very few salamanders, you remember, are live-bearing.

There is an old idea that a salamander is miraculously able to stay in the center of a fire. There is no truth at all in the idea—it is only a superstition.

Jefferson Salamander

Monterey Salamander

Texas Salamander

Large-blotched Salamander

Worm Salamander

Two-lined Salamander

Cave Salamander

Long-tailed Salamander

Red Eft (Newt)

155

Reptiles

The great days of the reptiles are over. They ended millions of years ago, when the last dinosaurs died. But there are still over 5,000 kinds. The reptiles of today are in four groups: the turtles, the alligators and crocodiles, the lizards and snakes, and, all by itself, the rare tuatara.

Turtles can be told from other reptiles by their shells. No other reptiles have shells. There are freshwater turtles, sea turtles, and land turtles.

These turtles are all freshwater turtles. They spend part of their time in water and part out of water. Since they breathe with lungs, as all reptiles do, they must be out of the water or at the surface to breathe.

The slider is our commonest pond turtle. As the pictures show, sliders hatch from eggs. All turtles do. The eggs, like those of other turtles, are laid on land. The parent turtles take no care of the eggs or of the little turtles that hatch from them in the fall. A new-hatched slider looks very much like its parents except for size.

Soon after it is hatched, a little slider makes its way to water. There it swims about, coming up to breathe and at times climbing up on a rock or log to sun itself. It does not have to look for any food, for inside it, it still has enough yolk left over from the egg it hatched from to last it till

Musk Turtle

Painted Turtle

spring. It spends the winter in the mud at the bottom of the water.

Sliders are often kept as pets. So are painted turtles. Painted turtles are named from the colored band bordering their shell. Mud turtles, as you would guess, live in ponds and streams with muddy bottoms. Musk turtles owe their name to their smell. One of their nicknames is "stinkpot."

The snapping turtle snaps at anything that disturbs it. It has no teeth—no turtles do—but its jaws are sharp enough to bite off a finger. Baby snappers, instead of hatching in the fall, may winter inside the eggs and hatch in the spring.

Mud Turtles

Snapping Turtle

Young Snapping Turtles

Box Turtle

The turtles called tortoises are all land turtles. So is the box turtle. Surprisingly enough, the box turtle, even though it lives on land, belongs to the freshwater turtle family that includes the slider and the painted turtle.

Tortoises are famous for their slow movement—everyone has heard the fable of the hare and the tortoise. They are also famous for their long lives. Giant tortoises may live to be over 100 years old. They rank at the top of the animal kingdom for length of life. These big land turtles of remote islands may weigh over 500 pounds.

The gopher tortoise is a medium-sized turtle of our southern states. The box turtle is more widespread. Unless it has eaten too many wild strawberries and mushrooms, this turtle can pull in its legs, head, and tail and shut itself up completely in its shell.

The hawksbill, leatherback, and green turtles all live in the sea. Their legs are paddles. Sea turtles have to come on land to lay their eggs. Green turtles sometimes come out, too, to sun themselves.

Tortoiseshell, once much used for combs and eyeglass frames, comes from the shell of the hawksbill. Green turtles are often caught for food. A full-grown one furnishes a great deal, for it may weigh 400 pounds. The eggs, too, are eaten. The leatherback's shell is covered with very tough skin. This turtle is not as big as some of the sea turtles of long ago, but it may be 8 feet long and weigh more than half a ton. By weight, the leatherback is the biggest reptile found anywhere in the world today.

Gopher Tortoise

Hawksbill Turtle

Green Turtle

Leatherback
Turtle

Giant Tortoise

American Crocodile

The tuatara lives nowhere in the world except on some small islands near New Zealand. This little reptile is another living fossil. It has been on the earth since before the days of the dinosaurs.

The tuatara lives in burrows in the ground. Usually it does not make its own burrow but lives in one made by a bird, a shearwater. The shearwater and the tuatara share the burrow.

The tuatara is carefully guarded by the government of New Zealand. People do not want this living fossil to disappear.

Although the largest alligator or crocodile is not as bulky as the largest leatherback, so far as average size goes the alligators and crocodiles are the largest reptiles. The longest may measure 24 feet and the smallest about 4. They all look much alike. On each side of its mouth, however, a crocodile has a long lower tooth which shows outside the upper teeth when its jaws are shut, and its snout is notched for the two teeth. A third member of this group, the gavial of India, can be told by its long, thin snout.

Alligators and crocodiles spend most of their time in the water. They have webbed feet but do not use them in swimming. They swim with their tails. In water flaps of skin protect their ears. On land an alligator or a crocodile usually lies sprawled on its belly, but it can lift itself up on its stout legs and run fast when it needs to.

The nostrils and eyes of an alligator or a crocodile stand up from its face. The reptiles can float with only their eyes and nostrils above water. They are hidden underwater and yet can breathe and see what is happening up on the bank or shore.

Most alligators and crocodiles live in warm waters near the equator. They cannot stand cold weather. The American alligator lives the farthest north. This reptile of our Gulf states often tells where it is by bellowing. It can be heard a mile away.

Alligators and crocodiles eat fish and many other kinds of animals. If their catch is too big to swallow whole, they can wring off the part held in their jaws by spinning themselves around fast.

Tuatara

160

Life History of American Alligator

All alligators and crocodiles hatch from eggs. The female reptile lays her eggs in a nest on land. The American alligator makes a nest of mud and plants. Heat from the sun and from the rotting plants keeps the eggs warm. When the little alligators are ready to hatch, they make a piping noise.

The mother, who has stayed nearby, then uncovers the nest. A baby alligator has a point—the "egg tooth"—on its head that helps it break out of its hard shell.

Alligators and crocodiles have very tough skin that is used to make beautiful leather for bags and shoes. So many of these big reptiles have been killed that there is danger that they will disappear. Now both the American alligator and the American crocodile are protected by law.

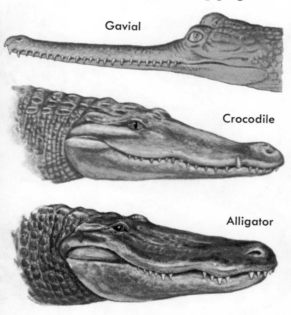

Gavial

Crocodile

Alligator

Caiman, a
Small Alligator

161

Flying Dragon

Common Chameleon

Glass Snake

Collared Lizard

Skink

162

There are lizards of many different sizes and colors and shapes. The skink is the shape we think of as the typical lizard shape. It is a small lizard. The flying dragon is about the same size and shape. But its wings, which are simply folds of skin that act as parachutes, make it look much like a big butterfly when it "flies."

Most lizards run or crawl on four short legs. But some can get up on their hind legs and run or leap. The collared lizard is one. And some lizards have no legs. The glass snake, in spite of its looks and name, is not a snake but a legless lizard.

Lizards eat food ranging in size from tiny insects to wild pigs. Some have remarkable tongues. The chameleon can shoot its tongue far out to catch an insect. The tip of its tongue is very sticky.

Not all lizards are meat-eaters. The marine iguana eats seaweed. Crested iguanas thrive on cactus. And chuckwallas eat the tiny leaves and flowers of greasewood.

A big marine iguana may be 5 feet long, but it is by no means the world's biggest lizard. Some of the monitor lizards of Asia may be twice as long and weigh 300 pounds.

The glass snake, like other lizards, has a remarkable way of keeping from being caught. If it is in danger, it simply breaks off its tail and runs away without it. Soon it grows a new, but shorter, tail. Some lizards

Chuckwalla

use their tails as whips to lash enemies away, and break off their tails only as a last resort. The armadillo lizard protects itself by rolling up with its tail in its mouth. It is as safe from its enemies as a closed-up box turtle. This tiny lizard looks flat enough to have been put through a wringer.

A few lizards are poisonous. But on the whole lizards are our friends. They help by eating insect pests and harmful mammals.

Most lizards hatch from eggs just as turtles, alligators, and crocodiles do. But some lizards are live-bearing.

Marine Iguana

Crested Iguana

Armadillo Lizard

Scarlet Snake

Plains Garter Snake

Hog-nosed
Snake

There are about 2,500 kinds of lizards and almost as many of snakes. Some snakes are much larger than others. The Indian python, for example, is a giant beside a garter snake. But all snakes are about the same shape. The only other reptiles that look like them are the legless lizards.

Since they have no legs, snakes cannot move in the way most other reptiles move. One way snakes move is by slightly lifting groups of the underside scales and moving them forward before putting them down. The snake's body flows forward in a straight line. A faster and more common way is to wriggle along. The snake pushes the curves in its body against tiny ridges of sand or soil made by the curves. Some desert snakes throw loops of their bodies forward to move themselves along when in a hurry. The trail left is not a continuous one but a series of parallel tracks at an angle to the direction the snake is headed. In addition to moving on the ground, snakes can swim, and many are good climbers or burrowers. The hog-nosed snake is a burrower.

Bull Snake

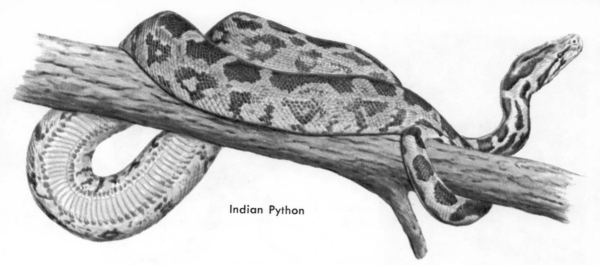
Indian Python

All snakes have skins covered with scales. As you can see, their coloring and the patterns the colors make may be beautiful. Snakes have the reputation of being slimy and unpleasant to touch. They are not; their scales are dry.

Snakes have many teeth, but they do not use them for chewing. Their teeth point backward toward their throats. They have long, slender tongues that are forked near the ends. The tongue may be black, red and black, yellow, green, or even some other color. A snake uses its tongue for feeling and as a help in smelling. The tongue, as it touches things, picks up traces that are then brought to the mouth, where they are smelled. Its tongue helps the snake find food and avoid enemies. It can dart in and out with remarkable speed.

Most snakes lay eggs. Some snakes, however, bear their young alive. The common garter snakes are live-bearing.

All snakes are meat-eaters. And they all swallow their food whole. Many of them eat animals that look much too big to be swallowed by a snake. The secret is that a snake's jaws are fastened together in such a way that the snake can open its mouth very wide. A snake's skin, moreover, stretches like rubber. One big swallow may be enough food to last for weeks.

As it grows, a snake has to shed its skin. Crawling out of its old skin is not easy.

The hog-nosed snake has several ways of protecting itself. When an enemy comes near, it raises its head, spreads out the skin of its neck so that it looks frightening, and hisses. From time to time it strikes at the enemy, but with its mouth closed. If the enemy is not driven away, the snake then plays dead. Most snakes protect themselves by running away. Some, you are sure to know, have poison fangs.

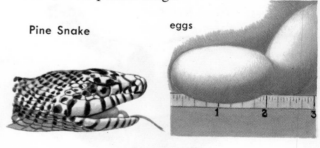
Pine Snake   eggs

Snake Shedding

Poison Fangs

Bushmaster

Many people are so afraid of snakes that they kill every snake they can. But most snakes do us no harm, and some are helpful. A few snakes, however, are dangerous. The dangerous ones, for the most part, are those with poison fangs. When these snakes bite an animal, poison runs through their fangs into the animal. The snakes pictured here are among the most poisonous ones in the world. The four shown below are found in the United States.

The water moccasin, nicknamed the "cottonmouth," the copperhead, and the eastern diamondback, which is a rattlesnake, belong to a group of snakes called pit vipers from pits between their eyes and their nostrils. The eastern diamondback is the largest of the country's poisonous snakes. Like all rattlesnakes—except for very young ones—it has a warning rattle at the end of its tail.

A coral snake's fangs are much shorter than those of the pit vipers. They do not, fortunately, go through heavy cloth or shoe leather. The cobras of the Old World are among this snake's many relatives.

The Indian cobra can be blamed for a great many of the deaths from snakebite in India. Another cobra, the king cobra of

Water Moccasin

Coral Snake

Copperhead

Eastern Diamondback

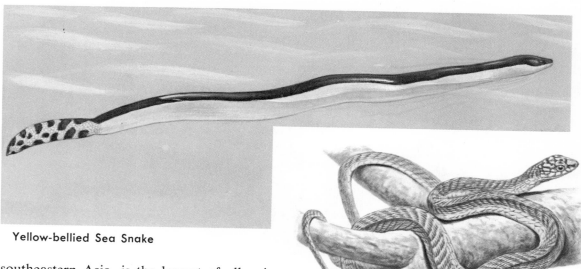

Yellow-bellied Sea Snake

Boomslang

southeastern Asia, is the largest of all poisonous snakes. It may be 20 feet long.

The tiger snake of Australia is a close relative of the cobras. A full-grown one has enough poison to kill 400 people. The mamba of Africa is another cobra relative.

South America can claim the largest poisonous snake of the Americas—the bushmaster. One may be 12 feet long—several more than a diamondback. Like the diamondback, the bushmaster is a pit viper. Another dangerous pit viper of South America is the fer-de-lance.

The Gaboon viper of Africa belongs to the family of snakes called true vipers. Its poison fangs may be an inch and a half long. India's tic-polonga is another true viper.

The boomslang of the African bush is the only one of the so-called rear-fanged snakes that is dangerous. As a rule it is mild tempered, but its poison is deadly.

Most snakes spend all, or at least most, of their time on land. But in the warm regions of the Pacific there are sea snakes, and they are very poisonous.

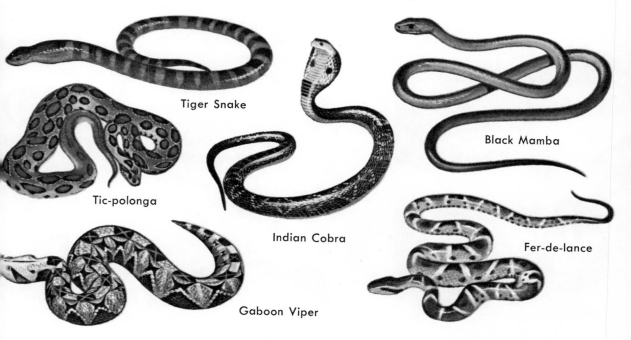

Tiger Snake

Tic-polonga

Indian Cobra

Gaboon Viper

Black Mamba

Fer-de-lance

Chimney Swift

Birds

Almost all the animals that fly are in two great groups, one without and the other with backbones. The two groups are, of course, the insects and the birds. In the days of the dinosaurs the birds had backboned rivals in the air, the flying reptiles. But times have changed. The only vertebrates besides the birds today that can fly are the bats, and birds outnumber bats ten times over.

Scientists have tried to find out how fast birds fly by timing some of them. The robin's speed is about 30 miles an hour. The chimney swift can fly twice as fast!

Having wings is one of the most important ways in which birds are fitted for flying. A flying fish can soar through the air for a long way. A flying dragon lizard can glide from tree to tree. But only creatures with true wings can really fly.

A typical bird's wings are powered by strong muscles. On the breastbone there is a projection called a keel to which the chief wing muscles are fastened. The wing feathers do much to make a bird's wings into wonderful flying machines.

A bird's light weight is a help in flying. A chimney swift weighs less than a mouse or lizard or toad of the same size. One reason a bird is so light is that, as with the flying reptiles of long ago, many of its bones are hollow and filled with air. Connected with

Robin's Nest and Eggs

Robin

its lungs a bird also has air sacs scattered through its body. The air sacs act like tiny hot-air balloons.

A streamlined body is another help in flying. One nickname of the chimney swift —"flying bow and arrow"—reminds us that this bird's body is streamlined.

Many birds use their power of flight to spend part of the year in one region and the rest of it in another. In the northern states the robin is one of the first signs of spring. For it goes south in the fall and returns north early in the spring. The chimney swift is a traveler, too. It leaves earlier than the robin in the fall, comes back later in the spring, and travels farther. Not all birds, however, have homes in two different parts of the world. Some stay in one place for season after season.

Kiwi

is trapped between them, feathers serve this purpose very well.

Just as there are some flying vertebrates that are not birds, there are a few birds that cannot fly. Since far back in the record of birds on the earth, there have been flightless birds. *Hesperornis,* you may remember, was an early one. Among the flightless birds of today are those pictured on these two pages. Still another, the emu, is pictured on page 176. Most birds, however, can fly for at least a short way, and many are remarkable fliers—they fly both fast and far.

With no tail, no wings that show, a rounded back, and short, thick legs, a kiwi is a strange-looking bird. Even though its

Besides being a great help in flying, feathers are an excellent protection for a bird's body. They shed water because they are a little oily and because the parts of each feather as well as the feathers themselves are very cleverly fitted together.

Feathers, moreover, help keep a bird's body warm. Since birds are warm-blooded animals, it is important for them to have a covering that will keep the heat of their bodies from escaping. Largely because air

Ostrich

Penguins

Jackass   Magellan   Little   Gentoo   Adelie   Rockhopper

legs are short, it lumbers along fast. Its long curved bill is good for pulling worms out of the ground. The kiwi is found only in New Zealand.

The ostrich, a native of Africa, is, as you know, the largest living bird. This giant bird is about 8 feet tall and runs faster than a horse. With each step it can cover 25 feet. In their native home ostriches often travel about in groups of 30 or more.

The cassowary is a bird of Australia and New Guinea. It is almost as tall as an ostrich. No one should find it hard, however, to tell the two birds apart. A cassowary has no beautiful plumes like those of an ostrich. And it has a strange crest on its head. The bare skin of its head and neck, moreover, is bright colored. Hanging down from the throats of some cassowaries are folds of skin called wattles.

The rhea is a bird of the South American grasslands. It is about 3 feet shorter than an ostrich, and, in spite of its broad look, not nearly so heavy. Its weight of 50 pounds, however, is greater than that of any other bird of the Americas. Its feathers make good feather dusters.

Many people think, when they see a penguin or a picture of one, that penguins have fur instead of feathers. Penguin feathers really are furlike. They make a good covering for these birds, many of which live on the icy shores of Antarctica and nearby islands. There are 15 different kinds of penguins, but all of them are alike in standing upright and in having paddle-like wings.

Rhea

Cassowary

171

Ruby-throated Hummingbird

Without any exceptions, birds hatch from eggs. Bird eggs all have hard shells very much like the shell of a common hen's egg. But they vary greatly in size. An ostrich egg is about 6 inches long. A hummingbird egg, in contrast, is only as big as a pea. As a rule the eggs are laid in nests built by one or both of the parents.

Some nests are wonderfully made. The ruby-throated hummingbird builds a beautiful little nest about the size of half a walnut.

The nest is lined with soft plant down and covered on the outside with moss, cobwebs, and lichens. It is built on a rather low limb.

The yellow warbler builds a small, stout nest of grasses and plant fibers. Some yellow warbler nests, like the one in the picture, have more than one story. The cowbird lays its eggs in the nests of other birds—often in the nests of warblers. When a yellow warbler finds a cowbird egg in its nest, it sometimes builds a new nest on top of the old one,

Yellow Warbler

leaving the cowbird egg to go uncared for in the "basement."

Birds have been on the earth for many millions of years longer than we have. The earlier birds could not build their nests near houses. But now many birds seem to prefer to do so. The house wren is one of them. This little bird will build its nest in an old tin can, a hole in a fence post, or the pocket of a discarded coat. It will also accept a man-made birdhouse. The amount of sticks and string and grass this bird will gather for its nest is amazing. A pair of wrens, once having chosen a birdhouse as its nesting

172

House Wren

place, may come back to the same one year after year to nest.

The purple martin is another bird that will accept a man-made birdhouse. Purple martins nest in colonies. A birdhouse provided for them usually has many separate "apartments," each with its own entrance. The Indians used to provide nesting places for martins by hanging hollow gourds from poles. Many farmers in the South still do so. People like having this bird nearby.

Each kind of bird has its own special kind of nest. A hummingbird never builds a nest like a wren's, or the other way around. A bird inherits its way of nest-building. It does not have to be taught how to build the nest, just as a honeybee does not have to be taught how to gather nectar and make honey, a spider does not have to be taught how

to spin its web, and a human being does not have to be taught how to walk upright.

Bird eggs, in order to hatch, have to be kept at a fairly steady temperature. As a rule the female bird sits on the eggs to keep them warm. With some kinds of birds the male shares or takes over this duty. Many male birds are much brighter in color than their mates. It is often an advantage, if the female does the sitting on the eggs, for her to be dull colored. She does not show so clearly.

Martin House

Bird Eggs

Pheasant

Robin

Hummingbird

Hen

Redwing

Ostrich

Sharp-shinned Hawk

173

New-hatched
Mockingbirds

The time that a bird's eggs must be kept warm, or incubated, before they hatch is different for different birds. A robin's eggs must be incubated for 12 or 13 days. A hen must sit on her eggs for about 21 days. The incubation time for an ostrich egg is twice as long and that for the egg of a wandering

Golden Eagle
and Nestlings

albatross about twice as long again. The tiny egg of a hummingbird hatches in 14 or 15 days.

Many birds, like the baby mockingbirds in the picture, are almost naked when they are hatched. They are so weak that they cannot stand up. Their eyes are shut, just as newborn kittens' eyes are. Their mouths are big, and their bills are rather soft. Such baby birds need to be kept warm and to be protected and well fed.

Baby birds like these eat an amazing amount of food for their size. Since they are warm-blooded, they have to eat not only enough to grow but also enough to help keep themselves warm. At night the mother bird, as a rule, hovers them to keep them from getting cold. Many little birds seem to be hungry all the time they are awake. A young bird, in fact, may eat its weight in food every day. A record kept of four baby robins showed that these little robins ate 16 earthworms in an hour—more than 5 feet of earthworm altogether. It keeps both parents busy from daybreak to dark finding enough food for a nestful of baby robins.

Some adult birds first swallow the food they get for the baby birds. Then they pump it up out of their stomachs into the wide-open mouths of the babies.

Baby birds grow fast. Even if they are naked when they are hatched, they are soon covered with soft downy feathers. Then bigger, stouter feathers begin to grow in.

While baby birds are still in the nest, they are often called nestlings. Young robins stay in their nest for 13 days or so. Little golden eagle nestlings like those in the picture have to stay in their nest for almost three months, for the nest is likely to be at the top of a steep cliff. The nest itself may be several feet tall. A pair of golden eagles usually uses the same nesting place year after year. Each year the eagles add more sticks to their nest.

Young birds like those pictured on this page are called fledglings. The mother and father birds may continue to bring them food for days, weeks, or even months.

Notice that the tails of all the fledglings in the pictures are short. Their tails must grow before the young birds can fly well and take over from their parents the job of getting food for themselves.

Fledglings, even when they are males, often look more like their mothers than like their fathers. A male scarlet tanager, for instance, does not take on its striking red-and-black coat until it is several months old. Probably dull-green coloring like the mother tanager's lessens the danger that the young birds will be caught by a cat or some other enemy.

Pine Warbler
Fledglings

Robin Fledglings

Male Scarlet Tanager
and Fledgling

175

Emu and Young

The four kinds of baby birds pictured here are not naked and helpless when they are hatched, as baby mockingbirds are. Instead, their eyes are bright and their bodies are covered with down. They are able to follow their parents about soon after their down is dry. As you see, these baby birds are much like little chicks.

Many other baby birds are like these in being able to fend for themselves soon after coming out of the egg. As a rule such birds stay in the egg longer than other birds of the same size. They have more time to grow there. In the eggs they hatch from, there is enough food to nourish the baby birds for the extra time.

The emu and the woodcock are land birds. Their babies run about on the ground. The swans and the Canada goose are waterfowl. Their babies spend much of the time swimming although they can walk on land.

The emu, a big flightless bird, lives on the dry plains of Australia. The eggs it lays are dark green and about 5½ inches long. One egg would be enough for scrambled eggs for a whole family.

Emu eggs must be incubated for about 60 days. The male emu sits on the eggs, and for the first few days after hatching he broods the babies just as a hen broods her chicks. Their conspicuous stripes make baby emus easy to identify.

Even baby woodcocks show some of the features that make adult woodcocks easy to tell from other birds. They have, for example, long bills with movable tips. A woodcock can push its bill into the ground and

Swans

Black-necked

Trumpete

Black

Mute

Woodcock Nestlings

feel about with the movable tip for an earthworm. It can open, if need be, only the tip. A woodcock's eyes, moreover, are set so far back that it can see all the way around its head.

The woodcock is a bird of forests and wet meadows. It has more than a dozen other common names. Among them are whistler, mud snipe, and timberdoodle.

Baby swans and geese—and baby ducks, or ducklings, too—are very much alike. Young swans are called cygnets, and young geese goslings. The goslings of the Canada goose need their coats of down to keep them warm, for they spend their babyhood far to the north.

Of course, the down with which all such baby birds are covered gives way to bigger feathers. Strangely enough, these birds have rather long babyhoods. The little birds hatched naked and helpless soon catch up with them. It is really no great wonder, for the little birds that are helpless when hatched are, as you know, stuffed with food. The down-covered birds do not eat so much in proportion to their size.

Canada Goose Nestlings

Ibises

Glossy

Sacred

Scarlet

White

There are about 8,600 kinds of birds altogether. Feathers make it easy to tell them from other animals. Bills and wings are a help, too, in telling whether an animal is a bird. But, although all birds are enough alike to be easily told from other animals, there are many differences among them. Birds range in size, for example, from the tiny hummingbird, which weighs less than a penny, to the ostrich, which may weigh 300 pounds. As you know, there have been in past ages birds even larger, but those bird giants are now extinct.

All birds have two legs, but the legs of one kind may be very different from those of another. Some are long, some short; some are strong, others weak; some are fastened farther back on the body than others.

The feet of birds are as different as their legs. Most birds have four toes. As a rule, three of the four toes point forward and one points backward. But some birds—the flicker, for example—have two toes that point forward and two that point backward. Some birds have webbed feet. Some have spreading toes or toes with sharp, strong claws. Some have feet so weak that the birds can barely walk with them.

You already know that the wings of birds are not all alike. You know, too, that a bird's bill—the woodcock's for one—may be peculiar. Bird bills come in many different shapes. Some are long and slender, some short and stout. Some are curved, some straight. Some end in sharp points and some are blunt. Bills are much more than mere mouths. They are also hands and tools. By imagining building a house and

Indigo Bunting

Flicker

Wood Duck

getting dinner with your hands tied behind your back, you can get an idea of how important to a bird its bill is.

A full-grown bird has several kinds of feathers—as a rule downy feathers, body feathers, and wing and tail flight feathers. It may have others, too, that serve special purposes. One bird's feathers may be very different in shape from another's. Notice the flicker's sharp-pointed tail feathers.

The common names of birds tell what a big range in color there is. We have, for example, the scarlet ibis, the indigo bunting, the cardinal, the purple gallinule, the brown thrasher, and the goldfinch.

Many differences in birds are related to the places where the birds live. Webbed feet help water birds swim. Long legs help shore birds wade. Strong legs like a robin's and a bobwhite's are good for hopping or walking about on the ground. Flickers, like all other woodpeckers, dig their nests in tree trunks. Their pointed tail feathers act as braces as the birds work. A flicker's sharp, strong bill is a good digging tool.

body feather

down feather

primary flight feather

secondary flight feather

tail feather

body feather

Feathers

Feet of Birds

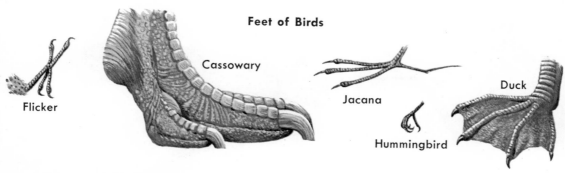

Flicker

Cassowary

Jacana

Hummingbird

Duck

179

Northern Shrike

A northern shrike would soon be very hungry if it had nothing to eat but the food a junco eats. A yellow-billed cuckoo could neither catch nor eat the food of a puffin. A nighthawk would not do at all well on the food of a tree sparrow. Most birds have their own food or foods. Many of the differences between birds have to do with the kinds of food they live on.

The northern shrike is sometimes called the butcher-bird. It gets this nickname because it often hangs up its "meat" just as a butcher hangs meat up on hooks in his market. A shrike's meat consists mainly of mice and big insects such as grasshoppers. The hooks it hangs its meat on are the thorns of a bush or tree or the barbs of a barbed-wire fence. Some people think, when they see food it has hung up, that a shrike kills other animals just for the fun of it. Probably, however, hanging up some of the mammals and insects it catches is just a way of storing up food for a rainy day.

The nighthawk eats nothing but insects. The insects, however, are not big insects like grasshoppers. They are small insects such as mosquitoes that the nighthawk catches as it flies about. It opens its mouth wide and scoops up insects from the air much as a fisherman gathers in fish with a net. Notice how small the nighthawk's bill is. A bill like a puffin's would get in the way of scooping in insects.

The slim, graceful yellow-billed cuckoo eats insects, but it does not catch them in the air. It eats many hairy caterpillars, a food most birds avoid.

All hawks are meat-eaters. The smallest hawks have to be content with insects, mice, and other little animals. Big hawks may catch mammals as big as rabbits and fast-

Nighthawk

Yellow-billed Cuckoo

Goshawk

Peregrine Falcon

Sparrow Hawk

Junco

Tree Sparrow

Puffins

flying birds as large as themselves. Catching such prey means that the hawk must fly very fast. And hawks do. The peregrine falcon, or duck hawk, is thought to be the fastest of birds. It sometimes reaches a speed of 175 miles an hour.

Vultures, close relatives of the hawks, are meat-eaters, too. But they are scavengers— they eat dead animals.

The junco and the tree sparrow for the most part eat seeds. As they gather the seeds they catch some insects, too. But they could live on seeds alone. Their stout bills are good for cracking small seeds. These two birds are built very differently from hawks. Since the seeds they eat, unlike animals, cannot try to keep from being eaten, there is no need for fast flight to get food. To gather seeds, moreover, there is no need for the hooked beaks and strong claws of the hawks.

Puffins are fish-eaters. One of the puffins in the picture, you notice, has several small fish hanging from its bill. A puffin that goes out to sea on a fishing expedition may bring back as many as 20 fish for the "pufflings" in its nest.

Some birds live on a wide variety of foods. The robin, for example, does. Earthworms, blackberries, cherries, and grubs are a few of the many things it eats.

Roadrunner

Great Horned Owl

Scientists have divided birds into more than 20 orders. The perching birds make up by far the largest order. More than half of all the thousands of kinds of birds are in it.

The birds pictured on these two pages belong in seven different orders. Although some of them are shown perching, none of them are in the order of perching birds.

The roadrunner is a bird of the desert land of southwestern United States and Mexico. It spends more time running about on the ground than flying. It can run faster than most horses. The cuckoos are in the same order.

Owls make up an order all their own. Many other owls have ear tufts like the great horned owl's "horns." The horns are not ears, but simply tufts of feathers. Owls do, however, have large ear openings and excellent hearing. They are birds of the night; bright sunlight blinds them. At night their eyesight is so keen that it enables them to catch such animals as field mice. The eyes of all owls face forward.

A peacock is a male peafowl. With its beautiful train of feathers, it is one of the handsomest of all birds. It often raises this train of feathers into a great fan as it struts about. In the order with the peafowl are all the pheasants, quail, grouse, and partridges, as well as turkeys and chickens.

The whippoorwill is one of the goatsuckers. The nighthawk is another well-known

Peacock

bird in this order. There is an old superstition that the goatsuckers can milk goats. There is no truth in it. Actually they eat nothing but insects. The whippoorwill gets its name from its call. The nighthawk looks like a hawk and flies about at dusk. It calls incessantly as it flies.

The wood stork is in an order that includes all the storks, herons, flamingos, and bitterns. Many of the birds of the order are long-legged shore birds. The wood stork is an American stork. The white stork of Europe and Asia is one of the most famous birds in the order. It often builds its nests on roofs of buildings. A stork's nest is supposed to bring good luck.

Gulls are water birds. They are a common sight along the shores of lakes and seas. They are fish-eaters. In the same order with the gulls are the terns, sandpipers, auks, puffins, plovers, and jacanas.

In the order with the Canada goose are all the other geese, the ducks, and the swans. They are all water birds and good swimmers. They are also good fliers: some of them can fly 60 miles an hour.

Whippoorwill

Wood Stork

Gulls

Canada Goose

183

Belted
Kingfisher

Emperor Penguin

Common Loon

Wandering
Albatross

Gannet

Yellow-headed
Amazon Parrot

Coot

184

These birds represent eight other orders of non-perching birds. The rails, cranes, and coots are all in the same order. The other birds are in seven different ones.

Penguins are in an order of their own, a very ancient one. The 3-foot-tall emperor looks almost human as it walks about.

A kingfisher's strong bill is good for catching fish. Kingfishers are in an order with the strange hornbills of Old World tropical lands. Page 199 shows a hornbill.

The wandering albatross has the greatest wingspread of any living bird. The distance from wing tip to wing tip is nearly 12 feet. This big bird spends most of its time far out at sea. It rides the winds high above the water for day after day. In the order with the albatrosses are the petrels and shearwaters. They, too, are sea birds that spend most of their time miles from shore.

Loons, like penguins, are in an order by themselves. There are only four kinds. All are expert swimmers and divers. They are good fliers, too, but they have trouble taking off. The common loon is famous for its eerie cries and wild "laughter."

The gannet is a common bird of the North Atlantic coasts. It is not as spectacular as some of the other birds in the same order, for the order includes the pelicans and the magnificent man-of-war, or frigate, birds. It also includes the boobies.

Parrots, too, form an order all their own, but there are many more kinds of parrots than there are kinds of loons or penguins. It is common knowledge that some parrots can be trained to talk. The yellow-headed Amazon parrot is a good talker. Some parrots are called cockatoos, others macaws, lovebirds, lories, or parakeets.

Of course you know that the bald eagle is the national bird of the United States. It was chosen for its strength and independence. In the order with the eagles are the vultures and hawks. Birds of this order are found almost all over the world.

The order that includes the cranes, coots, and rails also includes the gallinules. All are birds of shores or swamplands.

Sora Rail

Virginia Rail

Bald Eagle

Cranes

Crowned

Whooping

Sandhill

Demoiselle

185

Baltimore Oriole

The perching birds are divided up into many families. There are, for instance, thrushes, finches, and vireos, swallows and wrens. There are some 50 others besides. Many of the birds of America have close relatives in other parts of the world, but not all of them do. The birds pictured on these two pages belong to a truly American bird family—the blackbirds. No birds of the blackbird family can be found anywhere except in the Americas.

The blackbird family has nearly 100 kinds of birds in it. Many of them live near the equator, but several—all but one of the seven pictured—are common in the United States. The red-breasted blackbird lives in South America.

The handsome bronzed grackle, with its glossy black feathers, is one of the birds that gave the family its name. But grackles are not popular with people. They come together in big flocks and are noisy. Besides, they often drive other birds away.

The Baltimore oriole is a beautiful bird and a wonderful nest-builder. An oriole's nest is a gray bag. It hangs from the end of a limb high above the ground. The nest is woven of horsehair, strings, and plant fibers such as those which come from the outside of milkweed stalks. Grass and bark may be woven into the nest, too. Sometimes rags and bits of paper are used on the inside

of the nest. It is usually lined with hair. An oriole's nest must be strong, for it may have to hold as many as six babies. The female bird does the weaving. Of all blackbirds, orioles are the best singers.

The bobolink has a sweet, gay song. It has been called the "gladdest bird there is." The male bobolink changes his dress in the fall and spring. In the picture he has on his summer dress. In the winter he is dull brown, just as his mate is all the year round. The bobolink gets so fat before it flies south for the winter that it is sometimes called the "butter bird."

The cowbird gets its name because it is often seen in cow pastures. It eats insects the cows stir up. The cowbird is nicknamed the "lazybird." This name comes from its habit of laying its eggs in the nests of other birds instead of building a nest for itself. Often enough the birds the nests belong to take good care of cowbird eggs left in their nests and of the little birds that hatch from the eggs. But as you know, if you remember the yellow warbler's two-story nest, not all cowbird eggs are well taken care of.

The yellow-headed blackbird looks exactly as one would guess from its name.

The meadowlark can be told by its bright-yellow breast and black collar. This bird is found in fields and meadows. It builds its nest on the ground.

A well-known blackbird not pictured here is the redwing. It is a common swamp bird all over the United States. In many places there are so many redwings that the bird is a serious pest because of the damage it does to grain crops.

Bronzed Grackle

Bobolink

Red-breasted Blackbird

Yellow-headed Blackbird

Meadowlark

Cowbird

187

"Here are more blackbirds," you may think when you look at the crow and the raven. But these birds are not in the blackbird family. Not all black birds are blackbirds, just as not all blackbirds are black. A bird may even be called a blackbird without being in the blackbird family. In the Mother Goose rhyme of "four-and-twenty blackbirds" the bird meant is the European blackbird, which is a thrush.

Another member of the family that includes the raven and crow is the blue jay. All the jays and the magpies and nutcrackers, too, are in this family.

The birds of the jay-crow family are believed by many people to be the most intelligent of all birds. They appear to have good memories. Nutcrackers, for example, store nuts away during the summer and fall, and in the winter can go straight to where the nuts are hidden.

All the birds pictured on the next page belong to the tyrant flycatcher family. The tyrant flycatchers are active and daring. This family, like the blackbirds, is strictly American. There are flycatchers in the Old World, but they belong to another bird

Raven

Crow

Blue Jay

Vermilion Flycatcher

Scissor-tailed Flycatcher

Eastern Kingbird

Great Crested Flycatcher

Phoebe

family. There are more than 350 tyrant fly-catchers. As you can tell from the five in the picture, the members of the family differ considerably in size, shape, and color. They are alike in having good bills for catching insects.

Flycatchers eat flies. They also eat mosquitoes, grasshoppers, crickets, beetles, bees—in fact, almost every kind of insect there is. A few also eat small reptiles and amphibians, and one kind can catch fish.

Kingbirds are especially daring. They will attack crows or even hawks. The eastern kingbird is sometimes called the bee martin because it eats many honeybees. This flycatcher can be told easily by the orange-red patch on its head and the white band at the tip of its tail.

The scissor-tailed flycatcher is easy to identify by its very long, forked tail. It is the state bird of Oklahoma. The phoebe gets its name from its call, the vermilion flycatcher from its color, and the great crested flycatcher from its size and the crest on its head.

Bluebird

Redstart

Towhee

Goldfinch

Here are eight more perching birds. They represent four different families.

The goldfinch and the towhee belong to the finch family. So do the cardinal, the indigo bunting, the rose-breasted grosbeak, and the sparrows. The family is the largest of all bird families, but over half the birds in it are Old World birds.

The bluebird, the hermit thrush, and the wood thrush belong to the thrush family. This, too, is a big family, with over 300 birds in it. Not many of them, however, live in our country. Among the others that do are the robin and the veery.

The redstart belongs to the same family as the magnolia warbler. Both are warblers.

A name often used for this New World family of small birds is wood warblers. All the birds in the family are woodland birds.

The nuthatch is one of only four members of the nuthatch family found in our country. Nuthatches do eat nuts, but their chief food is insects.

A bluebird does not look much like its cousins, the wood and hermit thrushes. But it shows when it is young that it is a thrush. Baby bluebirds have speckled breasts. So do baby robins. Veeries have speckles all their lives. The thrushes are insect-eaters. They have short but rather sharp bills.

Redstarts get their name from the color on their wings and tail and from the quick way they hop about from branch to branch. The birds are almost never still.

A towhee spends most of its time on the ground—so much so that it is often called the ground robin. Another name for it is chewink. It gets this name from its call.

The goldfinch is sometimes called the thistlebird. As a rule it lines its nest with thistledown. It eats many thistle seeds, too. During the summer the male goldfinch is much brighter than the female. In the fall he changes his dress, just as the bobolink does. Then he looks like his mate.

The nuthatch is in its usual position in the picture—head down on the trunk of a tree. It has, you can see, a sharp bill. The bird uses its sharp bill to dig its insect food out of cracks in bark.

Of these eight birds, two are permanent residents in the places where they are found. They stay in one place, that is, the year round. These two are the goldfinch and the nuthatch. The others have winter homes in one part of the world and summer homes in another. In many parts of North America the redstart and the magnolia warbler are merely callers. They pay a visit for a day or two on their way south in the fall and on their way north in the spring. They winter in Mexico or farther south and nest in our northernmost states and Canada. The bluebird, the towhee, and the thrushes also nest in northern states. They winter in southern states or in Mexico.

White-breasted Nuthatch

Wood Thrush

Hermit Thrush

Magnolia Warbler

Some birds of other orders make pleasing sounds, but all the true bird songsters are perching birds. By no means every bird of this group, however, has a beautiful song. No one would call the starling, the crow, or the grackle a good singer, although they are all perching birds.

Saying that someone sings like a lark is paying the singer a high compliment. Larks have beautiful songs. Poems have been written honoring the skylark and its song. The only part of the United States, unfortunately, where you ever hear a skylark is Hawaii. The skylark has been carried from Europe and established there as well as in many other parts of the world. A lark more common in our country is the horned lark.

The robin has a pleasant song. As you know, it belongs to the thrush family, a family of famous songsters. Many people think that the hermit thrush is the finest songster of all the birds in the family. Others consider that the nightingale, an Old World thrush, has the most beautiful song. The nightingale's song, too, has inspired many poets and other writers.

Another bird that ranks high as a songster is the mockingbird. It may be heard pouring out a torrent of song at any time of the day or night or year. The mockingbird belongs to a family sometimes called the mimic thrushes. The mockingbird is truly a mimic; it imitates the songs of other birds. It often repeats over and over just one phrase of another bird's song.

The usual home of the mockingbird is in the southern states, Mexico, or the West Indies. This bird is seldom found as far north as the Great Lakes and New England. But in the northern states it has a cousin that is almost as good a singer and mimic— the catbird. The catbird has a black cap which the mockingbird does not have. A brown patch under its tail is another help in telling it from its relative. The call of a catbird is a mew that sounds much like a cat and gives the bird its name. In Mexico the blue mockingbird adds its songs to those of its better-known mockingbird cousin.

The brown thrasher is also in the mockingbird family. It, too, has a lovely song. It often does its singing from deep in a thicket of leaves and branches.

Canaries are famous songbirds. Although both the goldfinch and the yellow warbler are sometimes called the wild canary, only one, the goldfinch, has a family right to the name. The goldfinch and the canary

Horned Lark

Skylark

Blue Mockingbird

Mockingbird

Brown
Thrasher

Catbird

are close relatives. Another relative, the beautiful cardinal, is among America's best-liked songsters.

The ruby-crowned kinglet is a tiny bird—of North American birds only the hummingbirds are smaller. But it has a beautiful flutelike song. This small singer belongs to a large family known as the Old World warblers. The Old World warblers are better singers than the wood warblers.

Ruby-crowned
Kinglet

Cardinal

Purple Martin

Scientists have studied the food of birds carefully. Some birds are helpful and others are harmful because of the kinds of food they eat.

Birds help us by eating weed seeds, small harmful mammals such as field mice, dead animals, and insect pests. Weeds in a field or garden crowd the plants we are trying to raise and often take from the soil water and minerals the crop plants need. Field mice eat seeds and young plants. Dead animals would turn the earth into a great rubbish heap if there were no clean-up brigade. And insect pests, as you know, do harm to shade trees, fruit trees, crop plants, our tame animals, and even to ourselves.

Birds harm us by eating fruit, grain, and helpful insects. Some birds do harm, moreover, by eating the eggs of other birds and even small birds themselves. A few kinds of birds eat the buds of trees or drill into the trunks to get sap.

Of course, no bird is ever consciously helping us or harming us. We should not blame the birds that harm us any more than we should praise those that help us. They are simply eating the food they are fitted for eating.

Not many birds have records that make them entirely helpful or entirely harmful. We have to weigh the good a bird does against the bad.

The three birds pictured here are all beneficial. We count them as friends.

The purple martin, the biggest of the American swallows, earns practically a perfect score as a friend. Its food is almost entirely insects. Among these insects are several that are harmful to our fruit trees. A flock of martins in an orchard may save a fruitgrower the expense of spraying his orchard. Mosquitoes, too, are one of the martin's chief foods.

Chipping Sparrow

All the swallows are insect-eaters. Partly because of their help in destroying insects and also because they are attractive and friendly, the swallows are among the best-liked of birds.

The male rose-breasted grosbeak, as you see from its picture, is a beautiful bird. The female follows the common pattern among female birds of being mostly brown. She looks like a big sparrow. One nickname of the rose-breasted grosbeak is "potato-bug bird." As this nickname suggests, the grosbeak eats a great many potato bugs. It also eats weed seeds. Its short, strong bill is a typical seedeater's bill.

A close relative of the grosbeak, the cardinal, also ranks high as a friend. It eats some grain, but it does many times as much good by eating insect pests as it does harm by eating grain. In the South it is a great enemy of the cotton worm.

The chipping sparrow is another, but more distant, relative. This seedeater sometimes does damage to newly seeded lawns, but most of its food is wild grass seed and harmful insects. The field sparrow, the song sparrow, the vesper sparrow, and the tree sparrow are four more of the sparrows that rate high as friends.

One of the many other birds of our back yards that rate as friends because of the food they eat is the house wren. This little bird is strictly an insect-eater.

Rose-breasted Grosbeak

195

Red-tailed Hawk

Marsh Hawk

Swallow-tailed
Kite

because they furnish food for us. Centuries ago men found the meat of birds so good to eat that they began domesticating wild fowl of several kinds. We now raise millions of ducks, chickens, geese, and turkeys. Eggs, too, are important in our diet. There are still many wild game birds. Ducks, geese, quails, grouse, partridges, and pheasants are among them.

We use the feathers of some birds. Goose down, for instance, is excellent for pillows.

Bobwhite Quail

California
Quail

The bird friends you have just read about all belong in the order of perching birds. But there are many helpful birds in other orders. The quails are very valuable to farmers because of the weed seeds and the insects they eat. We get a great deal of help in fighting rats and mice from the hawks, kites, and owls. The vultures are our best bird scavengers. And the cuckoos, nighthawks, swifts, and woodpeckers destroy vast numbers of insects.

Some birds have a bad reputation which they do not deserve. The red-tailed hawk is a good example. This hawk occasionally kills chickens when its usual food is scarce. But it catches so few chickens in proportion to the mice and insects it eats that its common name of chicken hawk is unfair.

Of course, some birds are beneficial to us not because of the food they eat, but

Some perching birds, too, are valued for their feathers. Among them are the strange and colorful birds of paradise. To see one of them in its native home, you would have to go to northern Australia, New Guinea, or nearby small islands. Some birds of paradise live in mountain forests almost impossible to reach. Much of what scientists know about this family comes from studying birds of paradise in zoos.

All the birds of paradise pictured are male birds. Their wonderful display of feathers has to do chiefly with courtship.

For centuries plumes of birds of paradise have been used as ornaments in New Guinea. The first sight of them in Europe was when Magellan's ship "Victoria" came back to Spain in 1522 from its round-the-world trip with two bird of paradise skins brought as a gift to the king. They were so beautiful that the Spaniards said the birds must have come from paradise. The name "bird of paradise" has been used ever since.

Quetzal

All these colorful birds, too, are natives of tropical regions. The beautiful quetzal is the national bird of Guatemala. One of the coins of that country is called a quetzal. To the early Indians of Middle America, quetzal plumes were a sign of royalty. And even rather recently quetzals were being killed in large numbers for their plumes. Now the bird is protected.

Most of the more than 300 kinds of hummingbirds live near the equator. Many, like these three, have gayer colors or fancier feathers than our hummingbirds have.

Cockatoos are parrots of the Australia-New Guinea region. They can raise and lower their crests to suit their moods. These parrots do not do much talking.

Tropical Hummingbirds

Cockatoos

Toco Toucan

Emerald
Toucanet

Great Hornbill

Toucans are easy to recognize by their bills. With these enormous bills they gather fruits and catch insects, lizards, and even nestling birds to eat. The toco toucan is over 2 feet long, much longer than the emerald toucanet. Toucans clacking their bills make a great deal of noise.

The great hornbill deserves its name. It is 5 feet long and has a very strong, horny bill. This bird of Asia is famous not only for its size and strange appearance, but also for one of its habits. When the female is ready to lay her eggs, she climbs into a hole in a hollow tree. Then the entrance is walled up with mud, with only a narrow opening left. The mother bird stays walled in until the young birds that hatch from her eggs are ready to fly. All the while she is imprisoned, the male feeds his family through the small opening in the mud wall.

Dodo

Prairie Chicken

Great Auk

California
Condor

Once the dodo was common on a tiny island in the Indian Ocean. But this bird has been extinct since 1681. Sailors that landed on the island had a great deal to do with making the dodo disappear. They killed many dodoes for meat. The big bird could not fly and it did not know enough even to try to save itself by running away.

Another flightless bird now extinct because people killed too many is the great auk. This bird lived in the sea and nested on islands in the North Atlantic. Hunters trapped and killed the nesting birds for their meat and feathers. No great auks have been seen since 1844.

The passenger pigeon vanished more recently. The last one died in a Cincinnati zoo in 1914. Just 150 years ago the great flocks of passenger pigeons in America were one of the wonders of the bird world.

Cutting down forests where the pigeon nested had something to do with making it disappear. But hunters were more to blame. They killed enormous numbers for food. Nestlings brought higher prices than older birds and were easy to catch since there were often dozens of nests in a single tree. After a while there were millions of pigeons instead of billions, then thousands instead of millions. Finally none were left.

When people saw that the passenger pigeon was disappearing, laws were passed to protect it. But the laws were too late. Today a number of our other birds are in danger. At least some of them may be saved if the laws protecting them are obeyed.

Prairie chickens, once common game birds from the western prairies to the Atlantic coast, are now rare. One kind, the heath hen, is already gone.

Probably fewer than 50 of North America's largest bird, the California condor, are still alive. All that we know of live in a wildlife sanctuary in the mountains of California. Leaving the condor undisturbed is the best hope of saving it.

The story of the trumpeter swan is an encouraging one. This big white bird is the largest waterfowl in the world. Every year

Trumpeter Swan

big numbers used to be seen on their trips between their summer home in northern Canada and Alaska and their winter home in the southern half of the United States. Hunters found the trumpeter an easy target. In 1933, in spite of a law to protect it, only 66 were counted. But now it is increasing in numbers. By the last count there are nearly a thousand.

In recent years the draining of its swampland homes has threatened the roseate spoonbill. Wildlife refuges now established to insure it a place to live may save this beautiful bird for us.

The whooping crane makes headlines every spring and fall. Birds arriving from the north in the fall and from the south in the spring are counted carefully. The latest count showed the bird just holding its own.

Steps to save the ivory-billed woodpecker may have failed. In the past several years only one ivorybill has been reported. Once an animal is extinct, it is gone forever. There is no way to get it back again.

Roseate Spoonbill

Eurasian Spoonbill

Mammals

Of the animals pictured on this page, the koala and platypus clearly are mammals. Their fur announces that they are. The spiny anteater is also a mammal, but its stiff, sharp spines keep it from looking furry. Another name for this strange-looking animal is echidna.

The platypus and the spiny anteater belong to an order of mammals called *monotremes*. The monotremes differ from other mammals in that they lay eggs. All other mammals are born alive. After monotreme babies are hatched, however, they are fed with milk from the mother just as other mammal babies are. Monotremes are found only in Australia and some nearby islands.

Another name for the platypus is duckbill. When early settlers in Australia sent some platypus skins back to England, scientists there thought it was all a joke. They thought that the bills of ducks had been sewed to the skins of some furry animal.

The platypus is like a duck not only in having a bill and laying eggs, but also in having webbed feet. Platypuses are very much at home in the water. They use their stout bills to dig worms and shellfish out of the mud at the bottom of streams and ponds. The animals live in long burrows dug in the banks. The female makes a nest of weeds at the far end of a burrow and lays two or three eggs. Young platypuses are undeveloped and very tiny when they hatch. The mother helps hold them in place with her tail as they nurse.

On their hind legs the males have poison spurs. The only other known poisonous mammals are shrews.

A female spiny anteater rolls up in a ball and lays her two eggs directly in a pouch on the underside of her body. The babies that hatch stay in the pouch for several weeks. When they get to be too prickly, the mother scratches them out.

The spiny anteater is well built for living on ants. It has stout claws that are useful in tearing ant nests apart, a long beak, and an even longer sticky tongue. There are other anteaters among the mammals, but none are at all closely related to it.

Koala

Platypus

Spiny Anteater

202

The koala is a pouched mammal, or *marsupial*. Marsupials do not lay eggs. The babies are born alive, but they, too, are undeveloped and very, very small. The mother carries them about—in most cases in a pouch on her underside—until they are well covered with fur and able to eat foods other than milk. Even after a baby marsupial is able to leave its mother's pouch it may climb back into the pouch when it needs protection.

Like all the monotremes, most marsupials live in the Australian region. The opossum is the one North American marsupial. Unlike most other marsupials, opossums have many babies at a time, often 12 or more, and sometimes as many as 18.

The marsupials are far and away the leading mammals native to Australia. There are many kinds. For a very, very long time they had the continent pretty much to themselves so far as mammals were concerned. Australia has been separated by the sea from the rest of the world since the Age of Reptiles. Few mammals reached it on their own.

Of Australia's marsupials that are widely known, the koala is second only to the kangaroo. This little native "bear" lives in

Opossum

Australia

Kangaroo

Koala

Glider

Platypus

Kangaroo

trees and eats chiefly eucalyptus leaves. Only one or two young are born at a time. A baby koala stays in the mother's pouch for about six months and then climbs on her back and rides pickaback for another year. Its rides must be exciting, for koalas, although they spend most of the day sleeping among the lower branches of trees, go hopping about in the trees at dusk, often making jumps of several feet.

A young kangaroo's rides in its mother's pouch must be thrilling, too, when it is old enough to sit up and watch what is going on. Kangaroos are famous for the long leaps they make. The leaps often measure 20 feet. Kangaroos are grazers and browsers. Many of them live where plant foods are scarce. It is an advantage to be able to cover ground fast.

The honeysucker, sugar glider, and Tasmanian devil are other marsupials of the Australian region. The Tasmanian devil is now found only in Tasmania.

The honeysucker, or "honey mouse," and the sugar glider are close relatives of the koala. The honeysucker is mouse size. It pushes its slender snout and long tongue into flowers and pumps nectar, pollen, and insects up into its mouth. Gliders, also known as flying phalangers, are many times as big as honeysuckers. They cannot really fly—

Honeysucker

Sugar Glider

Tasmanian Devil

Deer Mouse

they can only glide. The sugar glider lives on nectar, leaves and flowers, insects, and the sap of trees.

The Tasmanian devil is about the size of a big house cat. The sounds it makes are as ugly as its looks. The devil is strong enough to kill animals far bigger than it is.

Among the other marsupials of Australia are "pocket-mice," wombats, bandicoots, wallaroos, and wallabies. The wallaroos and wallabies are in the kangaroo family.

Scientists call all the mammals except the monotremes and marsupials *placentals*. The deer mouse, gray shrew, and blue whale are in this group. The young of placental mammals are kept inside the mother until they are much better developed than baby marsupials. Although the babies at birth are not so tiny and helpless as baby marsupials, they, too, need care for weeks or

months—in some cases even years—after they are born. It is easy to see that baby deer mice need to be taken care of.

"As big as an elephant" is a common saying, but a blue whale is far larger—it is, so far as anyone knows, the largest animal that ever lived. The gray, or desert, shrew is only 3 inches long including its tail. A blue whale may measure 100 feet! The lightweight among the mammals is another tiny shrew—the pigmy. It would take more than 50 million pigmy shrews to weigh as much as one big blue whale.

A shrew is a bundle of energy. It is so active that every day it has to eat more than twice its weight in food, mainly insects. As you know, the blue whale lives in the sea. It eats chiefly tiny crustaceans called krill. This whale does not have teeth. Instead, it has plates of whalebone. On the edges of the plates there are long bristles which strain the little animals out of the water. A blue whale eats less in proportion to its size than a shrew, but imagine how many millions of krill it has to devour in one day!

Gray Shrew

Blue Whale

Walrus

All these animals are mammals of the sea. The walrus and the seals are fin-footed mammals. They spend part of the time up on land. Although the fin-footed mammals are great fish-eaters, they eat many other kinds of animals besides. The walrus eats mostly shellfish. Along with the clams it digs up with its long tusks it gets some seaweed. The walrus and most kinds of seals live in cold waters.

In contrast, the manatee, or sea cow, lives in tropical seas close to shore and, often enough, in river mouths and freshwater lagoons. This gentle beast eats only plants. A manatee has no hind legs. Probably seeing the homely but human-looking sea cow holding her baby in her flippers gave sailors the idea of mermaids.

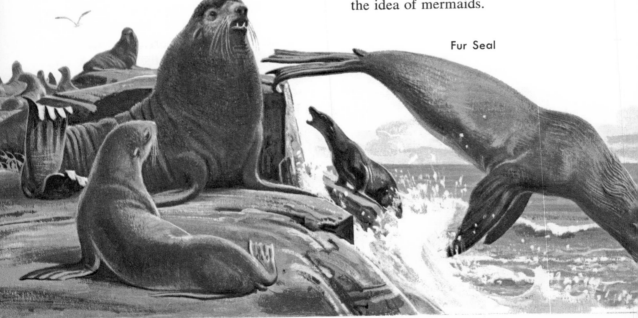

Fur Seal

The killer whale, porpoise, and dolphins are all toothed whales. The killer, which is only about a third as long as the blue whale, is the most terrible meat-eater of today. With its huge, sharp teeth it catches seals and smaller whales and often bites great chunks out of bigger whales. It has an enormous appetite. Most of the so-called porpoises in marine-life shows are really dolphins. Both dolphins and porpoises rank high in intelligence.

A sea otter often floats on its back. It sometimes uses its stomach as a lunch counter on which to spread out the crabs, clams, and sea urchins it has caught as food. A mother otter sleeps on her back holding her baby with her forepaws.

Manatee

Killer Whale

Dall's Porpoise

Sea Otter

Dolphins

Harbor Seal

Bottlenose

Common

Spotted

Big-eared Bat

Hoary Bat

Pika

These mammals all live on land. They belong in four different orders.

Bats form an order all their own. They are the only mammals that can truly fly. There are many kinds. The bats of the United States eat mostly insects. In Asia and Africa fruit bats are common. In tropical America there are vampire bats that bite animals and lap up the blood.

Jackrabbit

Cottontail

Anteaters

Giant

Pigmy

Lesser

Rabbits, hares, and pikas form another order. It is easy to tell rabbits and hares from other mammals by their looks, but it is not easy to tell rabbits and hares apart. Their common names do not help. Jack-rabbits, for instance, are hares. The common cottontail is a rabbit.

The small round ears of pikas make them easy to tell from their rabbit-hare cousins. These little animals make a lifework of gathering and storing food. They pile up stacks of grass and other plants near the entrances to their rock-crevice homes. When it rains they rush their stores inside.

The three anteaters pictured here are in an order that also includes the sloths and armadillos. The giant anteater, as you can see, is an awkward-looking creature. The claws on its front feet are so long that they interfere with walking. But they are wonderful for ripping open nests of ants and termites. The anteater laps up the insects with a sticky tongue 12 inches long. Its bushy tail makes a good sunshade or umbrella for the animal as it rests. The other two anteaters pictured live in trees just as sloths do. Their tails are good for hanging onto branches.

Moles are seldom seen, for they live underground. They belong in the order of

Mole

European Hedgehog

Common Tenrec

insectivores, or insect-eaters, an order that includes the shrews and the hedgehogs. Like the shrews, moles eat almost every minute they are awake. Their food is mostly earthworms, but they eat any insect or other small animal they find.

A hedgehog, too, eats many things besides insects. It will eat slugs, small birds and snakes, eggs, and even fruits, roots, and mushrooms. It does most of its hunting at night and sleeps during the daytime. When in danger the animal curls up in a tight ball with the sharp spines on its back sticking out in almost every direction. Its close relative, the tenrec, also has prickly spines. The tenrec is the largest animal of the order. It may be a foot and a half long. This creature has no tail at all. Another of its peculiarities is the number of babies born at a time. There may be more than 20 in a litter!

The giant pangolin is an anteater, but it is not put in an order with any of the anteaters you have already met. The pangolins, or scaly anteaters, are in an order of their own. They get the "scaly" in their name from horny scales that all but cover their bodies. In the picture of the giant pangolin you see no sign of hair. A pangolin has very little hair on its body, and what it does have is on its unscaled underside.

Giant Pangolin

To rest, pangolins curl themselves into a coil with the tail wrapped around the outside of the coil and hooked in place. They are remarkably strong. A giant pangolin can pull several people along. And if one is curled up, not enough men can get their hands on it to uncoil it.

A giant pangolin is not much of a giant. It measures about 6 feet from the tip of its snout to the end of its long tail.

The hyraxes and the elephants are also in orders by themselves. They are not alike in shape or in size or in habits, but the elephants are about the closest relatives hyraxes have. In Africa, where many hyraxes live, they have been called "little brothers of elephants." Both the hyraxes and the elephants are leftovers from groups once much larger and more important.

Hyraxes are mentioned in the Bible, but they are called conies there. These little animals look much like short-eared rabbits. They are quick to bite any animal that disturbs them. They have long front teeth that are as sharp as daggers. Hyraxes make amazing sounds. They chatter and whistle and scream as if in agony.

Some hyraxes live among rocks, usually in colonies. Pads on their feet that act as vacuum cups help make them as skilful at climbing steep rocky slopes as mountain goats are. A common name for these hyraxes is dassies. Other kinds live in trees.

No other animal of today looks enough like an elephant to be confused with it. An elephant's trunk alone serves to identify it. Almost every zoo has its elephants. They do well in captivity.

Elephants are the biggest land animals of today. The African elephant is larger than the Indian elephant and its ears are larger. The pictures show other differences between the two.

Indian elephants have long been tamed to do different kinds of heavy work. In ancient times they served as mammoth warhorses. African elephants, too, used to be used in wars, but they are not such common work animals today as Indian elephants.

Feeding peanuts to the elephants is part of the fun of going to a zoo. But wild elephants feed on grass and roots instead. Their tusks are a big help in digging up roots. In its mouth an elephant has four huge teeth good for chewing tough plants. As the teeth wear down new ones appear.

It is a common idea that elephants live much longer than people. On the contrary, few elephants live to be more than 70.

Hyrax

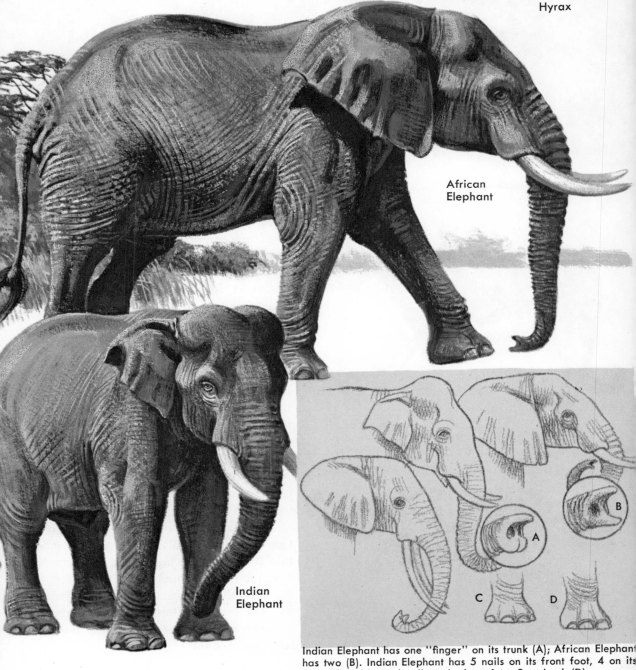

African Elephant

Indian Elephant

Indian Elephant has one "finger" on its trunk (A); African Elephant has two (B). Indian Elephant has 5 nails on its front foot, 4 on its back (C); African, 4 nails on its front foot, 3 on back (D).

Tiger Attacking Tapir

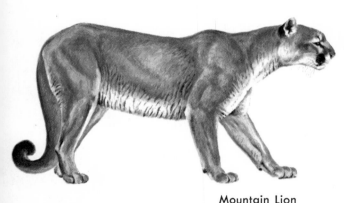

Mountain Lion

Jaguar

Except for the tapir pictured with the tiger, all these animals belong in the order of *carnivores,* or flesh-eating mammals. And they all live up to their name.

You have found out that there are food chains in the sea. In the same way, food chains can be traced in every region on land. In an area where there are oak trees, acorns are eaten by mice, and mice are eaten by owls. In parts of Africa, grass is eaten by zebras, and zebras are eaten by lions. In the Arctic, plants are eaten by insects, insects by the willow ptarmigan, and the willow ptarmigan by the arctic fox. A food chain always begins with green plants. As a rule it ends with a meat-eating animal, in many cases one of the carnivores. Some of the carnivores pictured here are the top meat-eaters in their home regions.

There are many families of carnivores. One is the cat family. The tiger, the mountain lion, and the jaguar are all cats. The lion, the leopard, the bobcat, the ocelot, and the cheetah are other members of the family. The tiger is often called the fiercest of the carnivores. But its cousin the leopard is fully as ferocious.

Dhole

Coyote

The dog family is another well-known group of carnivores. All these animals belong in it. You may never have heard of some of them. The dhole and the raccoon dog live in Asia. The dingo is a wild dog found only in Australia. It is the one large native Australian mammal that is not a marsupial or monotreme. Scientists are so sure that it is descended from the domestic dog taken to Australia by people in prehistoric times that they give it the same scientific name—*Canis familiaris*—with "dingo" added as its breed name.

Dingo

Red Fox Color Variations

Raccoon Dog

Gray Wolf

Ratel

Ferret, or Polecat

Civet

All these animals are carnivores, too. The ratel, the ferret, and the skunk belong together in the weasel family. The otters, too, are in this family.

The ratel is often called the honey badger. With its strong, sharp claws it can easily rip open a rotten tree trunk to get honey. The bird pictured with it is a honey guide. Honey guides find stores of honey and then lead ratels to them. The honey guides eat the honeycomb.

Ferrets are much like the weasels for which the family is named and are in the same genus. So are minks. The ferret pictured is often trained to help hunt rabbits.

Skunks are well known for their way of protecting themselves. They shoot out a liquid with a disagreeable smell. As a rule, however, they go their own way and pay little attention to other animals except for the small ones they capture for food.

Spotted Hyena

Striped Hyena

Civets are often called civet cats. They do not belong to the cat family, but they are rather closely related to the cats. Civets are so ferocious that they are hard to handle. A material "milked" from them is used in making perfumes.

Although hyenas are carnivores, their meat is often some that other carnivores have left behind. The striped hyena even digs up buried bodies for food. A spotted hyena's prey is, in many cases, a wounded or otherwise helpless animal.

Raccoons are easy to identify from their black masks. These carnivores are very well known in America. They are often called coons for short. In spite of being much hunted, raccoons have been able to hold their own, partly because they will eat almost any kind of food. As a rule a raccoon dips its food in water before eating it.

Bears are like huge, tailless dogs. The bear family is closely related to both the dog and the raccoon families. Like raccoons, bears will eat anything they can digest—fish, insects, berries, honey, and much else besides. Bears can move much faster than one would guess from their usual slow and lumbering way of walking.

Raccoon

Striped Skunk

Black Bear

Hippopotamus

The story has already been told of how the horse, over millions of years, became a large animal that ran about on its middle toenails, which had developed into stout hoofs. There are many other hoofed mammals. Scientists call them ungulates.

All the hoofed mammals live on the ground. They are all plant-eaters.

Some hoofed mammals have either two or four toes on each foot. Since they have an even number of toes they are called *even-toed ungulates.* All the animals in these two pictures are in this order.

The group is tremendously important, for it has in it many of the animals that have helped man in his upward climb. It includes cattle and buffaloes, camels and llamas, pigs, sheep and goats, and deer, as well as hippopotamuses, giraffes, and antelopes.

No animals in the group differ more in appearance than the squat hippopotamus and the long-legged, long-necked giraffe. These two also differ greatly in habits.

"Hippopotamus" means "river horse." The hippopotamus is not a close relative of the horse, but it does spend most of its time in rivers. It is one of the least beautiful of all mammals. Like the elephant and the whale, it has almost no hair. The mouth of this big plant-eater is enormous. And the animal has an appetite to match—a bushel of grass is only a taste. Strong tusks help it dig up plants to eat.

Klipspringer

Springbok

Hippos, like many of the other hoofed mammals, form herds. A herd spends the daytime in the water, as a rule, and moves out at night to feed in the lowlands.

A hippopotamus often floats in the water with only a small part of its face above the surface. Its beady eyes are raised above the rest of its face. So are its nostrils. Its ears stick up above the water, too. It is easy for the animal to breathe and to hear and see what is going on.

A baby hippopotamus is always a big attraction in a zoo. It looks tiny indeed beside its bulky mother.

The widespread toes of the hippopotamus are well suited for walking on muddy river bottoms. The hippopotamus can also swim well. It is, in fact, one of the best swimmers of all the land mammals.

A giraffe is an unbelievable kind of animal. Its legs and its neck are so long that they make the giraffe the tallest animal in the world today—18 or 19 feet tall.

This "animal on stilts" looks very awkward drinking at a water hole. It has to spread its front legs apart to get its head down to the water. But its long legs are a big help to it in eating leaves from trees and in galloping away from danger.

Fortunately for the giraffe, it has a remarkable ability to go for long periods without water. Of course, it gets some water in the leaves it eats.

The checkerboard pattern on the giraffe's skin helps the animal hide. It is a little like the pattern made by sunlight or moonlight shining down through trees. The lion is the chief enemy of the giraffe. If there is no chance to run away, a giraffe defends itself by kicking. With its powerful thigh muscles and big hoofs, it may kick hard enough to kill even a lion.

The klipspringer, springbok, and gnus are antelopes. Their horns are a help in telling antelopes apart. The klipspringer is one of the pigmy antelopes. The springbok belongs to the group of antelopes called gazelles. A gnu is a deer antelope.

Giraffes

Brindled Gnu

White-bearded Gnu

Mule Deer

The mule deer, as you would expect from its name, is in the deer family, a very large group of the even-toed ungulates. Almost all over the world deer are among the commonest of wild animals. As you see, the mule deer has antlers. Most male deer and a few female deer do. The antlers are different from the horns of the buffaloes, the yak, and the Barbary sheep in a number of ways. One is that they are branched. Another is that they are shed each year. For the first several years, the new antlers that grow are larger and more branched than those of the year before.

Antlers can be so big that they are a handicap. A giant deer—the "Irish elk"—once lived in the Old World. The antlers of this deer were the largest known. Except for fighting other males, they must have been a nuisance and a burden to carry about. The big deer died out.

Deer chew a cud. These animals depend chiefly on their speed to protect themselves from their carnivore enemies. A deer some-

Cape Buffalo

Water Buffalo

times has to get its food "on the run." It swallows the food without chewing it. The food goes down into one division of the animal's stomach. Later, when the animal can rest, the food comes back into its mouth as a cud. Many of the even-toed ungulates chew a cud. Giraffes, camels, and all the cattle family do.

Throughout the centuries deer have proved very useful to man. They have furnished food and skins for clothing. No deer has been more helpful than the reindeer. It is hard to see how the people of the Far North could have lived without it.

Yaks, buffaloes, and sheep are in the cattle family. This big family also includes goats, antelopes, and all those animals called cattle and oxen. The Cape buffalo is well known as a fierce attacker. The water buffalo has served as the workhorse of southeastern Asia for centuries. The yak is as important to the dwellers in the highlands of Tibet as the reindeer is to the people of the Far North. The Barbary sheep, or aoudad, lives in mountains in Africa and is a remarkable climber.

The wild boar is in the pig family. It is a dangerous attacker. The killer whale is the only mammal with a worse bite.

The alpaca is a camel. The camels, like so many of the even-toed ungulates, have been a great help to man. The vicuña, a small camel, has hair so soft and silky that in the days of the Incas only royalty was permitted to wear robes woven of it.

Yak

Barbary Sheep

Wild Boar

Alpaca

Young Fox Squirrels

The odd-toed ungulates are the remnants of a once much larger group. Today they are greatly outnumbered by those with an even number of toes. The horse, as you know, is odd-toed. It runs on the middle hoof, or toenail, of each foot. In the order, too, are the asses, the zebras, the rhinoceroses, and the tapirs.

The asses and zebras are very close relatives of the horse. They belong in the same genus. They are all descendants of *Pliohippus,* the "more-like-a-horse" of some 10 million years ago. The asses are found in Asia and Africa. They live mainly in desert or mountainous areas. The zebras are animals of the African grasslands.

Zebra

The rhinoceroses have had a long history. There were, you remember, many woolly rhinoceroses in North America in the days of the mammoths and mastodons. And *Baluchitherium,* the biggest mammal ever to live on land, was a rhinoceros. Now the only rhinoceroses are found in Africa and southeastern Asia.

A rhinoceros is easily told by the horn or horns on its nose. A rhinoceros horn is not made of real horn as a cow's horns are. It is a closely packed bundle of hair instead. The skin of a rhinoceros is very tough, so much so that "as tough as rhinoceros hide" is a common expression. A rhinoceros has three hoofs on each foot.

India is the home of the great one-horned rhinoceros. The white rhinoceros lives in Africa. Among land mammals this big animal is second only to the elephant so far as dimensions are concerned. Weightwise the hippopotamus takes second place.

Zebras can be identified readily by their stripes. These stripes make the zebras hard to see in tall grass or against a background of bushes. But they do not keep them from being the chief food of the lions of Africa.

Tapirs, one of which you saw in a picture on page 212, have three hoofs on each foot. Tapirs are found in southeastern Asia and in the Americas from Mexico southward. The broad, silvery-white band around the tapir pictured would seem to make the animal conspicuous, but actually it serves as a protection. This plant-eater feeds at night. On moonlight nights it is harder to see than if it were all dark or all light.

Squirrels belong in the order of *rodents,* the gnawing mammals—by far the largest of all the mammal orders. More than half of the thousands of kinds of mammals living today are in it. In addition to there being many kinds of rodents, there are often tremendous numbers of a kind. Rodents multiply fast. A fox squirrel, for instance, may have two litters a year, with four or five babies in each. Some rodents grow up fast enough to have babies of their own when they are only six weeks old.

Fox Squirrel

Rodents are found almost everywhere except in the seas. Some live on the ground, some under the ground, and some in the tops of trees. Some live in the water of swamps and streams. And some are so well fitted for living in desert lands that they never have to have any water to drink. Some hop, some scamper, some tunnel, and some are excellent swimmers or climbers. The flying squirrels even have flaps of skin which let them glide through the air.

These animals are well fitted for gnawing and grinding tough food. They can move their jaws sideways and fore and aft as well as up and down. Their two pairs of front teeth have such sharp edges that they are like chisels. Their back teeth grind up the food their front teeth have cut off. Even steel chisels wear down. The rodents' sharp front teeth would soon wear down if they were like ours. But they are not. They keep growing at the base.

Great One-horned Rhinoceros

White Rhinoceros

Chinchilla

Some of these rodents you are almost sure to recognize. Rats and mice and chipmunks are common, and you may very well have had a hamster as a pet. You probably know the porcupines by their quills.

Chipmunks look much like squirrels, but they are ground dwellers rather than tree dwellers. As a rule they live in cracks in

Hamster

Voles, or Meadow Mice

rocky walls or in burrows in the ground. A chipmunk's burrow may be several yards long and have a good-sized pantry for storing food. Chipmunks can carry a remarkable amount of food in pockets they have in their cheeks. It is always fun to feed them nuts and watch as they stuff one nut after another into their pockets.

The muskrat and the prairie dog live in quite different kinds of places. The muskrat builds homes in water, most often in marshes. The prairie dog lives in underground burrows in dry areas.

Of these rodents, the porcupine is the largest. But it is not the largest of all the gnawing mammals. The largest is the capybara. This pig-sized rodent lives in marshes and along streams of Central and South America. It eats plants growing in the water and along the banks.

Porcupines would never win any prizes for beauty or for playful ways. A common belief is that a porcupine shoots its quills when an enemy comes near. It has no way of doing so. But the quills come loose easily. An enemy attacking finds itself full of the barbed quills, which are almost impossible to pull out. With such a defense, a porcupine can be slowgoing, and it is.

Some rodents are valuable furbearers. The fur of squirrels is pretty but not durable. Ranking much higher as furbearers are the chinchilla, muskrat, and beaver. Another, the coypu of South America, is the source of the fur called nutria.

The villains among the rodents are the mice and rats. They destroy an enormous amount of food every year. Homeowners have to wage a never-ending war against them in their houses. Farmers have to fight them in their storage barns and fields. Rats not only destroy property but also carry disease. The black rat spreads bubonic plague. To keep rats from traveling by ship from one country to another, all big ships are equipped with rat guards to stop these dangerous pests from coming aboard by running up the ropes that moor the ships to the docks.

White-footed Mouse

Muskrat

Black Rat

Chipmunks

Prairie Dog

Canadian Porcupine

Mediterranean Porcupine

223

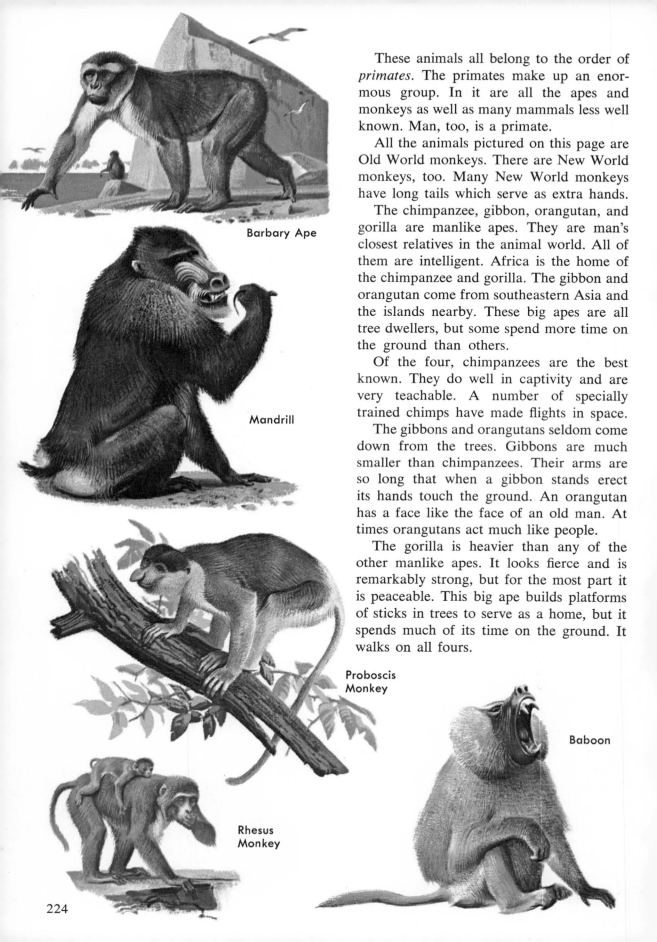

These animals all belong to the order of *primates*. The primates make up an enormous group. In it are all the apes and monkeys as well as many mammals less well known. Man, too, is a primate.

All the animals pictured on this page are Old World monkeys. There are New World monkeys, too. Many New World monkeys have long tails which serve as extra hands.

The chimpanzee, gibbon, orangutan, and gorilla are manlike apes. They are man's closest relatives in the animal world. All of them are intelligent. Africa is the home of the chimpanzee and gorilla. The gibbon and orangutan come from southeastern Asia and the islands nearby. These big apes are all tree dwellers, but some spend more time on the ground than others.

Of the four, chimpanzees are the best known. They do well in captivity and are very teachable. A number of specially trained chimps have made flights in space.

The gibbons and orangutans seldom come down from the trees. Gibbons are much smaller than chimpanzees. Their arms are so long that when a gibbon stands erect its hands touch the ground. An orangutan has a face like the face of an old man. At times orangutans act much like people.

The gorilla is heavier than any of the other manlike apes. It looks fierce and is remarkably strong, but for the most part it is peaceable. This big ape builds platforms of sticks in trees to serve as a home, but it spends much of its time on the ground. It walks on all fours.

Barbary Ape

Mandrill

Proboscis Monkey

Baboon

Rhesus Monkey

Chimpanzee

Gibbon

Orangutan

Gorilla

Warthog

Armadillo

Babirusa

You may never have heard of some of these strange mammals. Most of them are from other parts of the world.

Two—the armadillo and the sloth—you may remember as relatives of the giant ant-eater. Armadillos are well armored. They can curl up in their armor if in danger. Armadillos eat chiefly insects. Sloths spend most of their lives hanging from branches of trees. They feed on the leaves. Tiny plants growing in their fur make these slow-moving creatures hard to see in the trees.

The warthog and babirusa are pigs. It is not easy to say which one is uglier. The warthog lives in Africa, the babirusa in islands of the East Indies. The okapi is a close relative of the giraffe. Its home in Africa is in regions so long unexplored that a hundred years ago no one knew of this large animal's existence.

"Aardvark" means "earth pig." Sometimes aardvarks are called ant bears. But they are neither pigs nor bears. They belong in an order all their own. They are found only in Africa. Aardvarks live in burrows and seldom come out except to find food. Although they may be 6 feet long, they live mainly on termites. Their strong claws help them rip apart termite nests.

The flying lemur pictured lives in the forests of southeastern Asia. Flying lemurs are not lemurs and cannot fly. They are often put in an order of their own. But some scientists group them with the moles and shrews. Although flying lemurs cannot fly, they can glide more than a hundred feet.

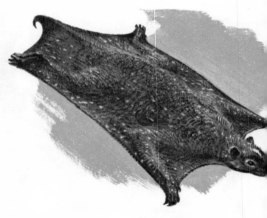

Aardvark

Flying Lemur

The giant panda and the ringtail are carnivores. The panda lives in high bamboo forests in Asia. Most carnivores, as you know, eat other animals, but the panda in its native home eats only bamboo shoots. The ringtail does eat flesh. It is a close relative of the raccoon. So, it has been thought, is the giant panda. Now scientists think it may be just what it looks to be—a bear.

The slow loris of Africa and the aye-aye of Madagascar are primates. They are, then, cousins of the monkeys, apes, and man.

Two-toed Sloth

Giant Panda

Ringtail

Okapi

Slow Loris

Aye-aye

Man is proud of the great dams he has built. He has a right to be. But he cannot claim to be the first dam builder. Beavers were building dams long before there were any people. By damming small streams they form ponds that provide building places for their homes. Colonies of beavers work together in building dams. With their sharp, strong teeth they fell trees near the water's edge, cut them into pieces, and float them into place. They then plaster the logs together with mud.

Early settlers in North America found the thick fur of beavers very useful for making warm clothing. Trappers killed beavers by the millions and made fortunes from the skins. It seemed that there were enough beavers to last forever. People had the same idea about other animals of the land. But this idea proved to be wrong. The beaver and many other mammals once common are now scarce. The bison, which roamed over much of North America in enormous herds before the coming of white settlers, all but disappeared. So, too, did the pronghorn, another hoofed mammal once almost as numerous as the bison.

Moose do not form big herds as the bison and pronghorn do. They were never seen in such numbers. But they, too, used to be much more common than they are now. Cutting down woods took away many of the places where moose made their homes, and hunters killed too many. Almost the only places in our country where moose are a common sight today are national parks such as Yellowstone.

The mass killing of beavers had some results which people did not connect with beavers for some time. By damming up small streams to form ponds, beavers make the water from heavy rains and melting snow run off much more slowly than it would otherwise. With few beavers left to build dams, the water raced down the streams into the rivers, carrying away much good soil and causing floods in the lowlands. The value of the land ruined was far greater than the value of the beaver skins. Now beavers are being encouraged in many places as a way of saving our soil and preventing floods.

The story of the American bison is another story we are not proud of. When

Beaver

Pronghorn

American Bison

Moose

229

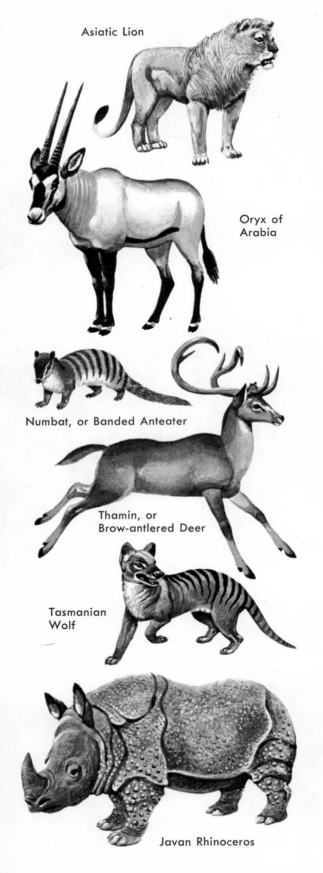

Asiatic Lion

Oryx of Arabia

Numbat, or Banded Anteater

Thamin, or Brow-antlered Deer

Tasmanian Wolf

Javan Rhinoceros

early settlers moved westward over the Great Plains the killing of bison—or, as they are commonly called, buffaloes—by the thousands began. Buffalo robes kept many people warm in winter. The meat of the buffalo made good food. The tongue was considered a special delicacy. Buffaloes were so plentiful that sometimes when one was killed only the tongue was eaten.

At the same time that bison were being killed by the thousands for their hides and their meat, their homes and food were being taken away from them by the plowing up of the plains where they roamed. Big herds were brought down to little herds and little herds were brought down to nothing. But just in time reservations, where buffaloes could live undisturbed, were set up for them. Now there are thousands of bison in the herds on reservations.

Others of our wild mammals have been killed in great numbers for fun or for fur or for food. Fortunately, there are now game laws, and they are helping our wild mammals to hold their own.

The pictures on this page show a few of the mammals in other parts of the world that are in danger of disappearing.

The Tasmanian wolf, found today only in the mountains of Tasmania, is perhaps the rarest mammal in the world. It is a marsupial and therefore not a wolf at all. At times it bounds away like a kangaroo.

Another marsupial in danger of extinction is the numbat of Australia. Unlike most marsupials it has no pouch for its young.

All the Javan rhinoceroses left are on a government preserve. People for centuries killed the rhinoceroses and made the horns into powder for medicines.

In a forest in India the only remaining Asiatic lions are being protected. The natives used to kill lions because they were a danger to their livestock. Besides, Indian maharajas hunted lions for sport.

The oryx is an antelope. Today it lives only in the almost lifeless desert of Rub' al Khali. And even there it is being hunted from automobiles and airplanes.

Polar Bear

The thamin of Burma has been killed in great numbers for food. Besides, its homes have been taken away by settlers.

The polar bear has been a successful dweller of the Far North with its perpetual ice and snow. Sportsmen long found the region where it lives difficult to reach. Now, however, they can fly in airplanes over the polar bear's forbidding homeland and hunt it down. This big bear is in grave danger of being killed off.

The sperm whale is a living oil tank. Oil it produces from its food is stored in its tanklike head. This whale had a great deal to do with the success of the New England colonies, for it furnished oil for lamps and fat for candles. Hundreds of whaling vessels went out each year to hunt it. Sometimes the whalers found ambergris, a waxy substance produced by sperm whales suffering from indigestion. Ambergris is used in perfumes. With the discovery of petroleum the need for whale oil lessened. A number of nations banded together, moreover, to try to save the giant whales. Even so, these mammals may well be fossils of the future.

Sperm Whale

Horses

Thoroughbred

Hackney

Arabian

Percheron

Our early ancestors lived very simply. Their best weapons were crude axes made of stone, they depended on the skins of wild animals for clothing, and their only way of getting food was to gather wild plants and hunt wild animals. But their whole way of living was changed when they at last found that they could domesticate some plants and animals and raise them as they needed them. No longer did they have to spend practically all their time in search of food.

Without question most domesticated animals were first thought of as a source of food—even the horse may have been raised first for its meat and milk. But they served many other purposes, too. They furnished skins and wool for clothing, they helped with hunting and with tilling the soil, and they carried people and their burdens from place to place. Besides, they guarded property and were friends and companions.

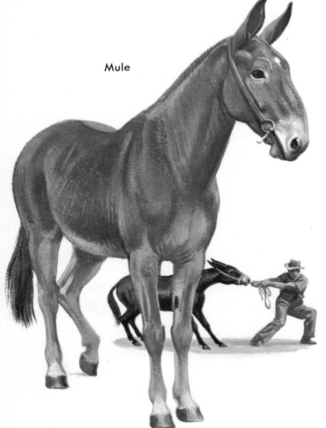

Mule

Shetland Pony

Ayrshire

Dairy Cattle

Guernsey

Brown Swiss

Jersey Calf

Holstein

No one knows the exact order in which animals were domesticated. The order in which our common domesticated mammals were tamed is believed to be this: dog, pig, cow, sheep, goat, donkey, horse, cat.

In the several thousand years since these animals were first domesticated, man has changed them in many ways. He has developed different breeds of the animals to serve special purposes or to suit them for living in particular regions.

The many breeds of horses can be classed as draft horses developed for size and strength, light horses developed for speed and beauty, and small horses, or ponies. With the coming of the automobile, horses, especially workhorses and carriage horses, lost much of their importance. The horse breeders in the United States today are most interested in racehorses, gaited saddle horses, and hunters and jumpers.

Arabian horses are the oldest of the breeds of light horses. And almost all of our modern breeds have Arabian somewhere in their ancestry. Many people, when they hear that a horse is a Thoroughbred, think that it is simply a horse with good breeding. But Thoroughbred is the name of one distinct breed. Most horses that take part in running races are Thoroughbreds. Man o' War, Swaps, and Buckpasser, horses that have set world records, are famous examples.

The mule is a cross between the horse and the donkey. Such a cross is called a hybrid.

Cattle have been developed along two lines: better meat production and better milk production. The pictures show five popular breeds of dairy cattle. The oldest breed is the Brown Swiss. Its ancestry can be traced back to the cattle raised by the Swiss Lake Dwellers of the New Stone Age. Among the best beef breeds are the Angus, Hereford, Shorthorn, Brahman, Africander, and Charolais. The Red Poll and the Milking Shorthorn are two popular breeds developed to furnish both milk and beef.

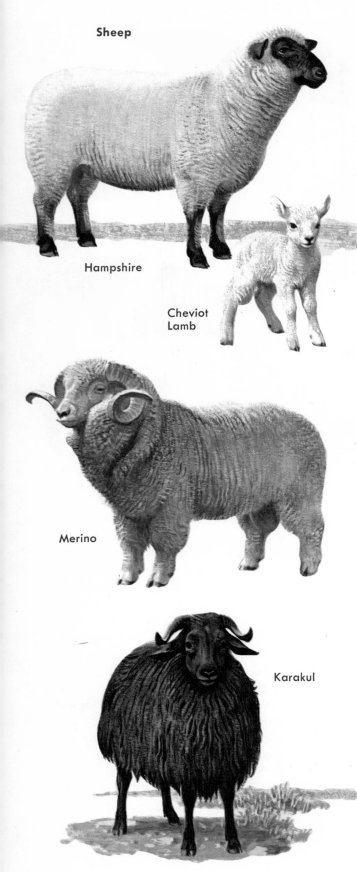

Sheep

Hampshire

Cheviot
Lamb

Merino

Karakul

For tens of centuries shepherds and their flocks have been an important part of the life of many lands. There are still, especially in regions in Asia, shepherds and flocks. But most sheep today are on farms and ranches.

Probably man first tamed sheep for their milk and their skins. Later he found that without killing the sheep he could shear the wool and weave it into cloth. He found, too, that the flesh of sheep is good to eat.

There are now many breeds of sheep. Some are raised chiefly for their wool. The world uses more than 2½ million tons of wool a year. Some breeds furnish fur. And some are raised mostly for meat. The meat from a sheep less than a year old is called lamb. That from an older sheep is mutton.

The Hampshire, Cheviot, and Merino are among the breeds raised in the United States. The Hampshire and Cheviot are raised chiefly for meat. Their wool is only a few inches long. The Merino is raised chiefly for its wool, which is several inches long. It is also finer than the wool of most other breeds of sheep.

The Karakul is a breed common in parts of Asia. The skins of lambs of this breed are made into the furs called caracul, Persian lamb, and broadtail.

Many of the sheep raised in Asia and northern Africa have long, heavy tails. They are known as fat-tailed sheep because they store a great deal of fat in their tails. The Karakul, in fact, is a fat-tailed breed. Its tail, however, is not nearly so long as the tails of many sheep in the group.

Fat-tailed sheep can be raised in regions that are dry and barren for long periods. When food is scarce the animals live on the fat stored in their tails. The fat is important to the people who raise these sheep for still another reason. The fat from the tails is made into a kind of butter when the sheep are killed.

Goats are much like sheep. Some are raised chiefly for their milk, others for their hair and wool. The Kashmir, a long-haired goat, furnishes the soft wool used for the expensive cashmere sweaters and coats.

234

Hogs

Spotted Poland China

Hampshire

Chester White

Tamworth

There is a saying in the part of the United States called the corn belt that most of the corn raised there walks to market. The saying means that the corn belt farmers, instead of hauling the corn to market, feed it to hogs and then herd the hogs into the marketplace.

The pictures above show four breeds of pigs, or hogs, popular with American farmers. Until about 25 years ago all hog breeds were divided into two groups, lard hogs and bacon hogs. The lard hogs were those that fattened easily. Their fat was made into lard, once much used in cooking. The bacon hogs were those that had less fat and therefore leaner meat. Today cooking fats made from the seeds of such plants as corn, soybeans, and cotton have largely taken the place of lard. Now, therefore, almost all hogs are raised chiefly for their

meat. The four pictured are all good meat animals. At agricultural experiment stations, today's breeds are being crossed to produce even better ones. Ways of keeping hogs free from disease and making them grow fast are being worked out, too.

Bacon is only one of the meats we get from hogs. Ham, pork chops and roasts, and sausage are others. The popular frankfurter, or hot dog, is usually part pork.

A football is often called a pigskin. Pigskin makes good leather for gloves, luggage, jackets, belts, billfolds, saddles, and many other things as well as footballs. Hog bristles are used in brushes. In parts of Europe and Asia hogs are trained to root up truffles, delicious mushrooms that grow underground. But few farmers anywhere would raise hogs if it were not for the meat these animals furnish.

Gray Dutch
Rabbit

Guinea Pigs

Short-haired

Rough-haired

Long-haired

Blue Persian

Many breeds of rabbits have been developed as food animals. Rabbits are popular pets, too. The white rabbit often seen as a pet is an albino. An albino is an animal

Cats

American Shorthair Tabby

Siamese

Black
Manx

Red Tabby
Persian

which for some reason has its natural pigment, or coloring, missing. As a rule, the eyes are pink. Many rabbits are raised for their fur or for the making of felt.

Guinea pigs, which are not at all closely related to pigs, are small tailless rodents that make good pets. They are among the easiest of pets to take care of. Guinea pigs are also used by scientists in experiments and tests. They have been so much used in this way that "being a guinea pig" means being used in an experiment.

Cats have been developed almost entirely as pets. They are good mouse catchers, but breeders have done nothing to develop better mousers. They have put all their effort on getting more interesting-looking and beautiful cats. Cats can be divided into long-haired and short-haired varieties.

The Persians are long-haired cats. Some of them are often called Angoras. They have been developed in more than 20 different color types. The American shorthair and the Manx, both short-haired cats, also come in many colors. Cats of all three of these breeds may have stripes called tabby markings. Manx cats are tailless. The aristocratic Siamese, with its beautiful markings, the Abyssinian, the Burmese, the Havana brown, and the Russian blue are other shorthairs.

There are well over 115 breeds of dogs—more than of any other domesticated animal. Visitors at dog shows are almost always surprised at the number of breeds on exhibit. The wild ancestors of our dogs of today, scientists think, were wolflike. Some of our modern breeds look more like wolves than they look like certain other modern breeds of dogs. A German shepherd dog, for instance, looks more like a wolf than like a Chihuahua.

Probably we have so many breeds because dogs serve so many different purposes. They guard property, help in hunting, pull loads, guide the blind, destroy rats, herd sheep and cattle, help find persons that are lost, and make wonderful companions. Some are bred specially for racing.

Dogs

English Springer Spaniel

Smooth Coat Chihuahua

Poodle

Wire Fox Terrier

Basset Hound

Rough Collie

There are big dogs and little ones, long-haired and short-haired dogs, sedate dogs and playful ones, and dogs of different colors. There is a dog to suit the taste of almost everyone.

All the many breeds are classified into six groups: working dogs, toy dogs, sporting dogs, nonsporting dogs, hounds, and terriers. Of the dogs pictured here, the springer is a sporting dog, the Chihuahua a toy, and the poodle a nonsporting dog. The wire fox terrier belongs, as you would know, to the terriers and the basset hound to the hounds. The collie is a working dog.

Arabian Camel

Animal Adaptations

Every animal has its natural home. It is fitted for living there. The ways it is fitted for living there may make it entirely unfitted for living in another kind of place. A camel is not fitted for living in marshland any better than a sandhill crane is fitted for spending its life in a desert. A bat and a mole would certainly be misfits if they changed places with each other.

An animal's natural place of living is called its *habitat*. The ways living things are fitted for their particular habitats are called *adaptations to environment*.

The camel is fitted in many ways for life in a desert. It has been used for traveling across deserts, especially those of North Africa and Arabia, for so long that it is often called the "ship of the desert." Travel in such deserts is not easy. The places where there is water to drink are far apart. It is hard to walk in loose sand, and sometimes sand is blown about in terrible sandstorms. Desert plants, where there are any at all to serve as food, are small and often bitter and thorny. But such hardships are not too great for a camel.

Sandhill Crane

Little Brown Bat

Camels do not have to have water as often as most mammals do. They can drink a great deal at one time. Records show that a thirsty camel may drink 20 gallons or more. Some of the water a camel drinks is stored in special cells in its stomach for later use. After a camel has had all the water it wants, it can go for days without drinking. It does not lose water by sweating the way we do in hot weather.

Camels can store up food, too, in their bodies. Their food storehouses are their humps. The food stored is mostly fat. When there is nothing to eat, a camel can live on the fat in its hump.

A camel's lips are covered with tough skin, and its teeth are strong. It can eat desert plants unfit for most mammals.

Its spreading, thickly padded feet keep a camel from sinking into loose sand. The camel's hair is a protection from both heat and cold. Many people think of camels as animals of only hot deserts, but the two-humped, or Bactrian, camel of the desert regions of Central Asia often has to endure extreme cold. Long eyelashes keep sun and sand out of a camel's eyes. Hairs in its ears shut out sand. Its nose can be closed during a sandstorm.

The sandhill crane has none of these adaptations. The chief things that fit it for its habitat are long legs that allow it to wade in the water of marshes, a long neck, a long, strong bill suitable for catching fish and frogs and water insects, and strong wings that carry it over the water.

A bat is fitted for life in the air. Its wings are made of tough skin stretched between its back legs and tail and its very, very long fingers. Its wings are so big in proportion to its body that the little animal almost floats in the air.

A bat's legs end in sharp claws. With them it can climb rock walls or branches of trees. To sleep, a bat hangs itself upside down by its claws from the wall or ceiling of a cave, an old building, or a cavity in a tree trunk. Some bats often fold up their wings and run about on all fours.

Most bats do their flying about in search of food after dark and avoid bright light by sleeping during the daytime. Bats have beady little eyes good for seeing in dim light. There is no truth to the saying "blind as a bat."

But it is not their eyes that bats depend on for getting about at night. Instead, it is an astonishing adaptation—a sonar system. As it flies, a bat makes sounds too high for us to hear. But the bat can hear them, and the echoes of these sounds sent back by obstacles in the way keep it from bumping into things even in pitch-darkness.

Moles spend practically all their time underground, a little way beneath the surface. A mole has fur that is like thick velvet. This fur can be brushed forward or backward and still be smooth. It lets the mole move either forward or backward through the ground easily.

Mole

Mountain Goat

A camel's habitat differs from a sandhill crane's chiefly in the amount of moisture present. A bat's habitat differs from a mole's chiefly in its relation to the surface of the earth. There are many other important ways in which habitats can differ. Temperature, light, pressure, amount of oxygen, and the nature of the ground surface are among them. Plant and animal populations vary, too. It makes a great deal of difference to an animal what plants and animals share its place of living.

The two habitats pictured here differ in several of these ways. The mountain goat lives high in the Rockies, where mountain-sides are steep. The African animals shown live on plains in the heart of Africa.

The home of the mountain goat is higher above sea level than the home of these African animals. The air is rarer. With each breath it takes, a mountain goat gets less oxygen than it would get if it were breathing the denser air nearer sea level. The temperature in the home of the mountain goat averages much lower than on the African plains. The air pressure is lower, too.

Mountain goats live above the timberline. No large plants grow there. Not many other animals live there either. The mountain goat does not have to do much sharing of the food that can be had. Neither does it have to escape from many enemies.

The African animals would certainly be misfits in the habitat of the mountain goat. The mountain goat has a thick coat of hair. It is very surefooted. The elephant, on the other hand, has almost no hair and its heavy legs and big feet would not do at all for steep slopes. Neither the elephant nor the monkeys would be at home in a treeless region. And the lion could not live without such animals as giraffes and zebras for food.

Even in the sea, which is much more the same everywhere than the land, there is a great variety of habitats. But different as different parts of the earth are, there are some animals fitted for all but the very coldest and driest places and those made unfit by poisonous gases.

From its home in the ground a mole digs tunnels in all directions. It can dig a tunnel with no difficulty. Its pointed nose works a little like a snowplow. Its big front feet are excellent shovels. The long, strong claws on its front feet are a big help in digging, too. In a single night a mole, which is only about 6 inches long, has been known to dig a tunnel of nearly 100 yards. As it digs its tunnels, the mole finds insects and earth-worms for food.

Although most moles have eyes to see with, some have eyes covered with skin. Good eyesight is not especially useful to an animal that spends its life in the dark.

At a Water Hole
in the African Bush

White Pelican

Green Frog

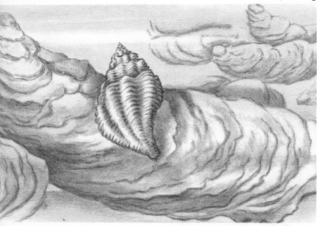

Oyster Drill and Oyster

Sea Anemone

Animals are built to live in different kinds of places. They are also built to eat food of different kinds and to get it in different ways.

The white pelican eats fish. It has a built-in fishing net. As it swims through the water, it scoops up small fish with the pouch fastened to its lower bill. It lets the water drain away and then swallows its freshly-caught fish dinner.

The pouch on its bill also serves as a soup bowl for the baby pelicans. The adult birds fill their pouches with a sort of fish soup from their stomachs. The baby birds stick their bills into the bills of the parent birds to drink the fish soup. A baby bird's head may be almost completely hidden inside a parent's bill.

The pelican has webbed feet that enable it to swim fast enough to catch fish. Its strong wings carry it to feeding grounds.

A green frog has a long, sticky tongue just as other frogs have. It is excellent for catching insects. The tongue is fastened at the front rather than at the back. It can therefore be flipped out a long way. When the frog flips its tongue back with an insect sticking to it, the insect is carried far enough down its throat to be easy to swallow.

Oysters are good food for many animals of the sea as well as for us. You may remember how starfish, with their tube-feet, pull open an oyster's shell a little way and then push their stomachs inside to eat the soft body of the oyster. Oyster drills, too, are great enemies of oysters. The oyster drill is a kind of sea snail. The way it eats oysters is quite different from the way a starfish does. The oyster drill does not have to pull on an oyster's shell to open up a crack. It could not possibly do so. Like all snails it has a long, filelike tongue, or radula. By means of its radula, the oyster drill can drill a hole through the oyster's hard shell. After it has drilled the hole, it scrapes out the oyster's body little by little and eats it.

The oyster itself is one of the animals that must wait for food to come to them. It strains bits of food material from the water that flows in and out of its shell.

The sea anemone is another animal that lies and waits. A sea anemone, unlike the oyster, does not lose the power of moving about, but it can move only slowly. An animal so slow would have a poor chance of getting enough food if it had to go after it the way a pelican does. Instead, the sea anemone uses its tentacles. It shoots out poison threads at any animal that comes close enough to touch a tentacle. Then its tentacles bring the paralyzed prey to its mouth. The anemone can even catch fish in this way.

Mussels also can creep slowly about, but most of the time they stay anchored in place by fine threads they secrete. They get food the same way an oyster does.

A lugworm in its burrow gets its food from the sand and mud at the bottom of the water. It swallows a lump of this bottom material every few seconds for a minute or so. Then it takes a short rest before beginning again. The worm digests the plant and animal material in the mud and sand it has swallowed and expels the rest. It spends most of the time eating.

A rock barnacle once settled in its stony prison cell never travels anywhere on its own. It uses its feather-like legs to kick tiny animals into its mouth.

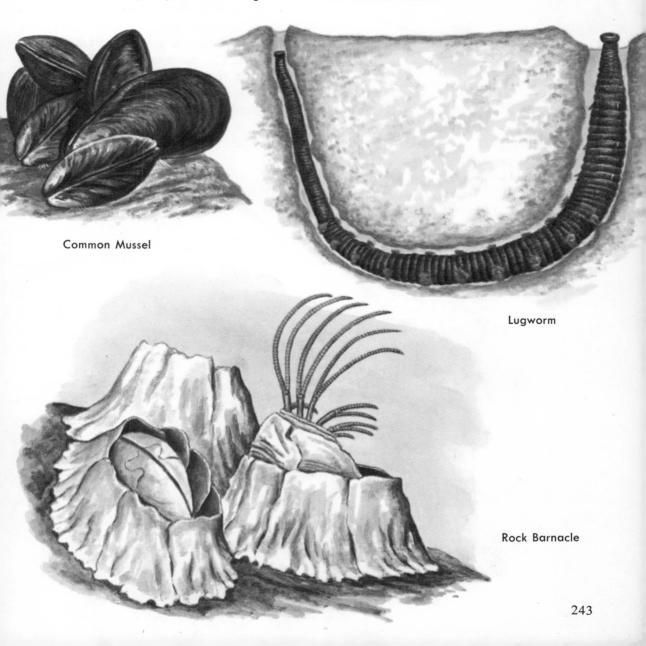

Common Mussel

Lugworm

Rock Barnacle

243

Bird Bills

Duck

Tern

Eagle

Kingfisher

Cardinal

Hummingbird

A hummingbird's bill is about as different from a pelican's as a bill could be. It is fitted for eating an entirely different kind of food. The hummingbird drinks nectar from flowers. Some of the flowers that produce nectar have their petals joined to form a tube. The nectar is at the bottom of the tube. The hummingbird's bill is long enough and slender enough to reach down into such flowers.

The tongue has its edges rolled inward so that it becomes a double "soda straw." The bird sucks the nectar up through it. The hummingbird often gets some tiny insects along with the nectar. They are important in its diet, too.

To drink the nectar the hummingbird must stay at almost the same spot for a time. It is able to do so by beating its wings up and down very fast—so fast that they make the hum that gives the bird its name. This bird is able not only to hover over a flower but also to fly backwards—a feat very rare among birds.

As you know, seeds, insects, toads and frogs, lizards, and small mammals are among the other things birds eat. Every bird has a bill fitted for getting the kind of food it needs. The pictures at the left show how different the bills of a duck, tern, eagle, kingfisher, and cardinal are from the bill of a hummingbird.

Ruby-throated Hummingbird

Both terns and kingfishers are fish-eaters. It may surprise you that their bills are not like the pelican's. The reason is that, instead of scooping up fish as the pelican does, they dive into the water and catch one fish at a time.

The duck pictured finds some of its food in shallow water and some on land. From the mud at the bottom of the water it gets snails and plant roots. It also eats leaves of floating plants. Waste grain and the seeds of wild rice furnish food for it, too.

The bald eagle has a bill good for tearing apart such animals as rabbits, squirrels, and mice. It is a typical bird-of-prey bill. The cardinal is a seedeater. Its short, thick bill is good for cracking seeds.

A flamingo eats a great assortment of food it finds in shallow water—tiny one-celled plants, worms, insect larvas, and crustaceans mixed together into a muddy soup. The bird holds its bill upside down as it takes in a mouthful of the soup. Then its lower bill and its tongue push down to squeeze out some of the water before the flamingo swallows the food.

Oxpeckers eat mostly ticks, spider relatives that bury their heads in the skin of animals and suck blood. It is not easy to pull out a feeding tick. An oxpecker has short legs, sharp claws, and pointed tail feathers that help it stay in place on an animal's back and sides as it pulls out ticks with its broad, thick bill. After it pulls one out and swallows it, it sips up the blood that comes from the wound. The oxpeckers pay the rhinoceroses and other African animals they get their food from by giving loud

Flamingo

warning cries when an enemy is approaching. Of course, it is also a help to an animal to get rid of its ticks.

In the animal kingdom we find countless other adaptations for food-getting. The long neck of the giraffe, the big pincers of the lobster, the trunk of the elephant, the giant anteater's long snout and very long, sticky tongue, and the spinnerets with which spiders spin webs that serve as insect traps are only a few of them.

Oxpeckers on Rhinoceroses

Mallard Ducks
Migrating

Many animals have habits which can be thought of as adaptations. Migration is one of them.

Ever so many birds, as you already know, have summer homes in one region and winter homes in another. They migrate, or make the journey between their two homes, twice each year. Many birds fly at night and are not seen as they migrate. Others are so small that no one notices them high in the air. But flocks of such big birds as ducks, geese, and cranes flying northward or southward are common sights of spring and fall, and their calls as they pass overhead are familiar sounds. Often migrating birds fly in a V pattern.

In their migrations birds may travel long distances. The arctic tern is the champion bird traveler. It nests as far to the north as there are islands in the Arctic. Healthy baby terns have been found in nests partly covered with snow. The bird winters far to the south, chiefly on islands off the Antarctic coast. The terns that nest farthest north and winter farthest south have to make an 11,000-mile journey every spring and fall.

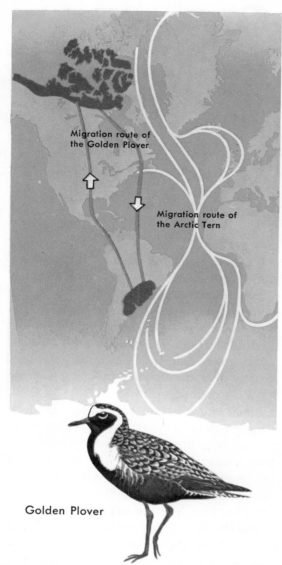

Migration route of
the Golden Plover

Migration route of
the Arctic Tern

Golden Plover

Arctic Tern

farther than others? What tells them where to go? And how do they find their way?

No one knows the answers to these questions. But one thing about migration is certain. It lets the birds that migrate live under better conditions than they could have if they stayed all year round in one place. Chimney swifts, which live almost entirely on insects, spend the whole year in regions where insects are plentiful. Mallards, which feed partly on plants of the marshlands, are able the year round to be where plants are growing. The arctic tern by its long journey gets more hours of daylight in a year than any other living creature. By migrating, birds also escape severe cold.

No one should think that birds run no risks in making long journeys. They meet many dangers in their travels—storms, enemies, and the chance of killing themselves by flying into obstacles. But the advantages may well outweigh the dangers.

The golden plover is another famous bird traveler. It spends its summers in northern Canada and Alaska, as the map shows, and then flies nonstop over the Atlantic to Argentina for the winter.

Some birds that migrate travel only short distances. The little house wren may go only between a northern and a southern state. There are other small birds that make long and difficult journeys. The ruby-throated hummingbird, for instance, flies without stopping all the way across the Gulf.

In many ways bird migration is a puzzle. How did it come about? Did the Ice Age start it? Why do some birds migrate while others do not? Why do some travel so much

House Wren

Monarch Butterfly

Although birds are the most famous animal migrants, many other animals travel periodically from one region to another. The monarch butterfly is one of them.

Toward the end of summer, monarchs gather in flocks and fly south. Their journey is leisurely, but some of them travel several hundred miles. In the spring they start moving northward one by one. But most of them fall by the wayside. The monarchs that arrive in the north are mostly young butterflies produced from eggs laid by the females on the northward journey.

Caribou

Caribou spend the summer in arctic regions north of the timberline. Their food is chiefly reindeer moss. In July they begin to move southward in large herds to the edge of the forests. In the spring they move northward again. The caribou push on even if they meet danger. Often great numbers of these deer are drowned in trying to cross flooded streams.

Bluefin tuna spend the winters in deep water out in the Atlantic. At egg-laying time, in the spring, they move into the Caribbean. They swim westward to the warm Gulf Stream and follow it northward. When they reach Nova Scotia it is fall and time to move out into deeper water once more.

The Pacific salmon and the eels are great travelers, too. Their round-trip travels, however, are not completed in one year. The Pacific salmon begins its life far from the coast in the branches of rivers that empty into the Pacific. Then it travels downstream and out into the sea. There it lives until it becomes adult and reaches the breeding stage. It now travels back up the stream it traveled down when it was young. It may have to cross dangerous rapids and leap up waterfalls. After it has gone far up the river, eggs are laid and fertilized. Then the salmon dies. It thus begins and ends its life in fresh water.

The story of the European and American eels is the story of the Pacific salmon turned around. Both eels begin life in the Atlantic in the region called the Sargasso Sea. Young

Pacific Salmon

eels all look very much alike. As you see from the picture, they are almost transparent. They differ greatly in shape, too, from adult eels.

When they are still too young to look very fishlike, they start swimming toward shore. The young European eels swim toward Europe and the young American eels toward America. What guides them, no one knows.

Their journey takes months or even years. When they reach shore they travel up rivers. They live for several years in fresh water. But sooner or later every eel gets a call to travel down to the sea. Many get the call at the same time. They travel to the Sargasso Sea and lay and fertilize their eggs. But they do not live to journey back to fresh water.

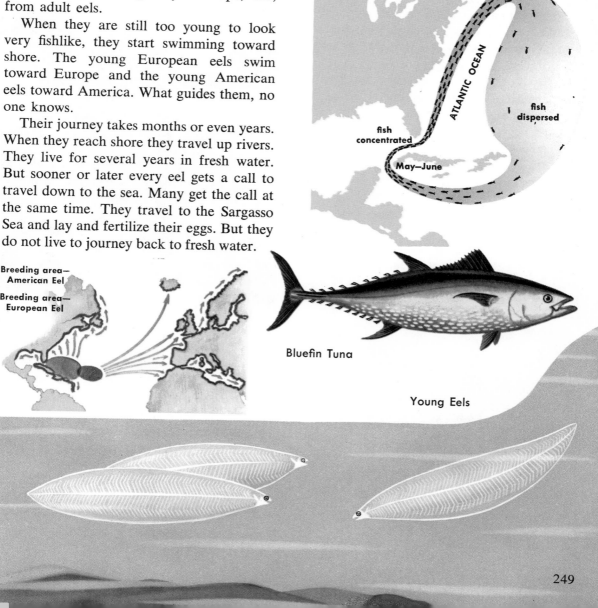

August—September

ATLANTIC OCEAN

fish dispersed

fish concentrated

May—June

Breeding area— American Eel

Breeding area— European Eel

Bluefin Tuna

Young Eels

Bear in Winter Sleep

so quiet that they need little oxygen. Their hearts beat very slowly.

Snakes and salamanders hibernate under rocks or old logs. Toads hibernate in the same kinds of places or in mud at the bottom of a pond. So do turtles. The buckeye butterfly hibernates in hollow trees. The queen bumblebee hides herself somewhere in the ground, in bark, or inside buildings. Earthworms crawl deeper in the ground.

But hibernation is not limited to cold-blooded animals. Almost no birds hibernate, but many mammals do. The woodchuck and the dormouse are well-known hibernators.

The little dormouse gets its name from the French word *dormir,* which means "to

Some animals are able to survive in regions of cold winters because they hibernate. Hibernation can be thought of as a kind of very deep sleep.

Many cold-blooded animals die when winter comes on, and leave only their eggs to endure the cold. Those that do live through very cold weather do so by hibernating. No one sees frogs or snakes or salamanders where ponds are skating rinks and snow covers the ground. No one sees earthworms, butterflies, or bumblebees either.

Frogs bury themselves in mud, often at the bottom of a pond. Before beginning their winter sleep they store food in their bodies by eating a great deal. While they are hibernating they eat nothing at all. They breathe only through their skins—they are

Woodchuck

sleep." It is well named, for it actually sleeps for about seven months of every year. A dormouse stuffs itself with nuts and insects during the summer so that it is very fat when it begins its hibernation in a hole in a tree or the ground. During its deep sleep it is so quiet that it looks as if it were dead. And its body is cold—only a little above freezing. In the spring it takes the dormouse hours to come wide awake.

Woodchucks follow the same plan. They eat a great deal before hibernation begins.

Chipmunk

Buckeye Butterfly

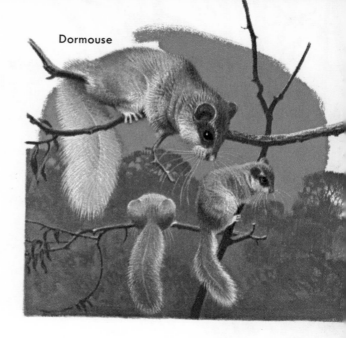

Dormouse

During its deep sleep a woodchuck is curled up in a tight ball and does not move; its heartbeat is slow and its body cold. It may breathe only once in five minutes.

A common superstition has to do with the hibernation of the woodchuck. If the woodchuck, or groundhog, so the superstition goes, comes out of its winter sleep and sees its shadow on Groundhog Day, there will be six more weeks of cold weather. The groundhog can have six weeks more to sleep. If it does not see its shadow, spring is just around the corner.

Many bears sleep through the winter, but their sleep is not like the deathlike sleep of the dormouse and the woodchuck. They may wake up from time to time and move about. Their temperature, their heartbeat, and their rate of breathing are about the same as during the rest of the year. Their winter sleep is a sort of half-hibernation. Chipmunks, too, are active from time to time during their winter sleep.

Many warm-blooded animals that do not hibernate have snug burrows or nests where they stay most of the time in winter. They come out only to look for food.

The African lungfish does not need to escape from cold. Its chief problem is to survive the drying up in summer of the ponds where it lives. When the water gets low, the fish crawls into mud. It then builds itself a cocoon by mixing the mud around it with a slimy material it secretes. This fish has both gills and lungs. While in its cocoon it breathes only with its lungs. A tiny tunnel close to the fish's mouth lets in air. The fish waits in its ball of mud till rains come again. Then it wriggles out into the water.

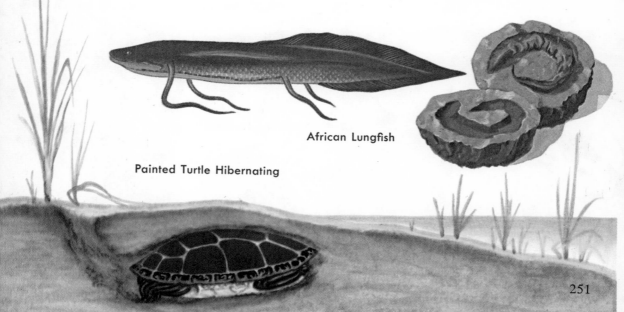

African Lungfish

Painted Turtle Hibernating

Bitterns

The main secret of survival among animals is being able to eat without being eaten. The color of an animal may be a great help. It may make the animal match its surroundings so well that it cannot be seen easily. Its color may be a great protection against its enemies. It may also be a help in getting the food it needs.

The polar bear is an example of an animal that is greatly helped by its color. The polar bear has no meat-eating enemies. It is a top carnivore in the Arctic, where it lives the year round. But food is not very abundant there. The big white bear lives chiefly on seals and fish. It also eats birds occasionally and birds' eggs. Since it matches its surroundings so well, it can often creep up on an animal it is trying to catch without being seen. It can pounce on a seal, for instance, before the seal knows that an enemy is near.

The pictures show a number of other animals with colors that match their surroundings. Of those at the bottom of this page, the arctic hare and the kangaroo rat are common prey of carnivores that share their habitats. How clearly these two would stand out if they were to change places!

The kit fox, the ermine, and the jaguar are carnivores. Matching their surroundings helps these animals get their food. Any of the three in the habitat of one of the others would be so easy to see that it would probably go hungry much of the time.

Many animals that live in tall grass, thickets, or forests are striped or spotted. As you see, the stripes and spots on their breasts help bitterns hide. These birds get protection, too, from their way of freezing into position with their long bills pointing upward when an enemy is nearby.

Ermine

Kit Fox

Arctic Hare

Kangaroo Rat

Jaguar

Fawns, with their spots, are protected from meat-eaters in much the same way. Their spots match the spots of brightness made by sunlight shining through the trees and keep them from showing clearly as they lie still on the forest floor. The spots and stripes of giraffes and zebras, too, as you already know, help hide them from enemies. The jaguar's spots, on the other hand, hide it from the animals it hunts.

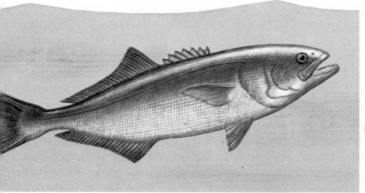

Bluefish

Praying Mantis

The general color plan of fishes is a good one for protection. A fish, as a rule, is darker above than below. Its picture shows you that the bluefish is. A fish-eating animal looking down at the water may not see a fish there because the fish's back matches the bottom or depths of the river or lake or sea so well. A fish-eating animal swimming below it may not see the fish because its light underside is not very different from the color of the sky as seen from underwater.

The praying mantis, you remember, has a great reputation as a destroyer of other insects. It would be much less successful if its color did not help it hide from approaching prey.

There is one puzzle about protective coloring. Why should an animal that matches the color of its surroundings almost perfectly have some differences in color that spoil the perfect matching? Why, for example, should the almost pure white arctic hare have black tips on its ears? And why should the kit fox and the ermine have black tips on their tails? Even the polar bear has a black nose!

Like the polar bear, many of the warm-blooded animals that live the year round in the Far North are white. Their color, in addition to helping them find food or keeping them from being eaten, helps in another important way. Being white helps an animal keep the heat of its body from escaping.

Some animals change the color of their coats with the seasons. The willow ptarmigan is one that does. In the spring this bird stays mostly in the remaining patches of snow until its brown summer coat takes the place of its winter white one.

Willow Ptarmigan

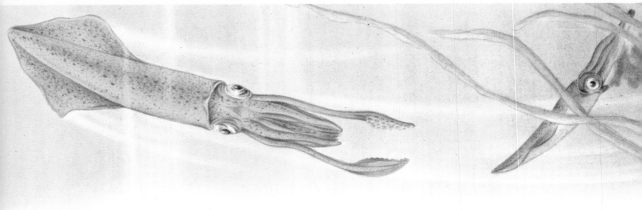

Squid

A number of mammals that live far to the north also change color with the seasons. The ermine, or shorttail weasel, is one. During the summer an ermine is brown. It matches the ground and dry leaves and grasses very well. It can creep up on the animals it eats without being seen easily by bigger animals that would welcome a weasel dinner. This little animal does not hibernate. It must be able to catch food all during the long northern winter. In the fall its brown hair drops out and white hair takes its place. The weasel then matches the snow almost as well as the polar bear.

Crab spiders change from white in the summer to yellow in the fall. Since many summer flowers are white and many autumn flowers yellow, the spider is protected by its color much of the time.

There are color changes in animals that have nothing to do with the seasons. Some have to do with moving from one environment to another. By changing color, an animal may make itself match new surroundings. The summer flounder is an example. It can make itself almost any shade of gray or brown. It can also give itself fine speckles that match sand and big speckles that match gravel.

Chameleons are so famous for color changes that ability to change color is the first thing one thinks of when he hears their name. But a chameleon's color changes do not always make it match its surroundings better. They have more to do with changes in light and temperature and with emotions. When a chameleon is cold it is usually brown. With temperature or light changes it

Ermine, or Shorttail Weasel

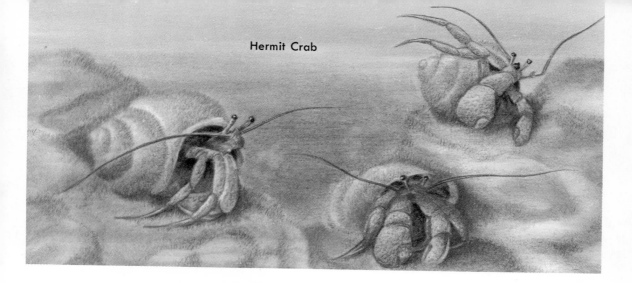

Hermit Crab

may turn green or a pale greenish-yellow. When it is excited it becomes bright green. If it has lost a fight with another chameleon it turns brown. Even though a chameleon's changes in color do not always make it match its environment better, it often happens that they do.

Unlike squids, which as you know can change color in a twinkle, it may take ten minutes for a chameleon to change. A squid's color changes may be due to emotions. They may be changes to match new surroundings.

Some animals are made to match their surroundings in the way shown by the picture of the hermit crabs. Here hedgehog hydroids—tiny colonial animals you will remember as relatives of the jellyfishes—are growing on both the rocks and the shells the hermit crabs are living in. The hydroids help the crabs by making them match their surroundings. In return they get a free ride from the crabs and have a better chance to get food than if they stayed in one place.

Although hermit crabs do find and fasten onto themselves sea anemones that serve as weapons for capturing prey, a hermit crab has nothing to do with camouflaging itself with hydroids. In contrast, the spider crab—pictured on page 86—does its own camouflaging. It sticks seaweed and small animals on its back and legs that make it match its surroundings. If the crab travels to a new home it may change its camouflage.

Ermine in Winter White

255

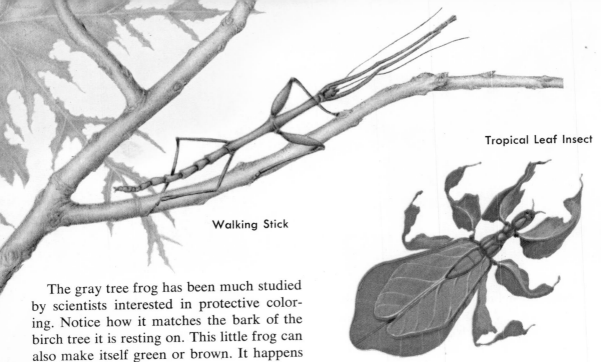

Walking Stick

Tropical Leaf Insect

The gray tree frog has been much studied by scientists interested in protective coloring. Notice how it matches the bark of the birch tree it is resting on. This little frog can also make itself green or brown. It happens that changing color frequently makes the frog match whatever it is resting on. But scientists say that such color matching is more accident than design. The changes are, they say, brought about largely by changes in temperature and moisture. Changing from one color to another takes the tree frog about an hour.

The walking stick shows a way of matching its surroundings that is called *mimicry*. The walking stick looks like a twig. Insect-eaters are likely to overlook it.

Sargassum Fish

A relative in Asia, the tropical leaf insect, is one of the very best examples of mimicry. As you see, the insect's two pairs of wings look exactly like two green leaves, one resting on top of the other. There are even "veins" that look like leaf veins. The insect's legs are green and are flattened out so that they look like bits of leaves. In places they have ragged edges as if other insects had been nibbling at them.

An angular-winged katydid resting on a green plant looks so like a leaf that it is scarcely noticed. Treehoppers are hard to tell from small leaves, buds, or thorns.

The viceroy butterfly is well known for its mimicry. It does not hide by looking like some part of a plant. Instead, it mimics the monarch butterfly, which is very easily seen. The viceroy is good food to many birds, while the monarch is not. The monarch may even give an animal that eats it indigestion. By looking almost exactly like the inedible monarch, the viceroy fools many an enemy and keeps from being eaten.

The bumblebee moth protects itself by copying the bumblebee—an insect with a well-known stinger. The moth has no stinger, but it looks so much like a bumblebee that enemies pass it by.

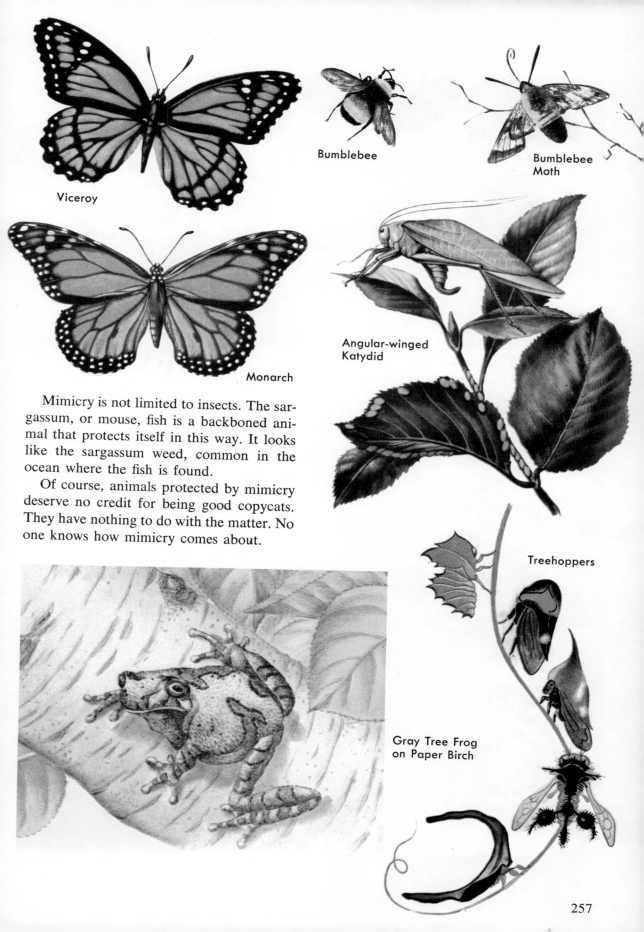

Viceroy

Bumblebee

Bumblebee
Moth

Monarch

Angular-winged
Katydid

Mimicry is not limited to insects. The sargassum, or mouse, fish is a backboned animal that protects itself in this way. It looks like the sargassum weed, common in the ocean where the fish is found.

Of course, animals protected by mimicry deserve no credit for being good copycats. They have nothing to do with the matter. No one knows how mimicry comes about.

Treehoppers

Gray Tree Frog
on Paper Birch

Whirligig Beetle

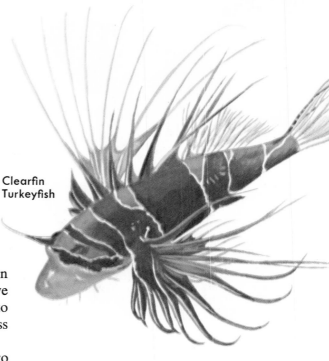

Clearfin Turkeyfish

Some animals are able to hold their own among their neighbors because they have good armor. Others owe their success to good weapons. Still others are helped in less conspicuous ways.

A whirligig beetle's eyes each have two parts. One part is above the surface of the water as the beetle swims about, the other below. The beetle can see an enemy approaching no matter whether the enemy is under the surface or above it.

The clearfin turkeyfish is one of the scorpion fishes. All these fishes have poisonous spines on their fins. A jab from one of the spines may cause terrible pain.

You already know about the bad-smelling liquid that skunks spray at their enemies. This liquid is an excellent weapon. But before the animals use it they give warning by lifting their tails or rearing up on their front feet.

The shell of a box turtle makes an especially effective coat of armor. Most turtles cannot shut themselves up in their shells as completely as the box turtle can.

Among the other well-armored animals you have met are the armadillos, the pangolin, the hedgehog, and a great many mollusks. The sword of the swordfish, the knives of the surgeonfish, the stings of bees and scorpions, the horns of the yak, the tusks of the wild boar, the quills of the porcupine, the poison fangs of the rattlesnakes, the

Striped Skunk

Spotted Skunk

Hog-nosed Skunk

Raccoon and Box Turtle

claws of a tiger, and the stinging cells of the jellyfishes and sea anemones are a few of the thousands of weapons animals use to protect themselves from enemies.

Many animals, as you know, protect themselves from the cold by migrating or hibernating. The picture of the arctic fox shows two other means of protection from cold. This fox, as you would guess from its name, lives in the Far North. It has a very heavy coat of fur. Besides, it has small ears. Since in winter there is not much warmth from the sun, one of the big problems of a warm-blooded animal in that season is to keep the heat of its body from escaping. Both the arctic fox's fur and its color serve to shut heat in. If its ears were big, much body heat would escape from them.

The fennec, a small fox of the hot, dry lands of Africa, does not need protection from cold. Notice how enormous its ears are. The kit fox lives in our warm South-west. It, too, is big-eared, but its ears are not nearly so large in proportion to its size as the ears of the fennec. Hares of one kind or another are found all the way from tropical regions to the Far North. The farther north a hare lives, the smaller its ears are.

Fennec

Arctic Fox

Kit Fox

Cheetah and Gazelle

Of course, their ways of moving about help fit animals for living where they do. Hard hoofs for running would be of no use to a whale nor would fins like a fish's be of help to a cardinal or a jackrabbit.

There are many big carnivores in the regions where gazelles live. Gazelles are able to run fast enough to have a good chance of escaping from most of their meat-eating enemies. But the speed of some of the meat-eaters is great, too. The cheetah, for example, can run faster than any other land animal. Speed clearly is a help to both the meat-eaters and the animals they prey on.

The gallinule is a shore and swamp bird. It does much walking about on the leaves of

Purple Gallinule

Three-toed Sloth, or Ai

Flying Squirrel

Spider Monkey

water hyacinths and water lilies. Very long toes fit it for doing so. They distribute the bird's weight so that it does not sink.

The sloth spends its life in trees. Day in and day out it hangs down from a branch. It has to move very little to get the leaves it eats. Its long legs and curved claws fit the sloth for its strange life.

The monkey is a tree dweller, too, but it is very active. A spider monkey's tail helps it swing from branch to branch.

Flying squirrels, like flying dragons and flying lemurs, cannot really fly. But they can glide from branch to branch.

The gecko, a lizard, can walk across a smooth ceiling to catch insects resting there. On its feet a gecko has pads that let it cling to very smooth surfaces, even glass. The pads are not, as many people suppose, sticky. Instead they have on them tiny hooklike cells that catch on any slight roughness. They let geckos hunt for food in places many insect-eaters cannot reach.

A spider can lower itself through the air by spinning a strand of silk to travel on. It can scurry back up the strand if it needs to. A tree frog has suction disks on the tips of its toes. It can hang from a twig by a single toe. A bug, the water strider, can live far out at sea and walk about on the water as if it were land. The story of ways in which animals get about and of other ways in which they are fitted for living in their surroundings could go on and on.

Gecko

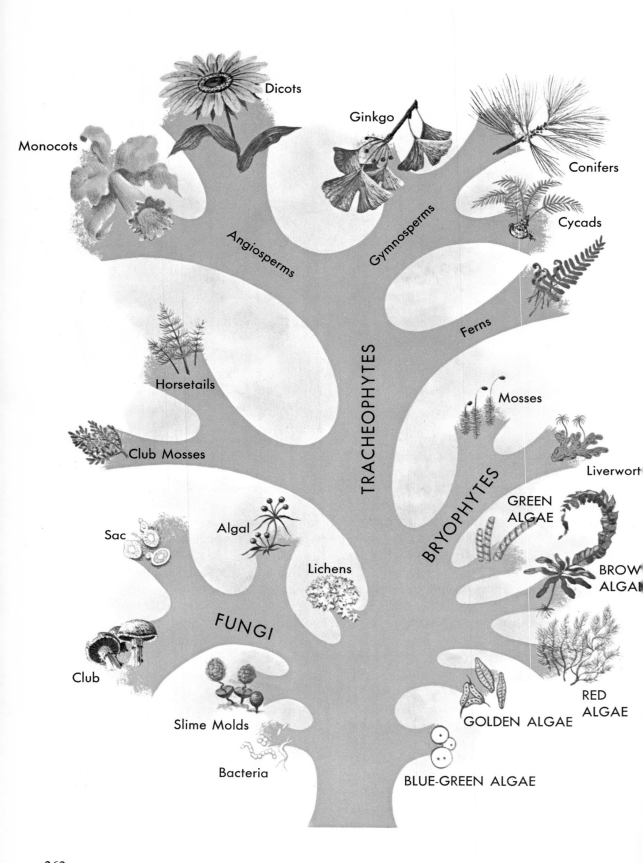

Dicots

Monocots

Ginkgo

Conifers

Cycads

Angiosperms

Gymnosperms

Ferns

Horsetails

TRACHEOPHYTES

Mosses

Club Mosses

BRYOPHYTES

Liverwort

GREEN
ALGAE

Sac

Algal

Lichens

BROW
ALGA

FUNGI

Club

RED
ALGAE

Slime Molds

GOLDEN ALGAE

Bacteria

BLUE-GREEN ALGAE

The Plant Kingdom

There are not nearly so many kinds of plants as there are kinds of animals—at least not nearly so many have been discovered thus far. Since some kinds of plants are very small and since there are still some little-known parts of the world, many more kinds of plants are sure to be discovered and named. But many more animals, as you know, are constantly being found, too. It is not likely that the number of kinds of plants will ever catch up with the number of kinds of animals. At present we know of roughly 350,000 kinds of plants as against about 1,000,000 kinds of animals.

Plants are classified very much as animals are. There are phyla, classes, orders, families, genera, and species. There are some subphyla, too, and some subclasses.

The common sunflower is a species of plant. It belongs to the sunflower genus. The sunflowers belong to the composite family. The composite family, a very large one, includes such well-known flowers as dandelions, daisies, and goldenrods. The family belongs to the order of bluebells. This order gets its name from the bluebell family, which it also includes. The bluebell order belongs to the subclass of dicots. The dicots are a part of a class called the angiosperms, or flowering plants. The flowering plants belong to the phylum of tracheophytes, or vascular plants—plants with "little vessels" for carrying water.

Every known plant has been given a scientific name just as every known animal has. The scientific name of the common sunflower is *Helianthus annuus*. The scientific name of the marsh marigold, a member of the buttercup family, is *Caltha palustris*. This small plant has several common names. In the same way, several different plants may have the same common name. From common names, then, it is not always possible to tell what plant is meant. But a plant has only one scientific name and no other plant has that same name.

The "tree" on the opposite page gives some idea of the whole plant kingdom. All the thousands of plants of today are supposed to have come from very simple one-celled organisms that lived back in the days when the earth was young.

Two branches near the bottom of the tree represent the bacteria and the slime molds. These groups of living things, you remember, are classed as protists by some scientists.

There are fewer plant phyla than animal phyla. Near the bottom of the tree there are several phyla called *algae*. There is also the phylum of *fungi*. The fungi and all the algae are plants with no true leaves, roots, or stems.

Above the algae and fungi on the tree are the *bryophytes*. Their name means "mosslike plants." In this group are all the mosses. In it, too, are the liverworts. Like the algae and the fungi, the bryophytes lack true leaves, roots, or stems.

The whole top of the tree is taken up by the phylum of *tracheophytes*. These plants all have stems in which there are water-carrying tubes. Notice that the tracheophytes branch into the horsetails, club mosses, ferns, gymnosperms, or cone bearers, and angiosperms, or flowering plants. Both the gymnosperms and the angiosperms, in turn, are still further branched.

The flowering plants were the last of the great groups of plants to appear on the earth. They were so successful that today there are many more kinds of flowering plants than of all the others put together.

Caltha palustris

Marsh Marigold
Cowslip
Kingcup
Soldier's Buttons
May Blob
Marybud

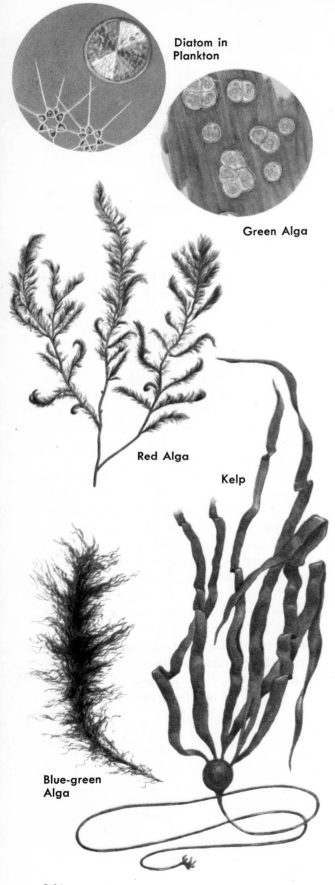

Diatom in Plankton

Green Alga

Red Alga

Kelp

Blue-green Alga

The plants pictured on this page represent the different phyla of algae. They are all water plants. Most algae are. Seaweeds are algae. So are pond scums. The algae that do not actually live in water live in moist places.

Some algae are so tiny that single ones cannot be seen without a microscope. Many of the green, blue-green, and golden algae are made of only a single cell. But by no means all algae are small. A giant seaweed, one of the big brown algae called kelps, may grow to be 150 feet long.

Diatoms are one-celled golden algae. They are plants with remarkable glassy walls like little pillboxes. They are an important part of plankton, the "sea soup" on which many animals of the sea live.

Mushrooms are fungi. Fungi do not have in them any of the green coloring matter that most plants have. Many of the fungi are either colorless or white. In the main they live on land.

Lichens are strange plants. They are made up of both fungus plants and green or blue-green algae. If you were to look at a bit of lichen through a microscope, you would see many tiny green dots (the algae) surrounded by white threads (the fungus).

A lichen is one of the best partnerships in the whole world of living things. The algae and the fungus help each other so well that the lichen can live on bare rocks where no other plants can grow. The algae furnish the fungus with food. The fungus stores up water from rain and dew and keeps the algae from drying out. The fungus also gives off an acid that eats down into the rock and helps the lichen anchor itself in place.

In time lichens make rocks start crumbling into soil. The places where they grow become fit for other plants. Lichens are plant pioneers.

Mosses are small. We often see them growing so close together that they form a velvety green carpet. They grow in many different parts of the world, even in very cold regions. Some live in water. Not many live where there are long dry spells.

Liverwort

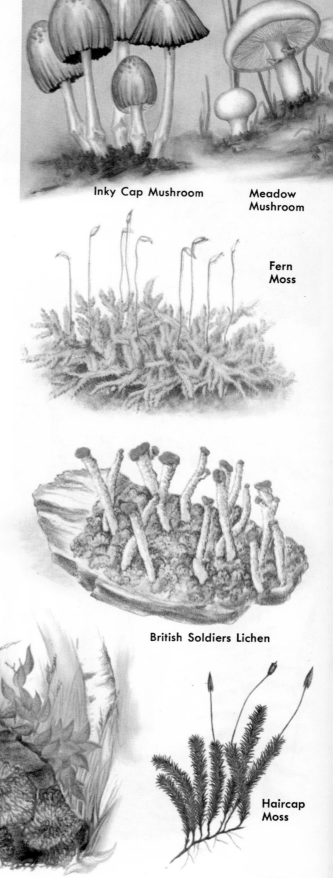
Inky Cap Mushroom

Meadow Mushroom

Fern Moss

British Soldiers Lichen

Haircap Moss

Mosses are not quite so common, however, as plant names might make you think. A number of plants are called mosses that do not belong to the group. Among them are Irish moss, long moss, and reindeer moss. Irish moss is one of the red algae. Long moss is a flowering plant, a cousin of the pineapple. Reindeer moss is a lichen.

The slender stalks rising from the moss plants pictured have spore cases at the top. Many of the plants that do not produce seeds are spread by spores. Spores are single cells. Some of the mosses are so much alike that it is hard to tell them apart. Often its spore cases give the best clues for identifying a moss you find.

The mosses are much better known than their fellow bryophytes the liverworts. Some liverworts look rather like mosses. Others are ribbon-like plants that lie close against whatever they are growing on. These liverworts are seen most often on the shaded walls of deep ravines.

Lichen on Rock

Wood Fern

Maidenhair Fern

Boston Fern

Tree Fern

Cinnamon Fern

Nodding Club Moss

Horsetail

All the plants pictured on these two pages are tracheophytes. They all have well-developed tubes for carrying water, which in turn carries food and minerals.

In the great forests from which coal was made, there were tree ferns, tree horsetails, and tree club mosses. They were the first really big land plants. Their water-carrying tubes made it possible for them to grow high up from the ground. But these groups of plants no longer play the leading role they once did in the plant world. Now there are no tree club mosses or tree horsetails. All the club mosses and horsetails of today are fairly small plants. There are still some tree ferns in warm, moist regions, but not many living ferns are more than a few feet high.

Today's horsetails are often called scouring rushes. They get this name because their

Spruce

Pine

stems are so gritty that they can be used for scouring pots and pans. For the most part horsetails grow in barren, sandy areas. They may not long be able to keep their foothold even there.

Today's club mosses grow close to the ground, often making a good cover for it. Some kinds are called "ground pine" and are used for Christmas greens.

Notice in the picture of the cinnamon fern that one leaf is rolled up like the head of a violin. This is a young leaf. It is following a pattern common among ferns. When it is young the leaf is rolled into a fiddlehead. It then unrolls from the base upward. There is a second way in which most fern leaves are alike. When a vein in a leaf divides, it forks into two equal branches.

There are many kinds of ferns. There are ten times as many species of ferns as there are of horsetails and club mosses together. But ferns are so far outnumbered by the plants that bear seeds—the cone bearers, or gymnosperms, and the flowering plants,

or angiosperms—that they make up only a tiny part of the whole plant world.

The pine and the spruce are conifers. The conifers rank high on the cone-bearer branch of the seed plants. Not all conifers are trees, but most are. They furnish much of our lumber.

You can see at a glance that the orchid belongs to the flowering plants. It ranks at the top of the monocots, one of the two branches of the angiosperms. No plants have flowers more beautiful or more complicated than those of orchids. Some orchids grow on the ground, but many, like the one in the picture, perch on the branches of trees in tropical forests.

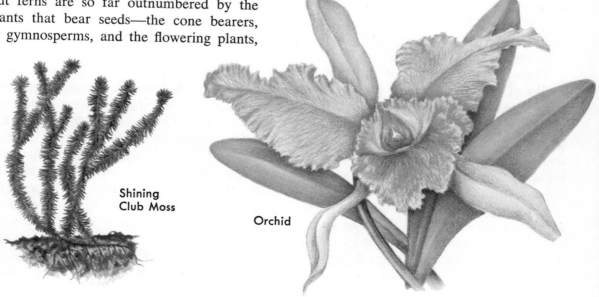

Shining Club Moss

Orchid

Sugar Maple

Plant Factories

In parts of the world where sugar maples grow, early spring is sugaring-off time. Holes are bored in the trunks of the maple trees, little troughs are put in the holes, and buckets are hung at the ends of the troughs. As sap begins to rise in the trees, some of it runs out into the buckets. The sap is mostly water, but it also has sugar in it. Sugaring off is boiling down the sap to make it into syrup and maple sugar.

The sugar in the sap was stored in the trunks of the trees through the winter. It is gathered up by the water rising in the trunks in the spring and if not drained out of the tree is carried to the parts of the tree that need it. New leaves and flowers and branches cannot grow unless they have food. Sugar is good food.

The story of how the sap of a maple tree happens to have sugar in it in the spring-time is thus a simple one. The story of how the sugar maple gets the sugar it stores in its trunk is more complicated.

A maple tree has only two places from which it can get materials it needs. One is the soil. The other is the air. There is no sugar in either soil or air. Since it cannot get the sugar from either the soil or the air, the maple tree must make it itself. It must make it out of materials it can get from soil or air. This idea has proved to be right. A sugar maple tree is a sugar factory.

A stalk of sugarcane is a sugar factory, too. Sugar maples and sugarcane, more-over, are not alone in making sugar. All green plants are sugar factories. They do not all make a great deal of sugar. Some use up what they make almost as fast as they make it. Some change much of what they make into other materials. But they all manufacture sugar as food for themselves.

Green plants use two common materials in making sugar. One is water. The other is carbon dioxide. The leaves are the chief sugar factories of most green plants—of all green plants, in fact, that have leaves.

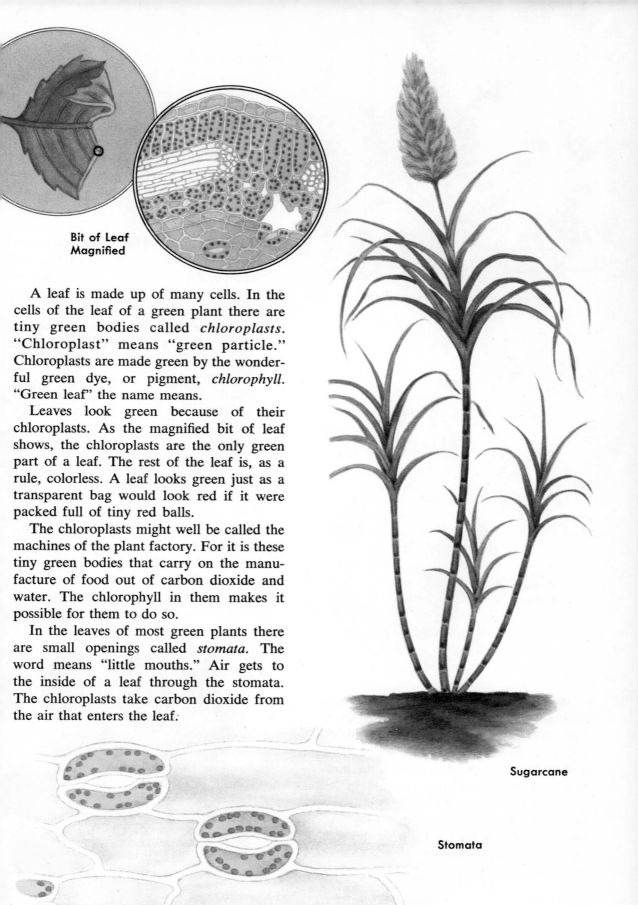

Bit of Leaf
Magnified

A leaf is made up of many cells. In the cells of the leaf of a green plant there are tiny green bodies called *chloroplasts*. "Chloroplast" means "green particle." Chloroplasts are made green by the wonderful green dye, or pigment, *chlorophyll*. "Green leaf" the name means.

Leaves look green because of their chloroplasts. As the magnified bit of leaf shows, the chloroplasts are the only green part of a leaf. The rest of the leaf is, as a rule, colorless. A leaf looks green just as a transparent bag would look red if it were packed full of tiny red balls.

The chloroplasts might well be called the machines of the plant factory. For it is these tiny green bodies that carry on the manufacture of food out of carbon dioxide and water. The chlorophyll in them makes it possible for them to do so.

In the leaves of most green plants there are small openings called *stomata*. The word means "little mouths." Air gets to the inside of a leaf through the stomata. The chloroplasts take carbon dioxide from the air that enters the leaf.

Sugarcane

Stomata

269

Oxygen Rising from Green Plant

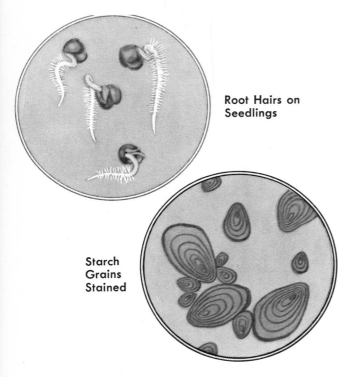

Root Hairs on Seedlings

Starch Grains Stained

water at last reaches the veins of the leaf. The veins carry it to the cells where the chloroplasts are.

Chloroplasts cannot work without light. Ordinarily, therefore, the making of sugar goes on only during the daytime. When they are making sugar the chloroplasts throw away oxygen. If plants are growing underwater, bubbles of oxygen can often be seen rising from them on sunny days.

After sugar is made it may be changed at once into starch. When grains of starch stained with iodine are examined under a microscope, it is easy to see that the grains have been built up in layers.

Green plants, after they have made sugar, can build it into still other kinds of food by adding minerals from the soil. Green plants cannot live on sugar and starch alone any more than we can.

Animals cannot make food for themselves. They have to get their food from plants or from other animals that eat plants. Plants that are not green, except for a very few plant protists, must get their food from animals or from green plants. The green plants are the world's food factories.

Much of the food made and stored by plants is for the next generation of plants. Seeds, for instance, contain food stored for the young plants that sprout from them. Nuts are seeds. They are only one of many kinds of seeds that people as well as many wild and domesticated animals use as food.

Cola

Water, even when there is a heavy rain, does not enter a leaf through the stomata. The "little mouths" as a rule are on the underside of the leaf so that it cannot. If a plant has roots, the water enters the roots. Near the end of a root growing in soil there is a little brush of root hairs. The root hairs cling to particles of soil. They soak up water. The water travels from the roots up through the stem and its branches. It goes in special water-carrying tubes. The

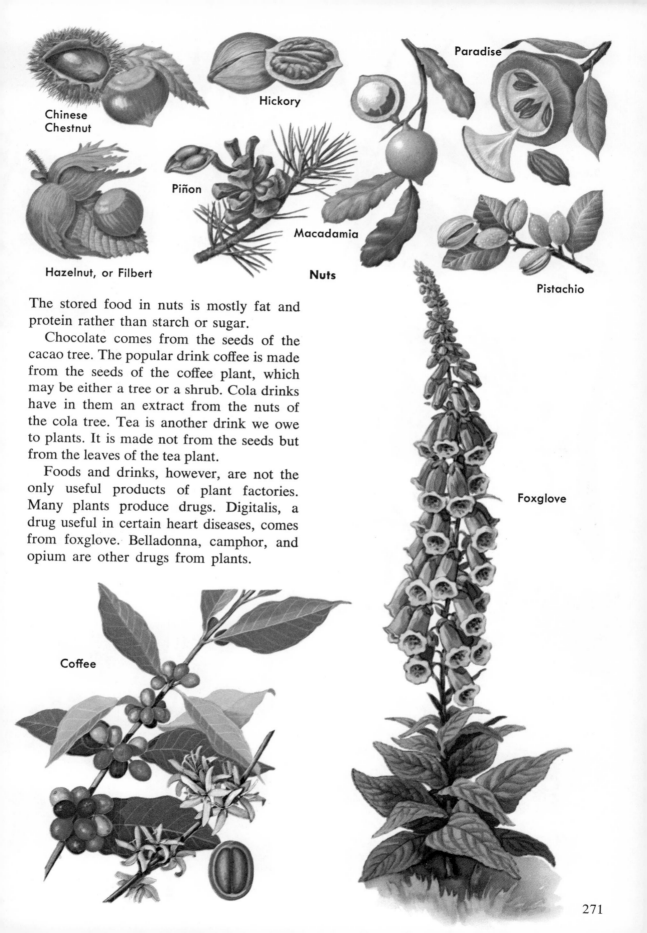

Chinese Chestnut

Hickory

Paradise

Piñon

Macadamia

Hazelnut, or Filbert

Nuts

Pistachio

Foxglove

The stored food in nuts is mostly fat and protein rather than starch or sugar.

Chocolate comes from the seeds of the cacao tree. The popular drink coffee is made from the seeds of the coffee plant, which may be either a tree or a shrub. Cola drinks have in them an extract from the nuts of the cola tree. Tea is another drink we owe to plants. It is made not from the seeds but from the leaves of the tea plant.

Foods and drinks, however, are not the only useful products of plant factories. Many plants produce drugs. Digitalis, a drug useful in certain heart diseases, comes from foxglove. Belladonna, camphor, and opium are other drugs from plants.

Coffee

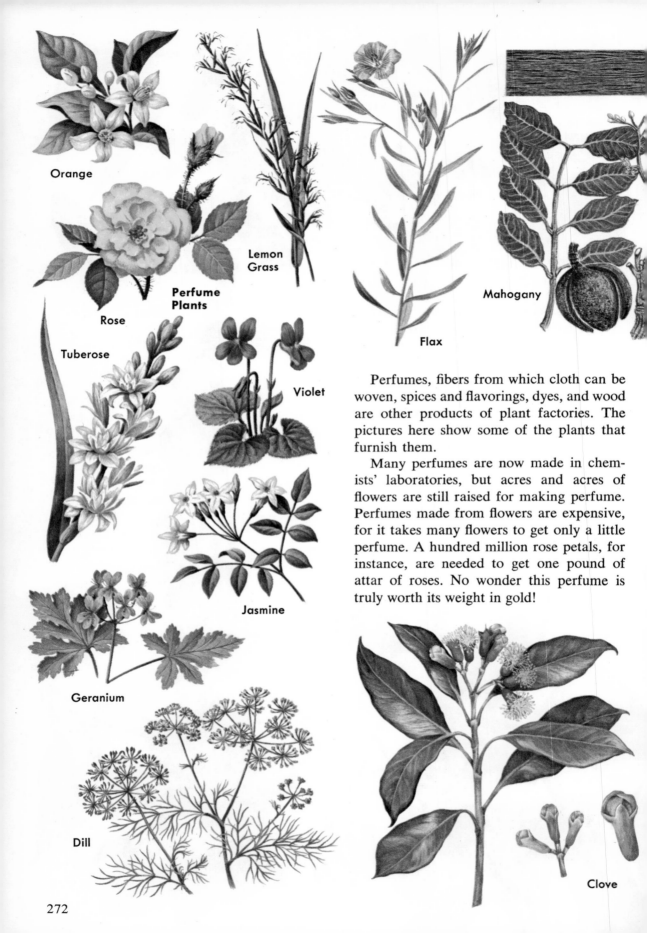

Orange

Rose

Lemon Grass

Perfume Plants

Tuberose

Violet

Jasmine

Geranium

Dill

Flax

Mahogany

Clove

Perfumes, fibers from which cloth can be woven, spices and flavorings, dyes, and wood are other products of plant factories. The pictures here show some of the plants that furnish them.

Many perfumes are now made in chemists' laboratories, but acres and acres of flowers are still raised for making perfume. Perfumes made from flowers are expensive, for it takes many flowers to get only a little perfume. A hundred million rose petals, for instance, are needed to get one pound of attar of roses. No wonder this perfume is truly worth its weight in gold!

Ebony

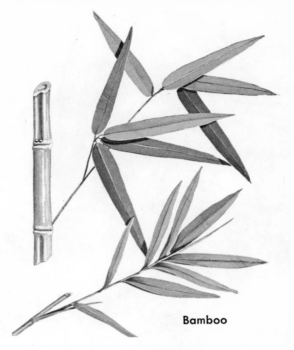

Bamboo

Linen is made of fibers from the stem of the flax plant. Cotton comes from fibers attached to the seeds of the cotton plant. Hemp and jute are other plants that furnish us with fibers.

The plants pictured at the bottom of these two pages all furnish us with spices or flavorings. Vanilla, a very popular flavoring for desserts, comes from an orchid. The dill plant furnishes the flavoring for dill pickles. Cloves and nutmeg are spices used in many foods. Saffron, from a crocus, is both a flavoring and a dye. It costs so much, however, that it is seldom used as a dye.

We owe wood to trees and shrubs. Ebony and mahogany are two of the most valuable and highly prized kinds. The stems of the giant grass bamboo are much used in place of wood in the Far East. They also serve as water pipes, carrying poles, and fishing poles. Split, they are woven into curtains, baskets, fans, and hats.

Rubber, turpentine, oil for soaps and paints, and chicle for chewing gum are among the other products green plants give us. Even if we did not depend on plants for food, we would go on raising many kinds for the other materials they manufacture.

Vanilla Orchid

Saffron Crocus

Nutmeg

Trees

Trees are our biggest plants. You may have the idea that trees are too big to be called plants, but this idea is wrong. A tree is built on much the same plan as a geranium or a rosebush; it is simply larger.

In the warm, wet regions of the world there are some tree ferns. All the trees of cooler regions are seed plants. But they are not all flowering plants. Many of them have cones rather than flowers.

Every tree represented in these pictures is a conifer, or cone bearer. Conifers all have narrow leaves. The leaves of some, like those of the balsam fir, are so narrow

that they are commonly called needles. Others, like those of cypresses, are scale-like. They overlap one another on the stems that bear them.

Some needles, like the fir's, are blunt at the ends. Some are sharp like those of pines. Notice that the pine needles are in clusters while those of the fir are not.

The leaves of a conifer, even though they do not have a leaflike look, serve the same purpose that other green leaves serve. They are the plant's food factories.

Most conifers have leaves the year round They are evergreens. The fact that they are green all the year round does not mean they never shed any leaves. They do, but they shed them a few at a time all during the year. The trees are never bare.

Not quite all conifers are evergreens. The tamaracks, or larches, and the bald cypress are among the few conifers that shed their leaves in the fall and send out new ones in the spring.

The conifers include some of our most valuable timber trees. They are often called softwoods, although that name is not an especially good one. The wood of some conifers is soft, but that of a few is hard and long lasting.

Even people who do not live near any conifer forests are familiar with a number of kinds of conifers. Many evergreens are planted as ornamental trees. And at Christmastime people buy small conifers and their branches for Christmas trees and greens.

The names of some conifers are confusing. The Port Orford cedar is not a cedar. It is, instead, as you might guess from its leaves, in the same genus with the Sitka and sawara cypresses. The Lebanon cedar

Lebanon Cedar

Jack Pine

Red Pine

Sitka Cypress

Port Orford Cedar

Sawara Cypress

Monterey Pine

Japanese Yew

275

Redwood

really is a cedar. Notice how different its leaves are. All true cedars are natives of the Old World. In the same way, the Douglas fir is not a fir, and the bald cypress is not a cypress.

Conifers flourished long before any trees with flowers appeared. In the past 60 million years, however, the group has been losing ground. But even now the tallest, the largest, and the oldest trees are found among the conifers.

The tallest trees are redwoods. Many are more than 300 feet tall. The record holder towers 368 feet into the air. It is in a redwood grove in northern California. The closest rivals of the redwoods are found among trees with flowers. They are eucalyptus trees of Australia.

The largest of all trees are giant sequoias, cousins of the redwoods. Another name for them is big trees. One giant sequoia, so famous that it has been given a name, has a diameter of 34 feet at the base and is over 272 feet tall—taller than a 20-story building. Inside its trunk there would be room for a church with a tall spire. This giant is the "General Sherman." There are other big trees almost as big.

The "General Sherman," scientists say, is probably about 3,500 years old. It began growing at about the same time that the alphabet had its beginnings far away at the eastern end of the Mediterranean Sea. The tree was already 3,000 years old when Christopher Columbus and his followers first reached the shores of America.

Tree Rings

Scientists cannot tell exactly how old the "General Sherman" is, but they do know how old some big trees have lived to be. They have been able to tell the age of these trees after they were cut down.

The age of a giant sequoia—and of most other trees, too—can be told from rings in the wood. In the trunks of most kinds of trees new wood is formed each year in a layer outside the old wood and beneath the bark. When the trunk of a tree is sawed across, each layer shows as a ring. The rings are called annual rings. Finding how old the tree is means simply counting the rings.

For many years the oldest giant sequoias were thought to be the oldest of all trees— the oldest, in fact, of all living things. Now some of the bristlecone pines, another conifer, are believed to be older than any sequoias. A bristlecone pine whose rings have been counted began growing nearly 5,000 years ago—before the days when the Egyptians were building great pyramids and over a thousand years before the "General Sherman" sprouted.

The leaves pictured on this page come from trees whose seeds are produced by flowers, not cones. Such trees are often called broadleaf trees. They are commonly spoken of as hardwoods, too, even though some of them have soft wood.

Many broadleaf trees drop their leaves in the fall and send out new leaves in the spring just as a few conifers do. During the winter months their branches are bare. Trees that drop their leaves in the fall are called *deciduous*. The name comes from the Latin word meaning "to fall off." As a rule the leaves of deciduous broadleaf trees change color in autumn.

It is a help to broadleaf trees to drop their leaves in the fall if they live in a region with cold winters. The living material in the cells of most conifer leaves is much better protected from the cold than the living material in the thin leaves of a broadleaf tree. But in regions where the winters are not cold, broadleaf trees can be evergreen. The live oak of the South is a good example.

Sugar Maple

Sassafras

Cottonwood

Ginkgo

The ginkgo is unique among the trees of today. It is a seed plant, but neither a flowering plant like the maples and cottonwoods nor a conifer like the cypresses and pines. As the tree of the plant kingdom on page 262 shows, the ginkgo is a gymnosperm. It is, therefore, closely related to the conifers, but it is in a group all its own.

A common name of the ginkgo is maidenhair tree. Ginkgo leaves have much the same shape as the tiny leaflets of the maidenhair fern. The tree bears plumlike seeds. The name "ginkgo" comes from the Chinese and means "silver apricot." The seeds have a silvery sheen. A much older name given the ginkgo by the Chinese meant "duck foot." The shape of its leaves earned the ginkgo this name.

The ginkgo is a living fossil. It has remained almost unchanged for more than 200 million years. Before the days of the flowering plants—back in the early days of the dinosaurs—the ginkgo grew in many parts of the world. It flourished in Europe, North America, and Asia. Today it has all but disappeared in the wild. For centuries, however, ginkgoes have been raised and planted in the gardens surrounding Buddhist temples of the Far East.

But millions of people have seen ginkgo trees who have never been in the Orient. Ginkgoes are now cultivated in other parts of the world as well and are fairly common along city streets and in parks. They are in favor partly because they are resistant to disease and drought and partly because they can stand the smoke of cities. But ginkgoes are not large or especially attractive trees. They are not likely to ever be as popular as maples and elms and oaks.

There are hundreds of kinds of trees. Some, like the ginkgo, are seldom mistaken for any other kind, but it is not easy to tell all trees apart. A tree's shape is a help in identifying it. The vase shape of the American elm, as you see, is very different from the broad spread of the live oak or the rounded head of the sugar maple. The almost circular crown of the mountain ash can be told at a glance from the slender triangle of a birch. If a tree is deciduous,

| Cottonwood | Birch | Mountain Ash | Bur Oak | Balsam Fir | Sugar Maple |

its shape is one of the best ways of identifying it in the winter.

A tree's shape has to do chiefly with the way it branches. Notice that the balsam fir branches so close to the ground that the trunk does not show. The American elm, on the other hand, branches many feet above the ground. The branches of the fir, moreover, are nearly horizontal, while those of the elm turn up. Some trees—weeping willow, for one—have drooping branches.

American Elm

Their leaves, of course, are a big help in telling trees apart. Every kind of tree has a leaf of a distinctive shape. Some leaves are narrow; some are broad. Some are very much larger than others. The edges, or margins, of some are smooth; those of others are toothed like a saw. Some leaves have lobes; others are entire—that is, unlobed.

Of the four kinds of leaves pictured on this page the elm and the beech have sawtoothed margins. The scarlet oak leaf is lobed, and the lobes end in sharp points. The live oak has a smooth margin and no lobes. The scarlet oak leaf is the largest.

Live Oak

Some trees play a kind of joke on people trying to identify them from their leaves. They have leaves of different shapes, all on the same tree. The sassafras is such a tree. Some sassafras leaves have lobes on each side like the one on page 277. Some are lobed on only one side; they are mitten-shaped. Others have no lobes. The mulberry also has leaves that vary in shape.

Scarlet Oak

Beech

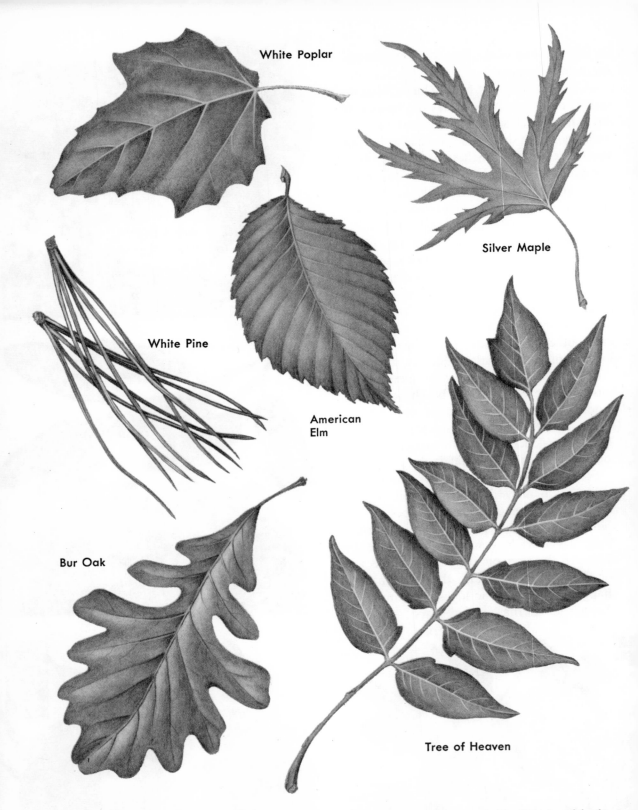

White Poplar

Silver Maple

White Pine

American Elm

Bur Oak

Tree of Heaven

It is easy to see that the leaves in these pictures all vary in shape and in margins. The pictures show some other ways, too, in which leaves of different trees differ.

It may surprise you to find that, with the exception of the clusters of pine needles, each picture shows a single leaf. Three of the leaves, however, are *compound*—they are made up of separate leaflets. The three are the tree of heaven, the buckeye, and the honey locust. The honey locust is doubly compound. Its leaflets are divided into still smaller leaflets.

Although the tree of heaven and the buckeye both have undivided leaflets, the leaflets are not arranged in the same way. Those of the buckeye spread out like the fingers from the palm of your hand. Those of the tree of heaven are arranged along a leaf stem. They remind one of a feather. We say that the buckeye leaf is *palmately compound* and that the tree of heaven leaf is *pinnately compound*. "Pinnate" comes from a Latin word for "feather."

The veins, or water-carrying tubes, of different kinds of leaves make different patterns. You cannot see the veins of the pine needles pictured, but the veins of all the leaves from broadleaf trees show clearly. Leaves may be palmately or pinnately veined. The maple leaf is palmately veined. All the other broadleaf leaves shown here have pinnate veining.

The stem of a leaf is called its *petiole*. The petioles of most leaves, if they have them, are round. The cottonwood leaf, on the other hand, has a flat petiole. It lets the leaf move very easily in the wind. The flat petiole explains why cottonwood trees rustle as they do in a breeze.

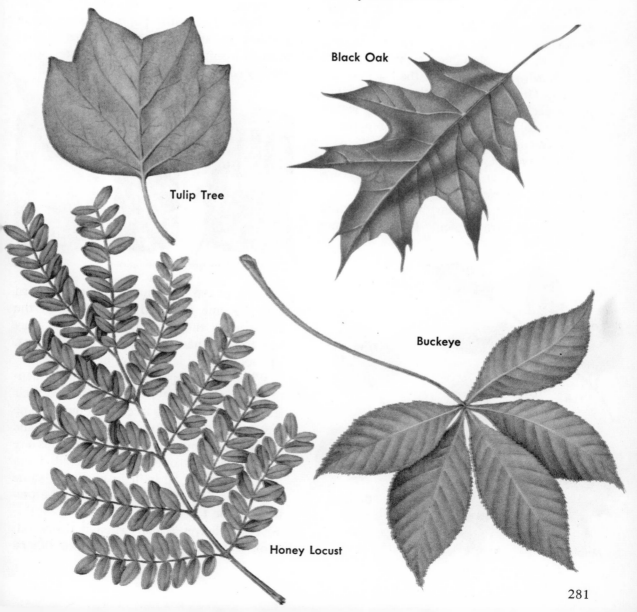

Tulip Tree

Black Oak

Buckeye

Honey Locust

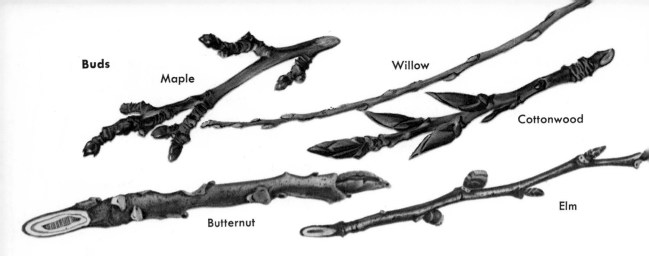

Buds

Maple

Willow

Cottonwood

Butternut

Elm

Different trees have their leaves arranged differently on their twigs. As you have already found out, pines have their needles arranged in clusters. But different pines have different numbers of needles in a cluster. Some have five, others only two or three. Piñon pine bundles vary from one to five.

The picture below shows three different ways hardwood trees have their leaves arranged. The maple has leaves that are *opposite* each other on the twigs. The leaves of all maples follow this plan of opposite arrangement. So do the ashes and buckeyes.

The leaves of the catalpa grow in rings of three each around the twig. They are said to be *whorled*.

The elm follows by far the most common plan of leaf arrangement. Its leaves come from first one side of a twig and then the other. They are, in other words, *alternate*.

Some leaves are smooth and glossy. Those of the live oak and the magnolia are good examples. Others are rather rough. Some are fuzzy. The white poplar gets its name because the underside of its leaves is covered with soft white down. The white shows clearly when the wind rustles the leaves.

Bark

Shagbark Hickory   Persimmon   Beech

Some of the leaf shoots of the hawthorn have become modified down through the ages so that they are now thorns. An easy way to tell a hawthorn tree is by its thorns. The locusts and acacias are also thorny.

When trees are bare, buds help to identify them. In the late summer, before their leaves fall, deciduous trees form buds. Some are flower buds. Most are leaf buds. The tiny flowers and leaves inside the buds are well protected from the winter cold. Even though they are all built in much the same way, buds do not all look alike, as the pictures at the top of the page show.

A leaf leaves a scar when it drops off. Some leaf scars are much larger than others.

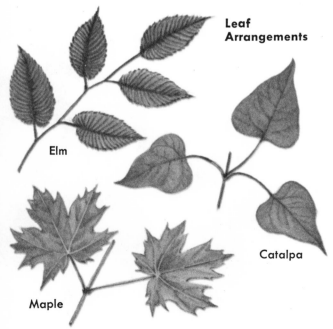

Leaf Arrangements

Elm

Catalpa

Maple

The leaf scars of different trees vary in shape, too. Of the twigs pictured, the leaf scars show most clearly on the butternut. There are two near the cut end of the twig.

Many people tell trees apart, especially in winter, chiefly by their bark. Notice how different the three kinds of bark pictured are. Not many trees have bark as smooth as a beech's. Not many have bark as shaggy as that of a shagbark hickory. The bark of most trees is more like that of the persimmon, but the pattern of ridges differs from one kind of tree to another.

The color of the bark varies, too. Graybrown is the usual bark color. But some is reddish-brown and some, as you see, is pale gray. The bark of the paper birch is white.

All conifers have cones of one sort or another that help to identify them. Even the cones of the different species in one group such as the pines are distinctive. Those of sugar pine, for instance, are long —often almost 2 feet long—while those of Jersey pine are oval. Two of the cones shown have already opened and lost their seeds. The cones of firs and larches are erect. Those of spruces hang down. Long pinecones, too, hang down, but most of those shorter than wide stand up.

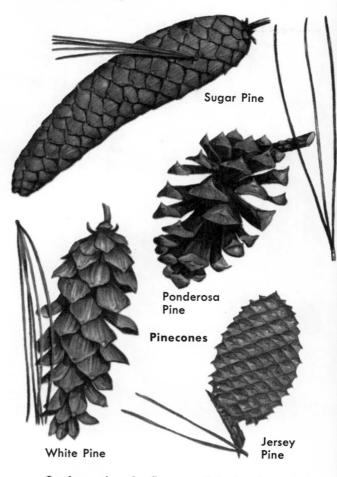

Sugar Pine

Ponderosa Pine

Pinecones

White Pine

Jersey Pine

In the spring the flowers of the hardwoods are a help in telling one tree from another. Later in the year the fruits and seeds are name cards to those who know trees well enough to read them. Acorns, for instance, grow only on oak trees, and every kind of oak has its own special shape and size of acorn. Notice how the cups as well as the shells of these acorns vary.

Live Oak

Acorns

Black Oak

Northern Red Oak

White Oak

Bur Oak

California Live Oak

Overcup Oak

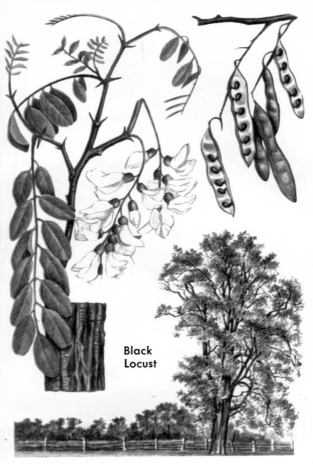

Black
Locust

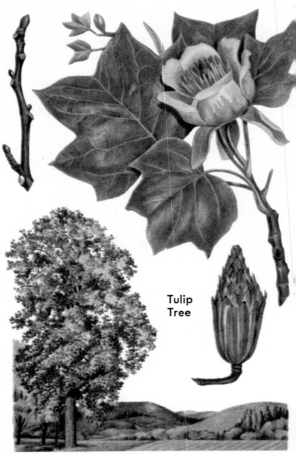

Tulip
Tree

Dogwood

Catalpa

edbud

Hawthorn

Our broadleaf trees belong to the great group of flowering plants, the angiosperms, but the flowers of many of them go unnoticed. No one would gather walnut or oak or maple flowers for a bouquet. Some trees, however, have large and showy flowers. The six hardwoods shown on these two pages are among them. They are often planted as ornamentals.

Most of our cultivated fruit trees, too, have showy flowers. No flower garden was ever more beautiful than an apple orchard in full bloom.

The flowers of the dogwood are showy only because of big bracts that surround clusters of them. The bracts are sometimes pink, sometimes white. They look like petals, but they are really not parts of the flowers. The flowers themselves are tiny.

For some reason which no one understands, one branch of the flowering plants—the dicots—produced many more kinds of trees than the other branch—the monocots. But there is one huge family of trees on the monocot branch—the palms. There are more than a thousand—there may even be several thousand—kinds of palms. To the people of tropical lands the palms are enormously important. They furnish shelter, food, drink, fibers, oil, and vegetable ivory.

The coconut palm is a common sight on the shores of warm seas. Although its flowers are small, its seeds—the coconuts—are among the largest of all seeds.

Palm trees do not have the solid woody trunks that dicot trees and conifers have. Their trunks are more like giant cornstalks. Bundles of woody water-carrying tubes are scattered through them with soft pith between. No one can tell the age of a palm tree by counting rings. There are no rings.

Coconut Palm

flowers

285

Banyan

All these trees are natives of other lands. Some of them, however, are planted in the United States.

The banyan, a "strangling" fig, is famous for its many trunks. The extra trunks develop from roots dropped down from branches. A famous banyan tree in India covers nearly two acres. The main trunk is 13 feet across. There are some 230 trunks more than 2 feet thick and over 3,000 smaller ones.

The silk tree of southern Asia has, you can see, doubly compound leaves and pink flowers. It is used as an ornamental. This tree, as you might guess from its leaves, is a cousin of the sensitive plant.

The monkey puzzle of South America is an araucaria, or Chile pine—a conifer but not a true pine. The way its branches bend at the ends reminds people of monkey tails.

The sausage tree of Africa is a relative of the catalpa. It is named for its sausage-shaped fruits.

The bottle tree gets its name from the shape of its trunk. This tree grows in the grasslands of Australia. Its trunk serves as a storage tank for water. The stored water tides the tree over dry periods.

Unfortunately, trees of all kinds have enemies. There are countless kinds of insects that live on the trees of our forests and orchards and the shade trees of our towns and cities. There are many tree diseases, too. One, for example, killed most of the chestnut trees in the United States. Another now being fought attacks elms.

Smoke is an enemy of trees, too. Many kinds cannot stand the soot of cities.

Fire is one of the worst enemies of our forest trees. Forest fires, many started by carelessness, have destroyed hundreds of millions of dollars' worth of good timber. Replacing a forest is a matter of years, perhaps of centuries. A forest fire may so damage the soil that trees cannot grow in it.

Trees are a great help to a city or town. But choosing shade trees for planting around our homes and on our streets is not easy. A tree that is likely to be killed by a disease or that is a prey to so many kinds of insects that a war against them will have to be carried on constantly is not a good choice. Neither is a short-lived tree nor one with wood so brittle that it breaks easily in storms.

Some trees are unpopular for city streets because they produce so many roots that they clog up sewers. Some are not well liked because their flowers have an unpleasant smell. Some litter up the ground under them with their flowers or fruits or seeds. But, although there are many questions to be asked about any tree that is being considered for city planting, there are many trees to choose from. Except in the very arid parts of our country, there are almost sure to be several kinds of trees that do well.

Silk Tree

Monkey Puzzle

Bottle Tree

Sausage Tree

Bacteria and Slime Molds

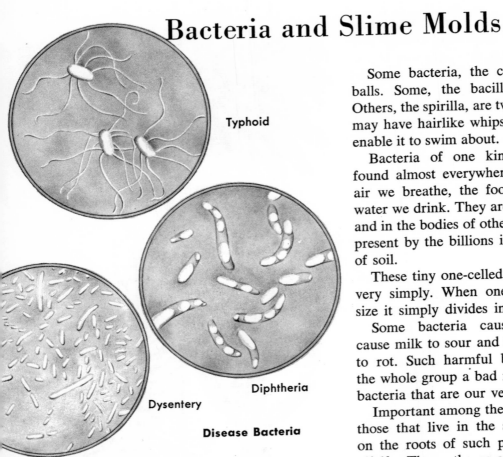

Typhoid

Diphtheria

Dysentery

Disease Bacteria

Some bacteria, the cocci, are like tiny balls. Some, the bacilli, are rod-shaped. Others, the spirilla, are twisted. A bacterium may have hairlike whips, or flagella, which enable it to swim about.

Bacteria of one kind or another are found almost everywhere. They are in the air we breathe, the food we eat, and the water we drink. They are in our own bodies and in the bodies of other animals. They are present by the billions in every square foot of soil.

These tiny one-celled organisms multiply very simply. When one reaches a certain size it simply divides into two.

Some bacteria cause disease. Others cause milk to sour and fruit and vegetables to rot. Such harmful bacteria have given the whole group a bad name. But there are bacteria that are our very good friends.

Important among the helpful bacteria are those that live in the soil and in nodules on the roots of such plants as clover and alfalfa. These, the so-called nitrogen-fixing bacteria, help keep soil fertile by taking nitrogen from the air and building it into compounds green plants can use.

Bacteria and slime molds, as you know, are called plants by some scientists and protists by others. They are certainly not much like the plants we are used to seeing. Bacteria are all far too small to be visible without a powerful microscope. It would take 50,000 of some kinds to make a row an inch long. Each bacterium is a single cell, but in many cases several may stay together and form a chain. Slime molds are much larger, but they are still tiny.

Early in its life history a slime mold is a creeping animal-like blob of protoplasm. Later it develops spores just as many plants do. The tiny spores scatter in the wind. Each then may start a new slime mold.

The spore cases of slime molds vary greatly in both color and shape. Those of the

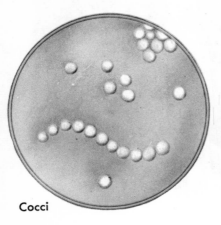

Cocci

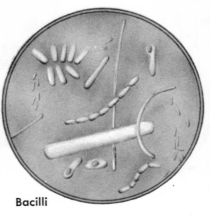

Bacilli

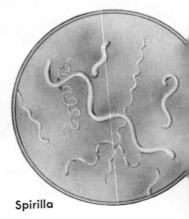

Spirilla

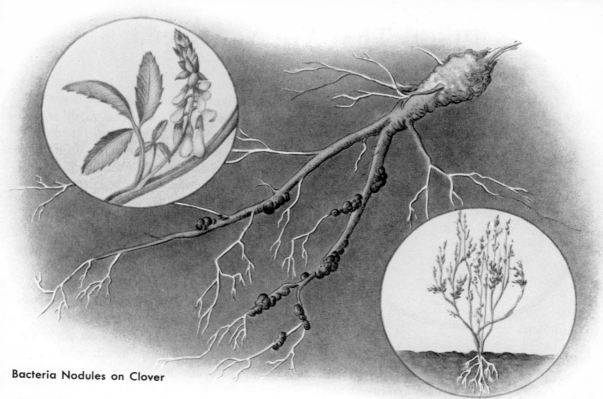

Bacteria Nodules on Clover

slime mold pictured here, you will notice, do not look much like those of the one pictured on page 63. Some slime molds have unstalked spore cases that lie flat on whatever the slime mold is growing on.

Slime molds are puzzling and fun to study. Scientists have found their animal-like stage useful in learning about protoplasm. These strange plant-animals, however, are far, far less important than bacteria.

Slime Mold

Plants That Are Not Green

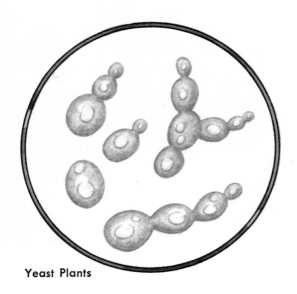

Yeast Plants

More than three-fourths of all the thousands of kinds of plants are green. With the help of their chlorophyll they can make the food they need. The other plants that make up the plant kingdom lack chlorophyll and cannot make food for themselves. Like animals, they must get their food ready-made.

Some plants that are not green take their food from other live plants or from live animals. Others get food from dead plants or animals or from such plant and animal products as flour, sugar, and leather.

Plants that must get their food ready-made are often called "dependent plants." More than 99 out of every 100 dependent plants are fungi.

Yeasts are one-celled fungi. They are larger than bacteria but they are far too small to be seen without a microscope.

Yeast plants depend chiefly on sugar for food. The sugar must be dissolved. As yeast plants use up sugar, they produce carbon dioxide and alcohol. When yeasts are at work in a solution, we say that the

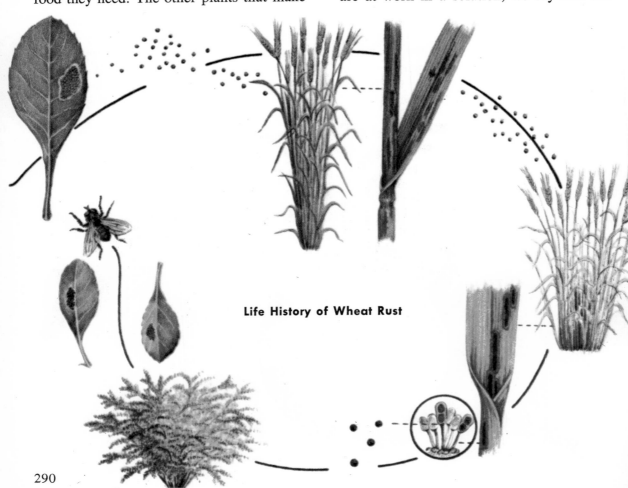

Life History of Wheat Rust

solution is souring, or fermenting. These tiny plants, like bacteria, float about in the air. They are likely to drop into any fruit juice or other sugar solution left uncovered and begin growing there.

The yeast plants floating about in the air are wild yeasts. Yeasts are cultivated for use in making bread and in making alcohol and alcoholic drinks. The cakes and packages of yeast used in making bread are made up of millions of yeast plants pressed together. In breadmaking it is the carbon dioxide produced which is important. The bubbles of this gas make the dough rise.

As a rule yeast plants multiply by budding. A small bud grows out of a cell. A wall soon divides it from the parent plant. In turn a bud may grow from it and another bud from that one. A whole chain may be formed. But at any time a chain may break apart into separate plants.

Molds are fungi, too. They are considerably larger than yeasts. The main part of a mold plant is a mass of colorless threads called a *mycelium*. From the mycelium tiny stalks arise which bear spores. Spores serve mold plants as seeds: new plants grow from them. Their spores give molds their color. Common colors among the molds are black, blue, green, brown, and pink.

Molds will grow on almost anything which comes from a plant or an animal. Molds growing on foods are usually a nuisance. But many kinds of cheese owe their flavor to molds growing in them. Molds growing on leather, cloth, or wood ruin it

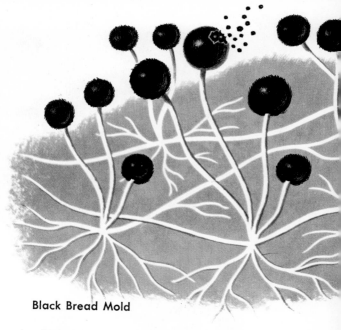

Black Bread Mold

in time. Some molds are a great help to us in fighting disease. The drug penicillin, for instance, is produced from a green mold.

Mildews are fungi, too. They are much like molds. The white powder one often sees on lilac or rose leaves is made of the spores of a powdery mildew. Late potato blight is caused by a downy mildew. The "mildewing" of books and paper and of belts, shoes, and rolled-up clothes in hot, humid weather is caused by molds rather than by mildews.

None of the fungi cause the farmer more trouble than rusts. They may ruin whole fields of grain. Rusts have complicated life histories. Many spend part of their lives on one plant and part on another. Wheat rust spends part of its life on barberry.

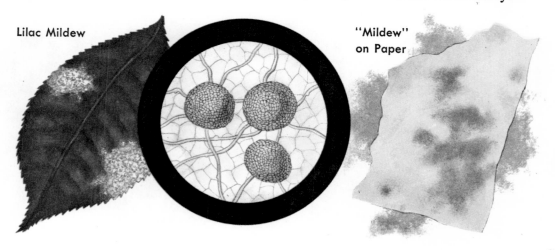

Lilac Mildew

"Mildew" on Paper

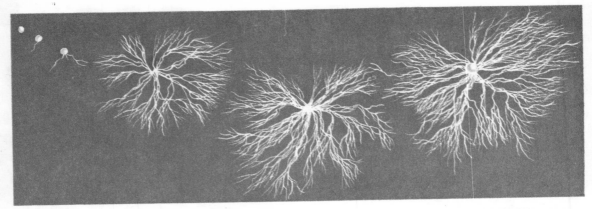

Mycelium Developing

Spore Print

Mushrooms are the largest of the fungi. The general plan of a mushroom is like that of a mold. The main body of the plant is a mass of colorless threads, or mycelium. Early stages of a mycelium are pictured above. Up from the mycelium grow stalks that bear spores. As a rule the mycelium is well hidden in whatever the fungus is growing on. The spore-bearing stalks of mushrooms are far larger than those of molds. What we usually call a mushroom is only the spore-bearing part.

Life History of Meadow Mushroom

Suppose the spore of a meadow mushroom reaches a good place for growing. A cobweb-fine white thread, the beginning of a mycelium, grows from it. It begins getting food from decaying plant materials in the soil. The young mushroom plant grows and branches. It spreads out in the soil. It may grow for many weeks underground.

At last tiny bumps the size of a pinhead appear on the mycelium. They are the beginnings of the mushrooms—the spore-bearing stalks. The little mushrooms get bigger. Soon they are large enough to push their way above the ground.

When a meadow mushroom first appears, it looks like a round white button. As the button grows, the top opens up into an "umbrella." The umbrella is called the cap. The handle of the umbrella is the stem. As the umbrella opens up, it leaves a collar around the stem. The cap may grow to be large. Meadow mushrooms with caps five inches across have been found. Usually the caps are smaller.

The underside of the cap is made up of many thin folds. These folds are called *gills*. They spread out from the center of the cap like the spokes of a wheel. The gills are pink when the cap first opens up. Later they turn brown and then nearly black. The top of the cap becomes darker, too.

The spores of the meadow mushroom are brown. When they are ripe the gills are covered with them. There are so many millions on a single mushroom that it would take 20 years to count them one by one.

Some of the spores fall to the ground. The wind blows some away. Any animal that brushes against the mushroom sends spores traveling. The spore print pictured was made simply by resting the umbrella of a meadow mushroom on a sheet of white paper and letting the ripe spores drop down on the paper.

The inky cap and the fairy-ring mushroom have gills just as the meadow mushroom has. The inky cap's gills are white at first. But when the spores are ripe the gills and cap turn to a black, inky liquid.

Inky Cap

Long ago people thought that the rings formed by the fairy-ring mushroom were actually made by fairies. We know now that the plant's mycelium spreads underground to form the circle. The mycelium in the center dies. Each year the ring is bigger than it was the year before. Another name for the fairy-ring mushroom is Scotch bonnet. This little mushroom's spores are white.

Sometimes mushrooms push their way up through hard-packed soil. It is difficult to see how they can do so, for they are not woody plants. They break through by taking in a great deal of water and swelling fast.

Fairy-ring Mushroom

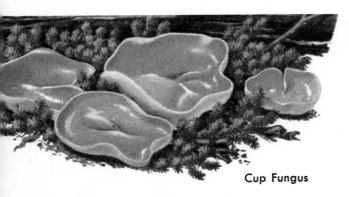
Cup Fungus

as much as 2 feet wide. The undersurface is white and fairly soft. Pictures can be drawn on it easily with a stick. Each mark is brown. Another common name for this bracket mushroom is artist's fungus.

The horn of the horn of plenty has an outer layer of spore-bearing cells. Its spore-bearing layer is not nearly so smooth as that of a cup fungus. The many branches of the coral fungus serve to spread out the spore-bearing layer of this mushroom. The delicate little hydnum bears its spores on soft, hanging teeth, or spines. This mushroom when young and pure white is considered one of the most beautiful of all plants. It is easy to imagine it as a winter scene in a dwarf forest. Later it turns brown.

The stinkhorn forms its spores underground in an egg-shaped case. When the spores are ripe, the case breaks open and with amazing speed a stalk grows up bearing a slimy cap of spores with a very bad odor. The odor attracts flies and other insects, which scatter the spores. Not all stinkhorns have the lacy veil that this one has.

The spores of puffballs are borne on a network of threads inside the balls. These mushrooms get their name because, when they ripen and open, clouds of spores puff out at the lightest touch. The number of spores puffballs produce is amazing even for mushrooms. A giant puffball may produce more than a thousand billion!

All mushrooms have histories much like that of the meadow mushroom. But they do not all bear their spores on gills. None of the mushrooms pictured here have gills. They have other ways of spreading out their spore-bearing surfaces. These mushrooms, too, produce spores in huge numbers.

The bright-orange lining of each cup of the cup fungus is the spore-bearing layer. Each pit in the cap of the morel is like one of the cups of a cup fungus. The lining of each pit bears spores.

The bolete and the shelf fungus are in a group called pore fungi. On the underside of the umbrella of a bolete and the shelf, or bracket, of a shelf fungus there are pores that open into slender tubes. The spores are borne on the lining of these tubes. When they are ripe, they fall out through the pores and are blown about.

Shelf fungi grow on trees of many kinds. This one, the common shelf fungus, may be

Bolete

Morel

Horn of Plenty

Puffballs

Hydnum

Shelf Fungus

Coral Fungus

Stinkhorn

Blewits

Honey Mushroom

Shaggy Mane

Rooting Collybia

Orange Lactar

Beefsteak Mushroom

Parasol Mushroom

Grape Coral

Oyster Mushroom

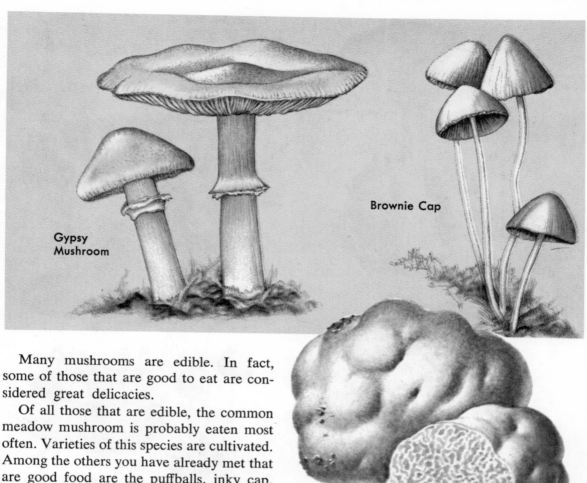

Gypsy Mushroom

Brownie Cap

Truffle

Chanterelle

Many mushrooms are edible. In fact, some of those that are good to eat are considered great delicacies.

Of all those that are edible, the common meadow mushroom is probably eaten most often. Varieties of this species are cultivated. Among the others you have already met that are good food are the puffballs, inky cap, fairy-ring mushroom, bolete, morel, hydnum, and horn of plenty.

All those pictured here can be eaten. The brownie cap, however, is so small that unless there are a great many close together it is scarcely worth picking. Its cap may well be only half an inch across.

In contrast with the little brownie cap, a truffle may weigh as much as two pounds. This mushroom grows wholly underground. As you already know, pigs are sometimes trained to sniff out truffles and dig them up. Poodles also make good truffle hunters. Many people consider truffles the most delicious of all mushrooms. Truffles are better known in Europe than in America.

There are many other edible mushrooms. Of those that are not good to eat, some are too woody or have a bad taste or smell. But some are not safe to eat. More than a few, in fact, contain deadly poisons.

Death Cap

Fool's Mushroom

Green Stropharia

Emetic Russula

Lurid Bolete

Mexican Sacred Mushroom

Fly Agaric

Jack-o'-lantern

Morgan's Lepiota

False Morel

298

All these mushrooms are poisonous. None of them can safely be eaten.

The death cap, fool's mushroom, and fly agaric are closely related. They are all amanitas. As you might guess from its name, the death cap is so poisonous that it is likely to kill anyone who eats it. The fool's mushroom is just as deadly. The poison in these mushrooms acts slowly. A person may not know until several hours after eating them that he has been poisoned. By that time it may be too late to do anything to fight the poison.

The poison of the fly agaric is not quite so deadly and it acts rapidly. In most cases the life of a person who has eaten it can be saved. This mushroom got its name because a growing one is likely to be surrounded by a circle of dead flies, killed by sipping juice from its cap. Its poison has been used to get rid of flies.

Amanitas always have a cup at the base of the stalk and a collar around the stem. Not all the amanitas are poisonous, and some are edible. But, since about nine-tenths of all people killed by eating mushrooms are killed by amanitas, any mushroom with a cup at the base and a conspicuous collar should be avoided "like poison."

Morgan's lepiota is a close relative of the edible parasol mushroom and looks much like it except that its spores are green. The poison of this mushroom causes indigestion but is not likely to cause death.

The lurid bolete also causes indigestion but is not deadly. Except for color this mushroom looks much like the edible bolete pictured on page 294. It deserves the "lurid" in its name. As you see, the stem is red shading into orange. The underside of the umbrella is vermilion at first and orange later. The flesh is yellow, but it becomes blue when bruised. The spores are greenish-gray.

Their beautiful colors help identify the stropharia and emetic russula. Their poisons usually cause indigestion.

The poison of the jack-o'-lantern acts like that of the fly agaric. This mushroom owes its name to the fact that it glows in the dark.

Eating the Mexican sacred mushroom has a strange effect. Its poison causes the eater to see visions and to stagger drunkenly.

The false morel, easily confused with morels we eat, is likely to have in it a poison that attacks red blood cells and may cause death. Strangely, this same mushroom may have no poison and be edible. But no one should take a chance with it.

Unfortunately, as you know from Morgan's lepiota, the lurid bolete, and the false morel, some poisonous mushrooms look very much like some that are edible. We should trust no one but an expert to tell us whether mushrooms found growing wild are safe to eat.

Many people think that mushrooms should not be called mushrooms unless they can be eaten. If they are not good to eat, these people say, they should be called toadstools. But "mushroom" to a scientist does not mean just a mushroom that can be eaten. Instead, it may mean any fungus large enough to be called fleshy. To many it means any mushroom that has gills. Still other scientists prefer the name only for those in the genus *Agaricus*—the genus of the meadow mushroom. "Toadstool" is simply a nickname for mushroom. Probably the "toad" comes from the unpleasantness of some of the mushrooms—some people call anything distasteful a toad. The stool-like shape common among mushrooms explains the rest of the nickname.

Jack-o'-lantern at Night

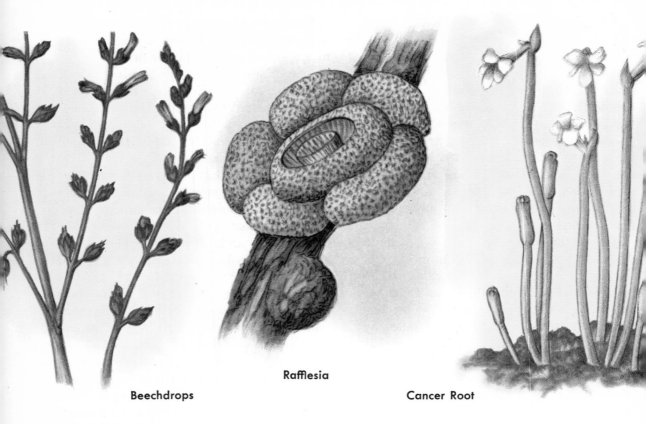

Beechdrops

Rafflesia

Cancer Root

Compared with the thousands of kinds of fungi, the other plants that are not green make up a very small part of the plant kingdom. All those pictured here belong much higher in the plant kingdom than the fungi. They are all flowering plants. But they have no green leaves to serve as food factories. The only green leaves in these pictures are those of the clover on which the dodder is growing.

Some dependent plants, it has been pointed out, take food from living plants or animals by growing on them or inside them. Such plants are called parasites. The rusts and mildews and a few molds are parasites. Shelf fungi that grow on living trees, many of the cup fungi, and a number of other mushrooms are parasites, too. There are also parasites among the flowering plants that have no chlorophyll.

Cancer root is one of the flowering-plant parasites. As you would guess from its name, it grows on the roots of other plants.

Suppose a seed of cancer root falls on the ground and begins to grow. The seed has enough food in it to keep the little plant growing for a time. But unless it finds a plant it can grow on before it uses up all its food, the little plant dies.

Beechdrops, a close relative of cancer root, grows on the roots of beech trees. As soon as a root of a beechdrops seedling reaches the root of a beech tree, it begins using food the tree has made for itself.

The biggest flowers in the whole plant kingdom are produced by a plant that cannot make its own food. The plant is a rafflesia, a member of a family of parasites that grow only in tropical regions. One blossom may be a yard across. But it is fleshy and not at all pretty. It has, moreover, an unpleasant smell. Rafflesias have no stems or leaves. The only part of them besides their flowers is inside the host plant.

Dodder twines around other plants. It, too, is a parasite. It sends suckers into the stem of the plant it is growing on. This vine does not have either roots or leaves. It must get water as well as food from the plant it twines around. Another name for dodder is love vine. Still others are devil's sewing thread and strangleweed.

There are more than a hundred different kinds of dodder, but they are all much alike. Some kinds must have one special kind of green plant as a host. One kind, for instance, will grow only on clover. But many kinds will grow on almost any kind of green plant within reach. Dodder is a close relative of the morning glory.

Once in a while an Indian pipe plant grows on the roots of another plant. But as a rule it is found growing in piles of dead leaves and branches in thick woods. There it has a mass of fungus threads around its roots. The fungus gets food from the dead wood and leaves, and the Indian pipe in turn gets food from the fungus.

Indian pipe is sometimes called a ghost flower because it is so white. Some Indian pipe plants, however, are not so ghostly as others. Some of them are pale pink.

Orchids are among our most beautiful flowering plants. But orchids may be almost colorless. Coral root and brunetta, both orchids, get their food like most Indian pipe.

Dodder on Clover

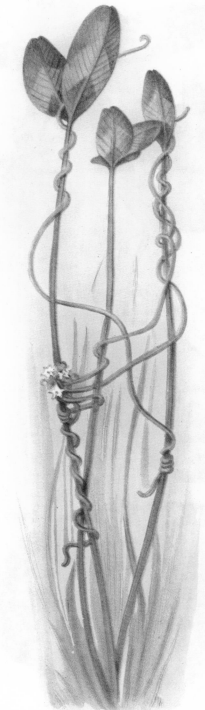

al Root   Indian Pipe   Brunetta

Vegetables

All vegetables are parts of plants—of green plants. They are storehouses in which the plants store up food they make and do not have to use up immediately. Different plants make different parts of themselves into storehouses. A vegetable may be any of several parts of a plant.

Roots are common storehouses. Carrots, turnips, beets, and sweet potatoes are all root vegetables. So are radishes, parsnips, and yams. Many of the root vegetables keep well. Before the days of swift transportation from one part of the earth to another, these vegetables stored away in vegetable cellars or other cool storerooms were almost the only fresh foods the people of northern lands had in winter.

The white, or Irish, potato is not a root, although it looks much like a sweet potato. It is, instead, an underground stem. Such an underground stem is called a tuber. The story is told that when potatoes were first raised in Germany the people did not know what part of the plant to eat. They first ate the green seedballs, which they found unpleasant. They were about to give up raising the potato when they learned that they were supposed to eat the tubers instead.

We eat the stems of asparagus and celery, too, but their stems are not tubers. They grow aboveground. Stalks of asparagus are the main stems of young plants. At the top are the beginnings, or buds, of leaves and branches. Stalks of celery are the stems of

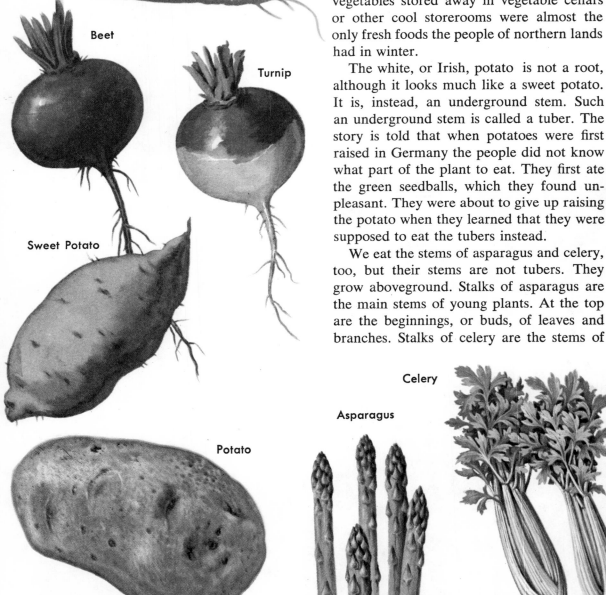

Carrot

Beet

Turnip

Sweet Potato

Potato

Asparagus

Celery

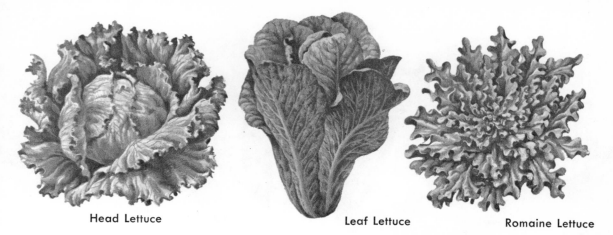

Head Lettuce   Leaf Lettuce   Romaine Lettuce

leaves. They have leaflets at the top. A bunch of celery is really a bundle of leaves. The fibers that make some celery and asparagus stringy are the water-carrying tubes.

When we eat lettuce or parsley we are eating the leaves of a plant. As you can see

Parsley

Onion

Leek

from the pictures, the leaves of lettuce may be curly or smooth. They may be quite free from one another or crowded into a head. Spinach, kale, endive, and cabbage are other leafy vegetables. The leaves of cabbage form a head like that of head lettuce. Brussels sprouts are tiny bundles of leaves. They are like cabbages except that they are much smaller. Some root vegetables have leaves as well as roots that are good to eat. Many people prefer the leaves of beets and turnips to the roots.

The part of the onion plant we eat is a bulb. A bulb is made chiefly of thick leaves that overlap one another. These leaves are

colorless because they are underground, away from the sunlight. A leek is a bulb, too. It is like a young onion.

A head of cauliflower is a bunch of flowers which have not yet opened out. We eat both the stems and the flowers of broccoli. The artichoke, which many people think ranks above all other vegetables for flavor, is a flower bud.

Artichoke

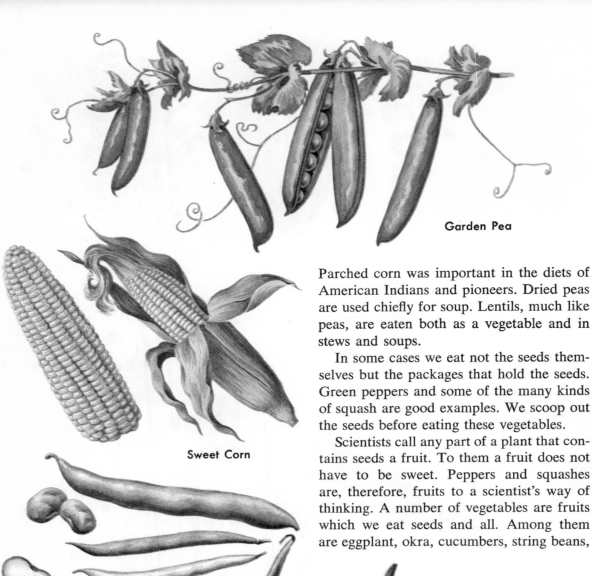

Garden Pea

Sweet Corn

Beans

Parched corn was important in the diets of American Indians and pioneers. Dried peas are used chiefly for soup. Lentils, much like peas, are eaten both as a vegetable and in stews and soups.

In some cases we eat not the seeds themselves but the packages that hold the seeds. Green peppers and some of the many kinds of squash are good examples. We scoop out the seeds before eating these vegetables.

Scientists call any part of a plant that contains seeds a fruit. To them a fruit does not have to be sweet. Peppers and squashes are, therefore, fruits to a scientist's way of thinking. A number of vegetables are fruits which we eat seeds and all. Among them are eggplant, okra, cucumbers, string beans,

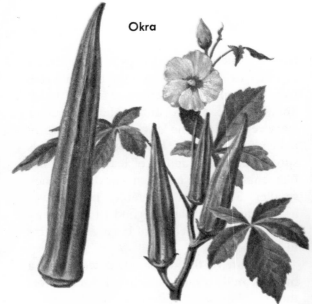

Okra

Many plants, as you already know, store a great deal of food in their seeds. Corn, peas, and beans are seeds we eat as vegetables. They are good canned or frozen as well as fresh from the garden. Seed vegetables have a big advantage over most other kinds—they can be dried and stored and still be good to eat long after they are picked. When dried they do not have to be kept cold. Dried beans of various kinds are staple foods in many parts of the world.

some of the squashes, and tomatoes. Tomatoes were raised in flower gardens long before anyone thought of eating them. They were called "love apples" and were believed to be poisonous. Now tomatoes have become one of the most popular vegetables.

One of the foods stored in many vegetables is starch. Another is sugar. This is not surprising, since sugar and starch are the foods which green plants make from water and carbon dioxide. The white potato is a storehouse filled mostly with starch. Some vegetables have enough sugar in them to taste sweet. Sweet corn is one. Sweet potatoes are another. Beets, peas, yams, carrots, and parsnips are still others even though "sweet" is not in their names.

Some vegetables have rather large amounts of protein. They can be used as substitutes for meat. Peas and beans are among the vegetables high in protein.

Perhaps more important than the starch, sugar, and protein stored in vegetables are the vitamins and minerals stored in them. Leafy green vegetables are one of our very best sources of iron and calcium, two minerals our bodies have to have. Green vegetables and tomatoes are excellent sources

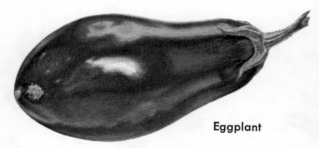

Eggplant

of vitamin C. Yellow vegetables such as carrots, corn, sweet potatoes, yams, and yellow squash furnish us with vitamin A. It is almost impossible to have a good diet without vegetables. A rule many meal planners follow is: Serve at least two different vegetables besides potato every day. One should be raw and one green or yellow.

Squashes

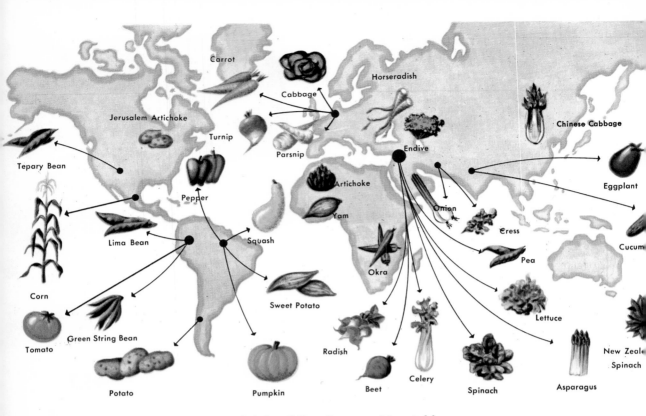

Origin of Our Common Vegetables

As the map shows, the vegetables now raised in the gardens of the United States came in the beginning from many different parts of the world. Very few of them are natives of North America. Our vegetable markets would look strange indeed if they had only vegetables that are natives of this continent. Of these, two—the Jerusalem artichoke and the tepary bean—you may never have heard of. But they would certainly be familiar to us all if vegetables had not been introduced from other lands. Of course, corn is well known.

You may wonder whether others of our wild plants could have been developed into vegetables to be raised in our gardens. Out in the country in the spring many people gather the leaves of such plants as dandelion and lamb's-quarters for greens. One of these —the dandelion—has in recent years been developed as a vegetable for marketing. We could doubtless raise other such leafy plants instead of lettuce and endive and spinach. But the list of wild plants that we

might have cultivated as vegetables is, so far as we know, very short. It is lucky indeed that vegetables that are not natives do well in our gardens.

A vegetable's name may give the wrong idea of its history. The so-called Irish potato is not a native of Ireland. The Jerusalem artichoke has no connection with Jerusalem. But, as an exception, New Zealand spinach is a native of New Zealand.

As the map shows, South America furnished some of our best-liked vegetables. But more than half of the kinds of vegetables we raise in our gardens were brought from the Old World. Many of them came from the lands near the eastern end of the Mediterranean Sea. These lands are sometimes spoken of as the cradle of civilization. Probably plants have been raised for food there longer than in any other part of the world.

The map does not show the origin of broccoli, cauliflower, Brussels sprouts, kale, collards, or kohlrabi. The reason it doesn't is that these vegetables are all descendants of the wild cabbage of Europe. They do not look much like their wild cabbage ancestor now. But the big heads of cabbage so common today do not look much like their wild ancestor, either. Would you guess from the picture of wild cabbage that any of the vegetables pictured with it were even relatives? Gardeners down through the centuries have been much interested in getting better vegetables from those they had.

The story of the Burbank potato illustrates one way in which improvement has been brought about.

Many years ago Luther Burbank, who became famous as a creator of new kinds of plants, saw a seedball growing on one of the potato plants in his garden. Usually potatoes are not raised from seed. Instead, a potato is cut into pieces with at least one bud, or eye, on each piece, and the pieces are planted. Some kinds of potatoes, in fact, seldom produce seeds. Burbank decided to watch over the seedball he had found and to plant the seeds when they were ripe. He was already much interested in ways of getting better plants. Perhaps by experimenting with potato seeds he would be able to get a potato better than any of the potatoes to be had at that time.

When he opened the seedball, Burbank found 23 seeds. In the spring he planted them in his garden. They grew. When the time came for harvesting the crop, he looked over the potatoes from each plant to see what they were like. Those from no two plants, he found, were identical. The potatoes from some were small and curiously shaped. Those from others had deep-set

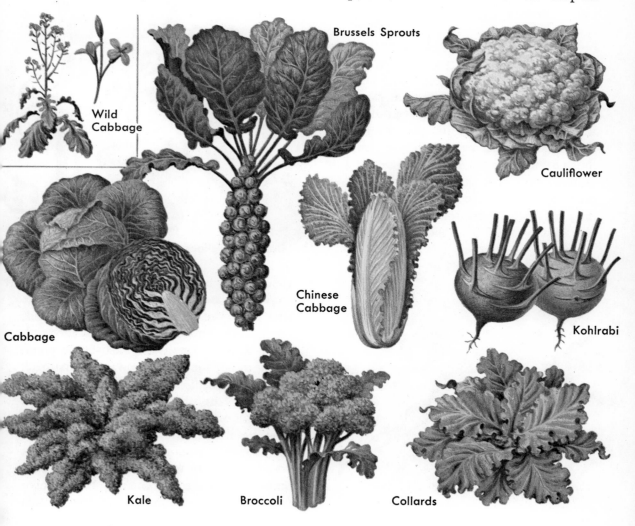

Wild Cabbage

Brussels Sprouts

Cauliflower

Cabbage

Chinese Cabbage

Kohlrabi

Kale

Broccoli

Collards

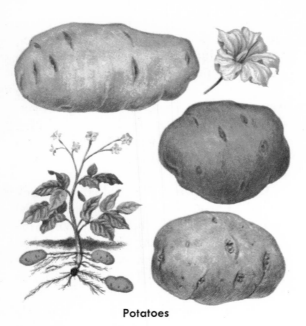

Potatoes

smooth potatoes. Soon he had enough of this new kind of potato to sell. Thus the Burbank potato was developed.

Burbank called his experiment with the potato his most important experiment because it was his first one. If this one had failed, he might have turned in discouragement to some other kind of work.

Careful selection of the plants from which new plants are to be raised is one way in which our vegetables have been improved and good varieties developed. From the story of the lima bean we see another way in which improvement may come about.

One day in the summer of 1850 a man who was walking along a country road in Virginia saw a dwarf lima bean plant by the roadside. He reported his find. At that

Peppers

eyes. Those from still others had rough skins. Clearly these potatoes were no improvement over the ones he had been raising. But some of the potatoes were good. Two plants produced large, smooth potatoes different from any then on the market.

Burbank examined these potatoes carefully. The potatoes from one of the two plants, he decided, were slightly better than those from the other. He saved the potatoes and planted them in the spring. They all produced big smooth potatoes. He selected the very best of these for raising new plants the next year. They, too, produced big

Radishes

time raising lima beans was a great deal of trouble because the plants were long vines and poles had to be stood up in the fields for them to climb on. This plant by the roadside was not a vine but a bushy little plant. So far as anyone knows, it was the first bush lima bean. Seeds of this plant were planted, and the plants that grew from them were dwarfs, too. A new kind of lima bean could now be raised. It soon became popular.

Close to the spot where the dwarf lima was found there was a whole field of pole limas. This dwarf lima must have grown from the seed of a pole lima. But it was very different from the parent plant. When a new kind of plant or animal thus suddenly appears that is changed in ways it can pass on to its descendants, it is called a *mutant*. The word "mutant" comes from a Latin word that means "to change." It is a good name for a plant or animal that differs noticeably from its ancestors.

Many mutants appear that are far worse than the parent plants they came from. But watching for desirable mutants and taking care of them when they do occur is another way in which our vegetables have been improved. All the many vegetables that have been developed from cabbage are thought to be mutants. The changes that gave us cauliflower were especially big ones.

Still another way of improving our vegetables has been to cross different varieties. A plant produced by crossing two different kinds of plants is called a hybrid. You have already read about hybrid animals. The story of exactly how plant hybrids are produced must wait for the discussion of flowers and the part they play in reproduction.

Just a glance at a garden catalogue gives some idea of the great number of varieties there are of our common garden vegetables. The pictures on the opposite page show a few of the many different varieties of potatoes, radishes, and peppers that we raise.

The picture of potatoes brings out the fact that varieties differ in color of skin.

The picture cannot show that different varieties are suited for growing in different kinds of soil and climate and for being cooked in different ways.

Not all the peppers shown are eaten as vegetables. Some are used chiefly to season other foods. They are too peppery to be eaten in large amounts.

As you see, radishes may be long or round, red, white, red and white, or almost black. Of course, you cannot see from the picture that some are much more spicy than others. Although radishes are usually eaten raw in the United States, they are often cooked in other countries. In the Far East radishes weighing several pounds are grown. These are cooked before they are eaten.

A way in which we have produced better vegetables, but not new varieties, is by fertilizing the soil in which they grow. Scientists have found that tomatoes, let us say, grown in one field may be richer in vitamins than those grown in another.

Some of the recent improvements in vegetables have been brought about through the use of growth regulators. Growth regulators are chemicals. Seedless tomatoes are produced by the use of a growth regulator. A seedless tomato is not altogether seedless, but it has fewer seeds than other tomatoes. Experimentation with growth regulators is being carried on with many different kinds of vegetables.

Seedless Tomato

Concord Grape

Fruits

In a fruit store of today there are sure to be fruits of many kinds. They come to the markets of the United States from all over the world. The demand for fruit is so great that it is brought to us by the boatload from other lands. Special machines have been invented for unloading bananas and other easily damaged fruits from fruit boats. Out of our own orchards and fruit farms fruit is carried to our towns and cities by train, truck, and plane.

A good diet calls for some fruit every day. But we would eat great quantities of fruit even if it were not an important part of a good diet. No other kind of food looks more attractive or, so many people think, tastes better.

The chief food stored in most fruits is sugar. Sugar is excellent energy-giving food. It is much better for us to get it in fruit, however, than in the form of granulated sugar, for in fruit we get vitamins along with the sugar, and some minerals, too. The citrus fruits, for example, are one of the best sources of vitamin C and the mineral calcium, while prunes are a good source of vitamin A and of iron and copper.

One vegetable, as you know, may be one part of a plant, another vegetable another. Fruits, on the other hand, are always the

310

same part of the plant. They are the packages in which the plants bear their seeds.

Although all fruits are packages of seeds unless they are seedless varieties developed by growers, fruits are built on a number of different plans. Some fruits have only a single seed. Some have several seeds. Some have a great many.

Each type of fruit has a name. The grape is an example of one type. In it several seeds are surrounded by a soft pulp. This pulp, in turn, is surrounded by a skin. The gooseberry, cranberry, blueberry, and currant are built on this same plan. No one commonly calls a grape a berry, but "berry" is the name scientists give to this kind of seed package. Oranges, queerly enough, are berries, too. So

Apple

are all the other citrus fruits. These fruits are different from other berries in that the pulpy part is divided up into sections.

The apple is a pome. The seeds are in a core in the center of the fruit. There are thousands of varieties of apples.

Citrus Fruits

Grapefruit

Orange

Lime

Tangerine

Lemon

Pears and quinces are pomes, just as apples are. They have their seeds in a core in the center of the fruit. There are many more varieties of pears than there are of quinces. Quinces are used mostly for making jellies and preserves. The pomegranate is the only fruit with "pome" in its name. Strangely enough, the pomegranate is not a pome. It is a berry instead.

Cherries and plums are one-seeded fruits. The seeds, moreover, have a very hard covering. One-seeded fruits of this kind are called drupes. Another name for them is stone fruits. Peaches are drupes, too.

Pears

Date Palm

There are cherries and peaches and plums of many different varieties just as there are many varieties of apples and pears.

Certain kinds of plums are often dried. They are called prunes.

You might expect the date, with its single seed, to be a drupe. Instead, it is a berry—one of the very few with just one seed.

Dates are the fruits of palm trees, the date palms. They have been an important food for the people to the south and east of the

Mediterranean Sea since before the dawn of history. Dates can be dried and kept for a long time.

An old saying is that date palms must have their feet in water and their heads in the sun. They thrive in warm, sunny desert regions where enough water can be furnished to the soil. Many, for example, are raised on irrigated lands along the Tigris and Euphrates and beside the Nile. Date palms are common in oases of the Arabian deserts and the Sahara. The raising of dates spread to our Southwest less than a hundred years ago. As you see, dates grow in big clusters.

Some fruits are called pepos. A pepo is a large fruit with a thick rind. Inside it there are many seeds, often hundreds. Pumpkins, squashes, and melons are pepos. Pumpkins and squashes are not sweet enough to be called fruits as the word "fruits" is commonly used, but melons are. The picture shows several kinds of melons that are good

Cherry

Quince

Plums

fruits for breakfast or for dessert. Another name for these melons is muskmelons. The "musk" in the name comes from the fruits' strong, pleasant odor. Of course, the banana melon owes its name to its shape and color. The watermelon is another popular fruit in the pepo group.

Banana Melon

Melons

Casaba

Persian Melon

Honeydew

Cantaloupe

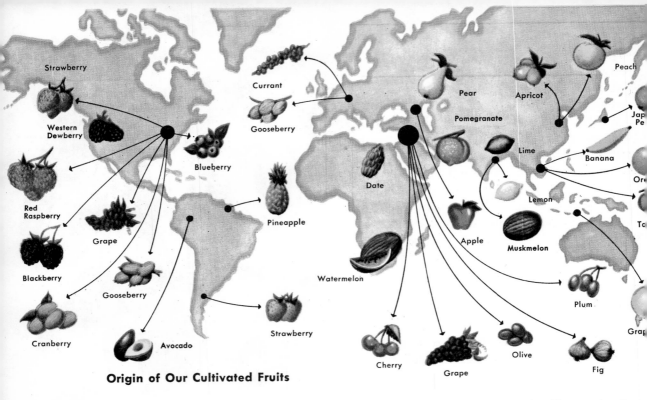

Strawberry

Western Dewberry

Currant

Gooseberry

Blueberry

Red Raspberry

Grape

Blackberry

Gooseberry

Cranberry

Avocado

Pineapple

Strawberry

Date

Watermelon

Pear

Pomegranate

Apricot

Peach

Lime

Lemon

Apple

Muskmelon

Banana

Jap Pe

Or

Ta

Plum

Gra

Cherry

Grape

Olive

Fig

Origin of Our Cultivated Fruits

A pineapple is made up of many fruits crowded so closely together that they seem to be one. It is a so-called multiple fruit. No seeds develop ordinarily in a pineapple. This seedless fruit can be raised only in warm, moist lands. It is one of the most important crops of Hawaii.

The fig, although it looks like a simple fruit with many seeds, is a multiple fruit, too. Many little fruits grow together to form a single fig. Figs, like dates, have been an important food in Mediterranean lands for thousands of years. Like dates, figs can be dried and kept for a long time.

Pineapple

Of the "berries" pictured below, the currant, gooseberry, and cranberry are true berries. The raspberry and the blackberry are made of many tiny drupes joined together. Each little round section has a single seed in it, just as does a cherry or a plum.

The strawberry is not a true berry, either. Its seeds are on the outside. The pulpy part of a strawberry is a cushion on which the seeds rest.

If we had to limit our fruits to those that are natives of North America, we would not fare too badly. Several of our berries and so-called berries are American. But most of the fruits we now raise in our orchards are natives of other parts of the world. The peach and apricot, as the map shows, came from China, the currant from Europe, and the watermelon from Africa. The grapefruit is a native of the East Indies, the banana and orange of southeast Asia, and the pineapple and avocado of South America. Australia is the only continent—except of course Antarctica—which has sent no fruits into our orchards and gardens.

A few fruits are shown by the map to be natives of two different regions. The grape

Fig

is one. Wild grapes grow in both the Old World and the New. The Concord grape came from one of our wild American grapes. Many of the other grapes we raise came from the wild grapes of Europe and the Near East.

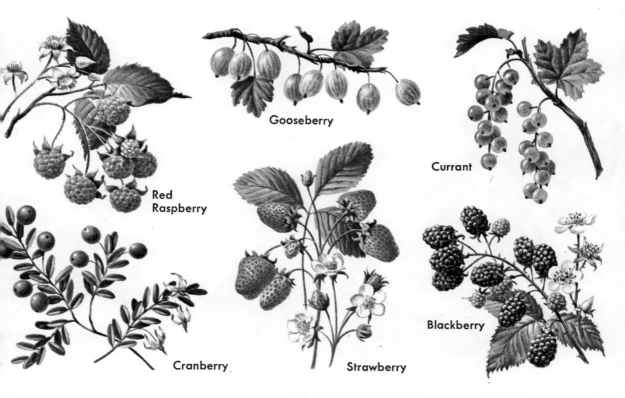

Gooseberry

Currant

Red Raspberry

Cranberry

Strawberry

Blackberry

Akee

Cherimoya

Barbados
Cherry

Soursop

Sugar A
or Swee

Mangosteen

Sapodilla

Surinam Cherry

Mango

Sapote

The banana is a tropical fruit known around the world. Great quantities are shipped to other lands from the regions where they grow. In contrast, few of the tropical fruits pictured here reach northern markets. You are not likely to know many of them.

The mango, an ancient fruit of India now raised in many tropical regions, is often called the most delicious of all fruits. The mangosteen of the East Indies—not like a mango in spite of its name—is also highly praised. It seems to melt in your mouth.

People of Hawaii and visitors to the islands know the papaya well. This fruit of tropical America thrives there as well as in warm regions of Asia, Africa, and Australia.

The cherimoya, sugar apple, and soursop are closely related New World fruits. They are large, with custard-like flesh. The akee of Africa has white pulp around shiny black seeds. Both the pulp and the seeds are said to be poisonous until the fruit is ripe enough to split open.

Barbados and Surinam cherries are natives of tropical America. So are the sapodilla and the sapote, or marmalade plum. The sapodilla comes from the tree that furnishes the chicle used in chewing gum.

Fruit gathered from wild plants made up much of the food of our early ancestors. But the fruit they ate was very different from the fruit for sale in our markets today.

We have improved our fruits, just as we have improved our vegetables, partly by raising them under better conditions than they had in the wild. We have raised new plants only from the best parent plants. And we have done other things, too.

Papaya

Loganberry

Occasionally mutants—or sports, as they are often called—appear among fruits just as they do among vegetables. Fruitgrowers have improved our fruits greatly by watching for sports and propagating them when they turn out to be desirable. They have produced many new varieties in this way.

The loganberry is thought to be a mutant. In 1881 Judge Logan of Santa Cruz, California, found growing among his blackberries a new kind of berry that was later named for him. The loganberry is shaped like a blackberry but it is red like a red raspberry. It grew, scientists believe, from a blackberry seed. The nectarine, a smooth-skinned fruit, is a mutant of the fuzzy peach.

Sometimes only one branch of a plant will bear fruit of a new and different kind. The navel orange, a freak because it is seedless, began in this way. Dozens of strains of the common varieties of apples have come about as branch sports.

Fruitgrowers have improved our fruits, too, by crossing different varieties. The boysenberry is a cross between the loganberry and the red raspberry. Many of today's varieties of fruits are hybrids.

The Golden Delicious apple is thought to be a chance hybrid—a hybrid that no one helped bring about. It may instead be a mutant. At any rate, a tree bearing this new apple was found growing in an orchard in West Virginia and was carefully protected. Thousands of Golden Delicious apple trees have been raised from this first tree.

Some hybrid fruits are crosses between two different kinds of fruit. The plumcot was produced by the "plant wizard" Luther Burbank. It is a cross between the plum and the apricot. The tangelo is a cross between

Apples

Delicious

Greening

McIntosh

Crab Apple

Jonathan

Golden Delicious

Rome Beauty

Navel Orange

Nectarine

the tangerine and the grapefruit. There have been many crosses of citrus fruits.

Attempts to cross different kinds of fruits are unsuccessful unless the fruits are fairly close relatives. The apple and the orange, for instance, cannot be crossed.

A new hybrid fruit is really as much of an invention as a new kind of machine. Our government, therefore, grants patents on distinctive hybrid fruits. It also grants patents on new varieties developed from sports. Nursery catalogues often call attention to patented plants they sell.

On the whole, fruits spoil rather easily. Refrigerator cars and trailers and cold-storage houses help fruitgrowers get their fruit to market in good shape. Fruitgrowers

have helped solve the problem of spoilage with some fruits by shipping them while they are still green. The bananas that reach our country are almost always green. They travel to us in refrigerated banana ships. From port cities they are carried by train and truck to centers of distribution all over the country. There they are ripened in special rooms, then delivered to fruit and grocery stores. Lemons and pineapples are other fruits that are harvested and shipped before they are ripe.

Another way of keeping fruit from spoiling before it reaches us is to coat it with an invisible protective chemical. Scientists keep searching for ways to furnish us with better fruits in better condition.

Banana

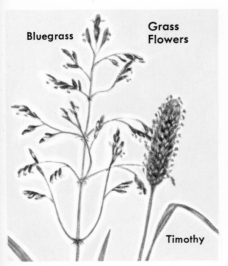

Bluegrass

Grass Flowers

Timothy

American Elm Flowers

Sugar Maple Flowers

Flowers

Learning to call by name all the kinds of flowers in the world would mean learning to know some 250,000 kinds, for there are that many different species of plants that bloom. Not all flowers, of course, are showy. It takes careful looking to find the flowers on some plants that are in bloom. Probably, moreover, most people see certain flowers without recognizing them as flowers. They may not know, for instance, when they find the walks on a spring morning littered with reddish catkins from cottonwood trees, that these catkins are clusters of tiny flowers.

A number of trees besides the cottonwood have flowers so simple that they are not easily recognized as flowers. The maple and

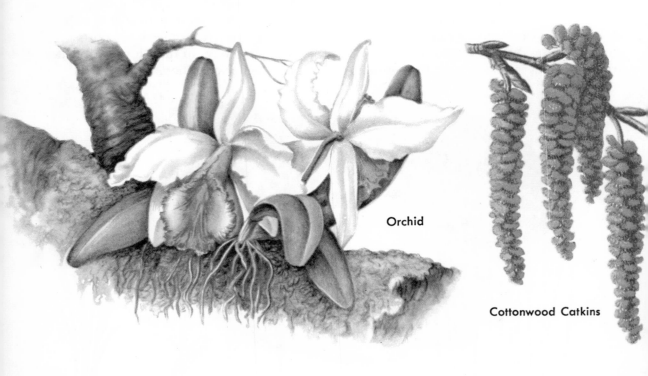

Orchid

Cottonwood Catkins

elm are among them. Grass flowers, as you see, are simple, too. In contrast, the orchid pictured is very showy.

The thousands of flowering plants are divided up into about 300 families. Flowers are the identification tags that tell to what family a flowering plant belongs.

Five different families are represented by the flowers on page 320. The cottonwood is in the willow family. The maple, grasses, elm, and orchid belong to the maple, grass, elm, and orchid families named from them.

All the plants pictured on this page are members of the grass family. This family is a very large one. About 10,000 different plants belong to it. It is, moreover, the most important to man of all the families of flowering plants, for it includes our most important cereal grains. Some of these grains have been cultivated since prehistoric times —Egyptian paintings 5,000 years old show farmers harvesting wheat!

The giants of the grass family are found among the bamboos. A stalk of corn may be

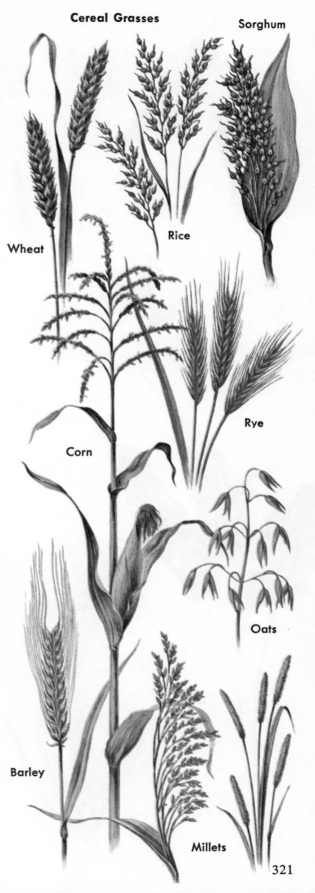

Cereal Grasses

Sorghum

Rice

Wheat

Corn

Rye

Oats

Barley

Millets

Bamboo

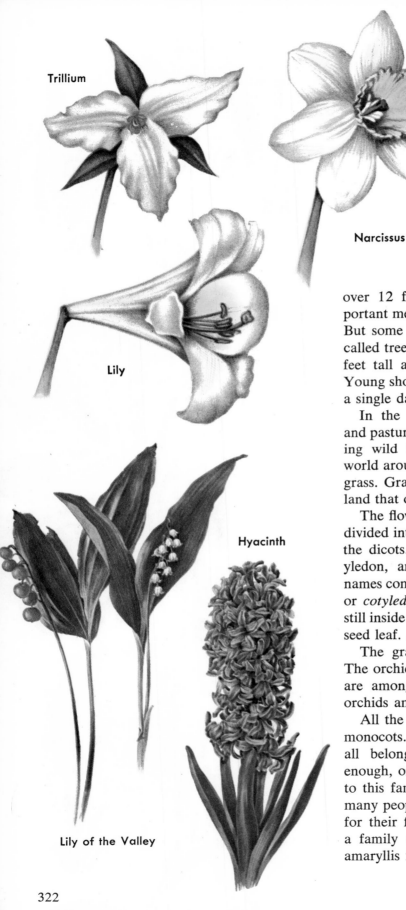

Trillium

Narcissus

Tulip

Lily

Hyacinth

Lily of the Valley

over 12 feet tall. Sugarcane, another important member of the family, is even taller. But some bamboos are large enough to be called trees. A full-grown plant may be 100 feet tall and have a stem a yard around. Young shoots may grow more than a foot in a single day!

In the grass family, too, are the lawn and pasture grasses as well as all those growing wild in meadows and grasslands the world around. Many food chains begin with grass. Grasses play much the same role on land that diatoms do in the sea.

The flowering plants, you remember, are divided into two groups—the monocots and the dicots. Monocot is short for monocotyledon, and dicot for dicotyledon. These names come from the number of seed leaves, or *cotyledons,* a baby plant has while it is still inside the seed. A monocot has only one seed leaf. A dicot has two.

The grass family is a monocot family. The orchid family is another. Grass flowers are among the simplest monocot flowers, orchids among the most complicated.

All the flowers pictured on this page are monocots. Except for the narcissus, they all belong to the lily family. Strangely enough, onion, leek, and garlic also belong to this family. So does asparagus. But not many people raise any of these four "lilies" for their flowers. The narcissus belongs to a family closely related to the lilies—the amaryllis family.

Daisy

Dandelion

Zinnia

Dahlia

These flowers are dicots. They all belong to the largest of plant families—the composites. The family is well named, for every so-called flower is composed of many tiny flowers, or flowerets. It is a whole bouquet.

The flowers of composites, however, are not all built on the same plan. The daisy is made of two different kinds of tiny flowers. Those around the edge are quite different from those in the center. The dandelion, on the other hand, is made up of flowerets all of the same kind. The zinnia and the dahlia follow the daisy pattern. Most of them have so many flowerets like those around the edge of the daisy that it is not easy to see those in the center. But one of the dahlias shows clearly that it is built like a daisy.

The willow, maple, and elm families also belong to the dicot group. Among other well-known dicot families are the pea family and the rose family. The pea family includes peas, peanuts, sweet peas, beans, and clover. The rose family includes not only our roses but also most of our fruits. Apples, plums, apricots, peaches, pears, strawberries, and raspberries are all cousins of the rose.

The chart on pages 372-75 lists 22 families of flowering plants and names several plants in each. It may hold some surprises.

323

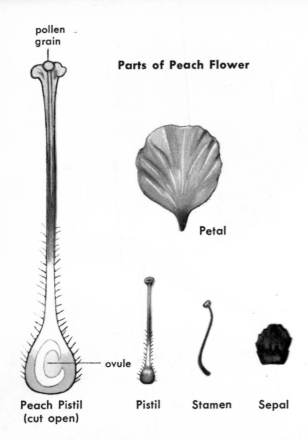

pollen
grain

Parts of Peach Flower

Petal

ovule

Peach Pistil   Pistil   Stamen   Sepal
(cut open)

The role of all flowers, whether they are simple or showy, is to produce seeds. The story of how a peach seed is formed will serve as an example of how seeds are produced by flowers.

A peach blossom has four sets of parts. In the center of the blossom there is a *pistil*. It looks like a tiny green vase with a long narrow neck.

Surrounding the pistil are many pinkish stems with sacs full of yellow "dust" at the top. They are *stamens*. The yellow dust in the sacs is *pollen*.

Outside the stamens are five bright-pink *petals*. The petals, of course, are the conspicuous part of a peach blossom. It is the petals that make a blossoming peach tree into a cloud of pink.

A ring of five reddish-green sepals surrounds the petals. They form a tiny cup for the rest of the flower.

Down inside the base of the vase-shaped pistil there are two small greenish-white bodies shaped like eggs. They are *ovules*. Ovules are the beginnings of seeds.

Ovules contain female cells, or eggs. Pollen grains contain male cells, or sperm. Male cells from pollen grains must reach the female cells in the ovules before the ovules can grow into seeds. The male cells and the female cells must join—the eggs must, in other words, be fertilized.

Fertilization in the case of a peach blossom comes about in this way: As soon as a peach blossom opens, bees come to it to get nectar. As a bee gets nectar, it brushes against the stamens. Some of the pollen from the pollen sacs sticks to its fuzzy body. When the bee rubs against the stamens it rubs against the pistil, too.

At the same time that the bee is getting pollen on its body it is rubbing pollen from the last peach blossom it visited off on the top of the pistil. The top of the pistil—the *stigma*—is sticky. It holds fast any pollen grains that reach it.

The picture far to the left tells the next step in the story. It shows a section down through the pistil of a peach blossom as it would look if it were greatly magnified. One of the ovules in the base of the pistil can be seen. A grain of pollen is resting on the top

Life History of Peach

of the pistil. Down from it a tube is growing. The tube grows till it reaches an ovule. Then all the living material from the tiny pollen grain enters the ovule. A male cell reaches and joins the female cell. The ovule is now ready to grow into a seed.

As soon as the egg in one ovule is fertilized, the other ovule in the pistil dries up. It does not develop into a seed. A single peach blossom produces only one seed.

After fertilization has taken place, the petals, stamens, and sepals wither and fall off. So do the neck and top of the pistil. Only the base of the pistil is left, with the tiny young seed inside.

The seed grows. While it is becoming a large peach seed, the wall of the part of the pistil that holds it is developing into the rest of the peach, the sweet, juicy part of the fruit that we eat.

When the peach seed is ripe, it is ready to be planted to grow into a new peach tree. The new tree will bloom, the blossoms will produce seeds, and the seeds will produce new peach trees. The circle of tree—blossom—seed is repeated over and over again.

All complete flowers have the same four kinds of parts peach blossoms have: pistils, stamens, petals, and sepals. But many flowers lack one or more of these parts. A flower must have, however, either stamens or pistils. It cannot play any part in producing seeds if it has neither.

Of the flowers that have already been pictured, the trillium shows best the four parts of a complete flower: In the center there is one pistil. You can just see its top in the picture. Surrounding the pistil are six stamens. Around them there are three white petals, and on the outside of the petals three green sepals.

Having three petals and three sepals is common among the monocots. The petals and sepals of the dicots more often come in fives or in fours. A peach blossom has five sepals and five petals. The peach, you remember, belongs to the rose family, which is one of the families of dicots.

Bumblebee in Columbine

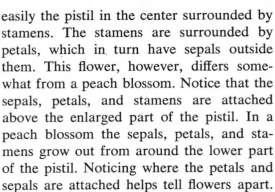

Mallow   Cosmos   Pollen   Petunia   Nasturti

Carnation   Rose

In some cases it is not easy to tell whether a flower has both petals and sepals. Petals and sepals may look very much alike. They do, for example, in a tulip. The only way of telling them apart is that the three that are sepals are outside the three petals.

Columbine is another flower with sepals and petals both brightly colored. But the petals can be told by their long spurs. The picture shows the spurs clearly.

In orchids the petals themselves differ in shape. And when the sepals as well as the petals are beautifully colored it is hard to tell which are petals and which sepals.

A flower does not have to be large to be complete. Even the tiny flowerets that make up a dandelion have sepals, petals, stamens, and a pistil. Five petals are joined together to make a yellow "strap." The sepals are white bristles. A pistil rises from the center of the flower. Joined in a cuff around it are five stamens.

This diagram shows a section down through a complete flower. You can see easily the pistil in the center surrounded by stamens. The stamens are surrounded by petals, which in turn have sepals outside them. This flower, however, differs somewhat from a peach blossom. Notice that the sepals, petals, and stamens are attached above the enlarged part of the pistil. In a peach blossom the sepals, petals, and stamens grow out from around the lower part of the pistil. Noticing where the petals and sepals are attached helps tell flowers apart.

In descriptions of flowers the words "calyx" and "corolla" are often used. All the sepals together form the *calyx*. The petals form the *corolla*. "Calyx" means "cup." "Corolla" means "crown."

The cottonwood catkins on page 320, you remember, are bunches of tiny flowers. Each flower is about as simple as a flower can be. It consists of many stamens fastened to a tiny cup-shaped disk. There are no sepals, no petals, and no pistils.

Stamens alone, however, cannot produce seeds. Cottonwood trees would never have seeds if they bore only flowers with stamens —*staminate flowers* they are called. As a matter of fact, the cottonwood trees that bear these staminate flowers never do produce seeds. Cottonwood seeds are produced on other cottonwood trees that bear catkins made up of only flowers with pistils—*pistillate flowers*. Each pistillate flower consists of a single pistil.

Of course, the staminate flowers are just as important as the pistillate flowers. Pollen from them must reach the ovules of the pistillate flowers if seeds are to form.

Scientists call the cottonwood tree a *dioecious* plant. "Dioecious" means "two households." The cottonwood gets this name because its pistillate flowers are on one tree

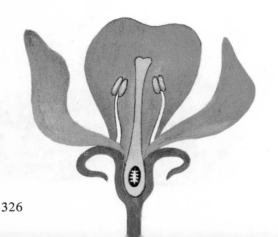

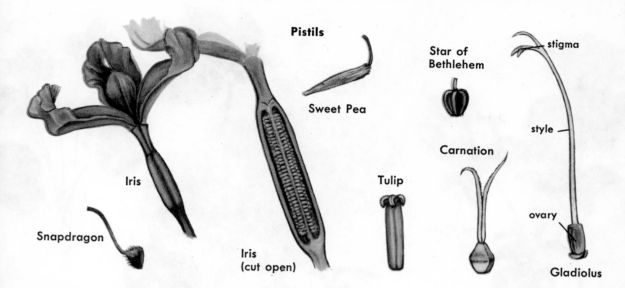

Pistils

Snapdragon

Iris

Iris (cut open)

Sweet Pea

Star of Bethlehem

Tulip

Carnation

Gladiolus

stigma

style

ovary

and its staminate flowers on another. The willow, a close relative of the cottonwood, is another two-household plant.

Some plants have two kinds of flowers—one with pistils and one with stamens—but bear both on the same plant. Corn is a good example. These plants are *monoecious*. The word means "one household."

Maple and elm flowers, which, you have seen, are not at all showy, are not as simple as willow and cottonwood flowers. But they are not complete flowers either. Both of them lack petals.

Even though flowers of all kinds have either stamens or pistils or both, the stamens of different flowers do not all look alike and neither do the pistils. The pictures on this page show some ways that stamens and pistils vary. An iris pistil, for example, has stigmas that spread out to look like petals. The stamens of anemones are squat, those of snapdragon long and curving. Even the pollen grains different flowers produce are different. The pictures of pollen grains show them greatly magnified.

You might expect that there would be no problem of fertilization for flowers that contain both stamens and pistils. But in many, many cases there is no fertilization unless pollen is brought from another flower, often from a flower on another plant of the same kind. Many flowers must, in other words, be *cross-pollinated*.

Wind blows pollen about easily. Many flowers are pollinated by the wind. But many flowers depend on insects, just as the peach tree does, to carry their pollen from blossom to blossom. Most plants without showy petals are wind-pollinated. Those with showy petals need the help, as a rule, of insects or other small animals. Red clover, for instance, depends on bumblebees. In the story of life on the earth, insects and flowering plants go hand in hand. Neither could have developed as they did without the help of the other.

Gay petals are signal flags—SOS calls to insects for help in carrying pollen from flower to flower. It is when the pollen sacs open up that the petals are freshest and brightest. The perfume of a flower helps call insects, too.

The bees, moths, and other insects that carry pollen do not know, of course, that they are helping the plants. To them the petals and perfume are simply dinner bells.

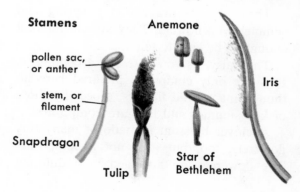

Stamens

Anemone

pollen sac, or anther

stem, or filament

Snapdragon

Tulip

Star of Bethlehem

Iris

Red Clover

Violet

Wild Rose

Daisy

These flowers are common spring and summer wild flowers. They are all different enough to be easy to tell apart.

The daisy, as you know, is a composite. It is the only composite pictured here although many wild flowers, especially those of late summer and fall, are composites.

A clover blossom is made of many tiny flowerets, too, but it is not a composite. The flowerets are arranged in a different way. All of them are alike, and each one is like a tiny sweet pea.

The petals of both the wild rose and the shooting star are pink, but the flowers are very different in shape. Notice how the petals of the shooting star bend backward.

The petals of both the bluebell and the Dutchman's-breeches are joined together. But they are joined in different ways. The yellow pollen sacs of the May apple are very conspicuous against its pure-white petals. And the color and petal arrangement of the violet tell what it is.

You probably know these wild flowers by sight. But you are almost sure to meet some wild flowers that you do not know. There are flower guides to use in identifying wild flowers. Most of them help by picturing many of the flowers. But it would take a very, very large book to picture all our wild flowers. You may very well have to identify a flower just by its description. If so, the

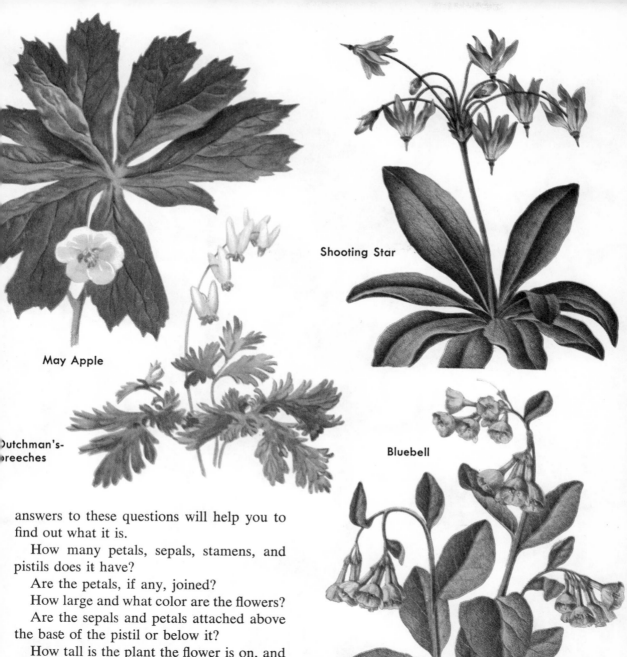

May Apple

Shooting Star

Dutchman's-breeches

Bluebell

answers to these questions will help you to find out what it is.

How many petals, sepals, stamens, and pistils does it have?

Are the petals, if any, joined?

How large and what color are the flowers?

Are the sepals and petals attached above the base of the pistil or below it?

How tall is the plant the flower is on, and where is it growing?

What time of year is it in bloom?

Many of our spring wild flowers are found in woodlands. They come into bloom before the trees are fully leafed out. Before there are leaves on the trees, sunshine can reach the floor of the woods. The spring woodland flowers take advantage of this sunshine. Some wild flowers are *perennials*. They live, that is, for several or many years. In bulbs or roots or underground stems they store up food which they use to come into bloom quickly. In the spring sunshine their leaves

make food which is stored for the next year's blooming.

Although many spring flowers are hardy perennials, as a rule nothing remains aboveground during the winter to show that the plant is living on. Instead of merely losing their leaves for the winter as elm trees and rosebushes do, the whole upper part of the plant withers and dies.

Wild Sunflower

Goldenrod

Butter-and-eggs

Cardinal Flower

Wild Aster

Black-eyed
Susan

Joe-pye W

The wild flowers on these two pages are
flowers of late summer and fall. They are
for the most part not woodland but roadside
flowers. Most of them are perennials. The
sunflower is an *annual* instead—it grows,
that is, from seed, blooms, and dies all in

one season. And the black-eyed Susan is a *biennial*. It lives for two years.

Some wild flowers have the word "weed" in their names. They are weeds in the sense that they can take care of themselves; they do not have to be planted and cultivated as our garden flowers do. But a better definition of the word "weed" is "a plant that grows where it is not wanted." Any plant can be a weed. Grass, for example, can be a real nuisance in a vegetable or flower garden. And violets and buttercups, although beautiful in the spring, do not help the appearance of a lawn later in the season.

The dandelion, everyone agrees, is a weed. But if it did not bother us so by getting into our lawns we would surely think of it as a lovely wild flower.

To the men who work to keep roadsides clear, many of the flowers pictured here are weeds. To most of the people who see them they are wild flowers.

Some of our wild flowers are in danger of disappearing. People have been too careless about picking them. If all the flowers are picked from a plant, it cannot make seeds to start new plants. To get its flowers, people often pull up a whole plant. Sometimes, too, they dig up plants to take home to their gardens. Many wild flowers die if they are transplanted.

We are killing off our wild flowers, moreover, by taking away their homes. We have cleared woodlands, plowed up prairies, and covered thousands of square miles with the concrete of superhighways. We are mowing or burning over our roadsides and our railroad embankments. We are keeping our fields clear of weeds. Our growing cities take over open country. Sooner or later many of our wild flowers are bound to disappear unless everyone does his share in protecting them.

Even now some of our best-liked wild flowers are very hard to find. The showy lady's-slipper is one of them. Anyone who finds a showy lady's-slipper should be careful not to pick it and should try to keep others from doing so.

Fortunately, some of our wild flowers have an amazing ability to live even under unfavorable conditions. After a good rain our Southwest deserts "come into bloom" so that they are worth going miles to see. The plants produce their flowers and seeds with great speed when conditions are good, then rest till such a time comes again.

Some wild flowers, and some cultivated flowers as well, have to be several years old before they bloom. The century plant, a native of Mexico, grows in our Southwest. It got its name because the time it lives before it blooms seemed to people like a hundred years. Actually a century plant may have flowers in 10 to 15 years. After the plant has bloomed it dies. In contrast, most of our perennials come into bloom year after year once they begin.

Day Lily

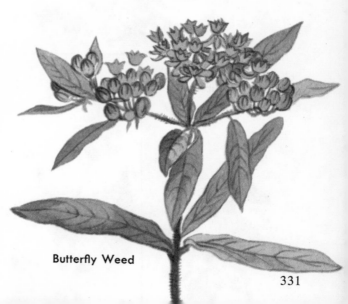

Butterfly Weed

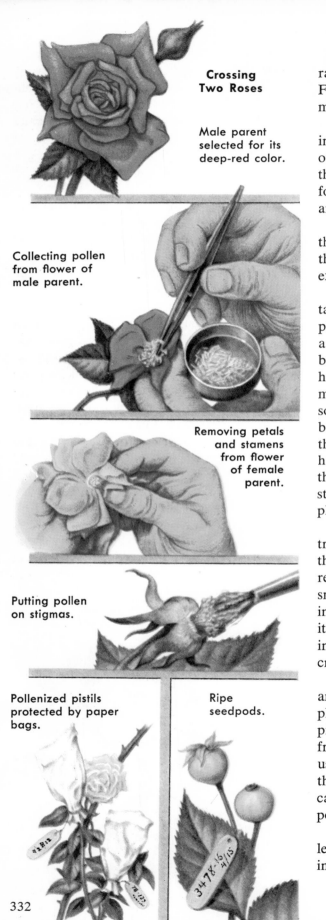

Crossing Two Roses

Male parent selected for its deep-red color.

Collecting pollen from flower of male parent.

Removing petals and stamens from flower of female parent.

Putting pollen on stigmas.

Pollenized pistils protected by paper bags.

Ripe seedpods.

Many plants—hundreds of kinds—are raised just for the beauty of their flowers. Flower catalogues list many varieties of most of them.

Plant breeders have gone about improving our flowers just as they have improved our fruits and vegetables. Carefully selecting the best plants for propagation, watching for sports and taking care of desirable ones, and producing hybrids are the chief ways.

The three roses pictured at the top of the next page are hybrids. Knowing about the parts of flowers helps us understand exactly how hybrids are produced.

Crossing two flowering plants means taking the pollen from the flower of one plant and putting it on the pistil or pistils of a flower of a different variety. Often a plant breeder has in mind some new characteristic he would like the new flower to have. He may have in mind some special color, or some special shape, or some certain number of petals. He may be thinking more of the plant itself and want an especially hardy one, or one that climbs well, or one that will thrive in poor soil, or one that can stand the attacks of certain insect pests or plant diseases.

The plant breeder may, let us say, be trying to get a very hardy climbing rose that has big bright-red flowers. He has a red rose of the color he wishes, but it is a small bush. He has a very vigorous climbing rose that stands cold weather well, but its flowers are pale pink. The two roses are in bloom at the same time. He decides to cross the two.

First he cuts away the petals and sepals and stamens of several of the roses of one plant. Let us suppose it is the plant with pink flowers. He takes some of the pollen from the red flowers of the other plant and, using a soft brush, puts it on the pistils of the pink flowers. Then he ties paper bags carefully over these pistils so that no other pollen can reach them.

Perhaps no seeds will develop. The pollen of the red rose may not be of any use in fertilizing the eggs in the ovules of the

Hybrid Roses

pink rose. If seeds do develop, some of the plants that grow from them may have the worst traits of their two parents. But perhaps one will have the characteristics the breeder is working for.

Obviously the plant breeder might cross the two plants the other way round. He might put the pollen of the pink rose on the pistils of the red one. The results might be either better or worse.

Every year new hybrid roses are listed in garden catalogues. Some of them are different enough from other roses to be given a patent by our government. The popular Peace rose is a patented hybrid rose.

Garden catalogues list hybrids of many flowers besides roses. Tulips, irises, peonies, marigolds, petunias, chrysanthemums, and zinnias are only a few of them.

Not all new varieties, however, are hybrids. Some of them are sports. Recently, for instance, a rosegrower found in a field of tea roses with big red flowers one rose that was growing twice as fast as any of the others. It kept on growing and turned out to be a climbing rose with flowers like those of the tea roses around it. Many plants were then raised from this one sport.

Organizations have been formed that rate the varieties of some kinds of flowers. They give each variety a grade. A certain kind of peony, let us suppose, is rated 9.8 on a scale of 10. Giving it this rating is the same as giving it a grade of 98 if the highest possible score is 100. A peony rated 9.8 is much better in at least some ways than one

rated 7.2. The peony pictured is one with a very high rating.

Daffodils, irises, and tulips are among the other flowers that are sometimes given a rating in flower catalogues. In choosing flowers for a garden, however, one should realize that the highest rated flower may not be the best one for his garden. It may take more care than he wishes to give it, it may not be as hardy as some he might choose, it may not bloom at the time he wishes, or its color may not fit in with the other flowers in his garden.

Walter Faxon Peony

Iris

Anyone interested in having a flower garden has dozens and dozens of flowers to choose from. Here are only a few.

Some of these flowers are hardy, just as many of our wild flowers are. They may die to the ground in the fall as the iris does. Or they may simply lose their leaves like the hydrangea. Others, like the nasturtium, live only through the summer.

Some, as you see, have their flowers arranged in spikes. Some bear them in heads. Some have single flowers.

Garden clubs and flower shows have done a great deal to interest people in producing lovelier flowers. Many cities take great pride in their gardens. One may celebrate tulip time each spring, another hold a lilac festival; still another may specialize in roses or azaleas. No one can have a pleasanter hobby than raising flowers.

Forget-me-not

Nasturtium

Stock

Snapdragon

Hydrangea

Candytuft

Phlox

Crocus

Sweet Pea

Canna

Larkspur

Tulip

Geranium

Wild Geranium

It goes without saying that the ancestors of all our cultivated flowers once grew wild. But even if we could see these wild ancestors the chances are we would not recognize them. Wild tulips like the one pictured below can still be found in western Asia. They do not look much like the gorgeous tulips we are used to seeing.

No garden flower has had a more exciting history than the tulip. Many of the tulips in our gardens today can trace their ancestry back to tulips brought from Turkey to Europe in the 16th century.

When tulips reached Holland they became very popular there. In fact, in the 1700's there was a tulip craze that came to be called "tulipomania." Enormous prices were paid for new varieties of tulips. A single bulb of a variety of tulip named Semper Augustus sold for what would be more than a thousand dollars in our money!

The craze ended, but tulip breeding is still important in Holland. New varieties are being developed in other countries, too. There are now hundreds of varieties.

The wild geranium pictured is one of our wild flowers. But the geranium we see most often came to us from South Africa.

In our flower gardens there are many other immigrants. The flowers that came from our own wild flowers rub shoulders not only with tulips and geraniums, but also with such foreigners as strawflowers from Australia, hollyhocks from Asia, snapdragons from Europe, nasturtiums from South America, and marigolds from Mexico.

Wild Tulip

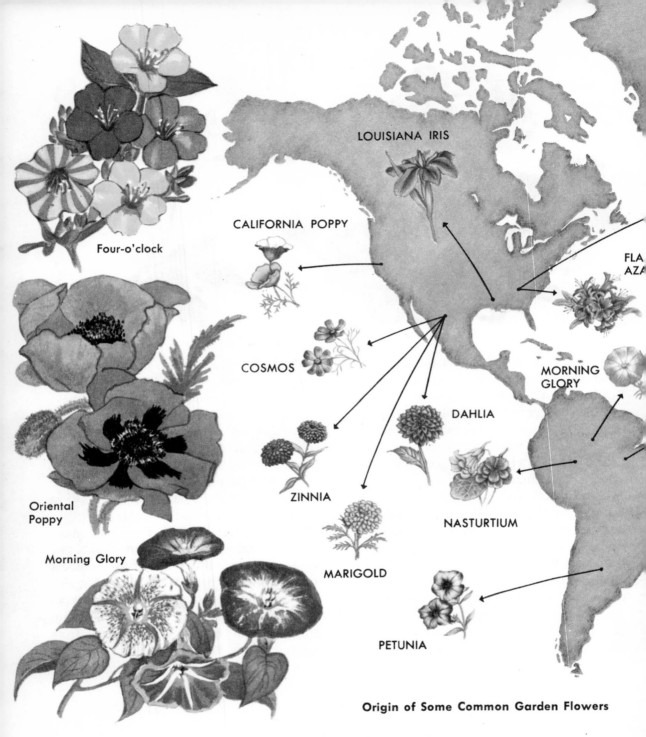

Four-o'clock

Oriental Poppy

Morning Glory

CALIFORNIA POPPY

LOUISIANA IRIS

FLA
AZA

COSMOS

DAHLIA

MORNING
GLORY

ZINNIA

NASTURTIUM

MARIGOLD

PETUNIA

Origin of Some Common Garden Flowers

A few wild flowers had to make a more roundabout journey to our gardens than one would guess. Some of our wild asters, for example, were carried to England. They came back to us as Michaelmas daisies.

This map tells us from what lands 30 of our common garden flowers came. Comparing it with the map on page 306 shows that

the petunia and the potato reached us from the same region of South America. It is not surprising that they did, for they are cousins. Both of them belong to a family especially common there—the nightshade family.

The morning glory and the sweet potato are both natives of another region in South America. They, too, are cousins; they belong

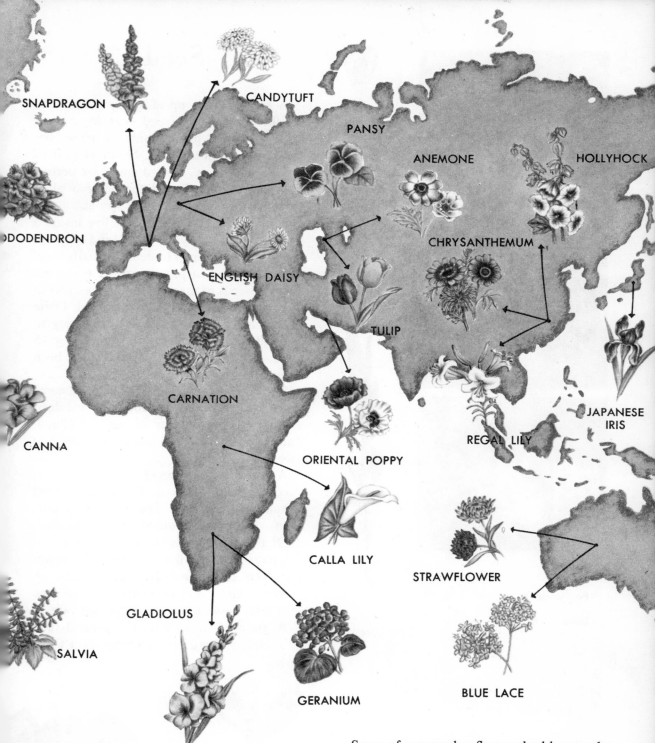

SNAPDRAGON

CANDYTUFT

PANSY

ANEMONE

HOLLYHOCK

RHODODENDRON

CHRYSANTHEMUM

ENGLISH DAISY

TULIP

CARNATION

CANNA

ORIENTAL POPPY

REGAL LILY

JAPANESE IRIS

CALLA LILY

STRAWFLOWER

GLADIOLUS

SALVIA

GERANIUM

BLUE LACE

to the morning-glory family. Asparagus, onions, and tulips were brought from southwestern Asia; they, as you know, are all members of the lily family. Candytuft and cabbage belong to the mustard family. They both came to us from Europe.

Some of our garden flowers had been cultivated for centuries before our country was founded. A trip through a flower garden of today may well take one back in imagination to the gardens of the ancient emperors of China or the monastery gardens of medieval Europe or the flower-bordered highways leading to Aztec temples.

Seeds

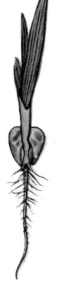

A seed is made up of a tiny plant, food for the plant, and a seed coat for protection. The tiny plant inside is sometimes spoken of as the *embryo*. No other part of the seed can grow. A seed may look perfect from the outside, but if the embryo plant has died the seed will never sprout.

How long a baby plant will live inside a seed depends partly on what kind of plant the seed came from. Gardeners usually want seeds produced in just the previous season. And the seeds of many plants seldom sprout if they are more than three years old. Quite a number of seeds, however, are likely to be good even if they have been stored for 15 years. And more than a few kinds have been known to grow after over 100 years.

The record for long life is held by some water lily seeds that were found buried deep underground in a layer of peat in China. They were about 1,000 years old when they sprouted!

A few plants, the cocklebur for one, produce two kinds of seeds. Those of one kind sprout soon, if at all. The others stay dormant—live but unsprouted—for a long time.

Of the three kinds of seeds pictured on this page, one—corn—comes from a monocot. The other two are dicot seeds. A monocot embryo, you remember, has one seed leaf, while a dicot embryo has two.

A grain of corn shows the general plan of a monocot seed. The embryo plant takes

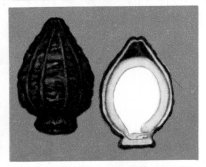

Corn

Four-o'clock

Lima Bean

Corn Sprouting

Lima Bean Sprouting

Petunia

English Walnut

Sweet Pea

up only a small part of the seed. It rests on the food that has been stored up for it. The tiny plant's one seed leaf never leaves the seed. When corn sprouts, the growing plant forces its way out of the seed coat. Through the seed leaf it takes in the stored food.

Although the four-o'clock and the lima bean are both dicots, their seeds are built on somewhat different plans. In the four-o'clock the two seed leaves are thin. They are wrapped around a ball of food. It is easy to take a four-o'clock seed apart and find the ball of food. It is mostly starch.

The embryo bean plant fills the whole seed. No food is stored beside it. Instead, the food is stored in its two thick seed leaves. When the bean sprouts, the stem of the young plant pulls the two seed leaves out of the seed coat and up out of the ground. Soon, after the food stored in them has been used up, they drop off the plant.

Some seeds are far, far larger than others. They range all the way from orchid and witchweed seeds, which are so tiny and light that it would take millions and millions to weigh a pound, to palm seeds that may weigh more than 40 pounds. These enormous seeds—sometimes called twin coconuts—are produced by palms of the Seychelles Islands in the Indian Ocean.

The flowering plants form by far the biggest group of seed plants. Most seeds, therefore, are produced by flowers. Some kinds of flowers are very much bigger than others. But big flowers and big seeds by no means always go together.

Petunia flowers are larger than sweet peas, but sweet pea seeds are far larger than petunia seeds. Walnut flowers are not nearly so large as sweet peas, but their seeds are much larger. The seeds of even the biggest, most beautiful orchids are like dust.

Seeds come in so many different sizes and shapes and colors that collecting seeds is an interesting hobby. It is easy to learn to tell many kinds of plants by the size and shape and color of their seeds. Can you pick out in the assortment of seeds pictured below the three corn, four bean, one pea, and two sunflower seeds?

Cottonwood

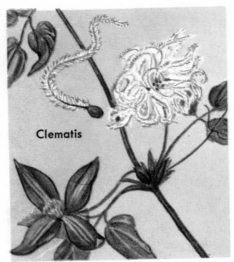

Clematis

Milkweed

Some plants form millions of seeds in a season. The cottonwood and sycamore are two that produce enormous numbers.

If all the seeds of a cottonwood or sycamore were to fall under the tree that bore them, they would not have a good chance to grow. Many of them might start growing, but one tiny tree after another would die because it was so crowded that it could not

Dandelion

get all the water, minerals, and sunshine it needed. It is important for every seed plant, if it is to hold its own, to have some way of getting its seeds scattered.

Many kinds of seeds travel by air. The smaller the seed, as a rule, the better it can ride the wind. The tiny seeds of orchids and witchweed are so light that during much of their journeys they are actually floating like tiny balloons in the air. The slightest breeze carries them a long way.

The pictures on these pages show a number of other seeds that are airborne. These seeds are all helped in their travels through the air by having parachutes of down. As you would expect, they, too, are small, light seeds. Only light seeds are equipped with parachutes. The parachutes may be tufts of silky hairs like those of the milkweed or feathery plumes like those of clematis.

In some cases the parachutes are fastened to the seeds themselves. In others they are fastened to a close-fitting covering around the seeds. Many so-called seeds are really one-seeded fruits even though the part of the fruit that surrounds the seed is not at all thick and juicy like that of a peach. The wall of the pistil the seed was formed in has become just a sort of extra seed coat.

A milkweed seed is a seed. A dandelion "seed" is actually a fruit. It does not make any difference so far as the scattering of the seeds is concerned.

Seeds that travel by parachute are sometimes called flyaways. A seed with a parachute may fall to the ground and then be picked up again and again to continue its travels. A single seed with a parachute may be carried more than a hundred miles.

Some kinds of plants whose seeds travel by parachute have spread for many thousands of miles. Each cattail of a cattail plant is made up of thousands of tiny one-seeded fruits with parachutes. Cattail plants now grow on the edges of swamps and ponds all over the world. The constant fight we have to carry on to keep our lawns free from dandelions is another sign that parachutes are a big help in getting seeds scattered.

The story of galinsoga is another proof of how well parachutes help scatter seeds. This little plant, sometimes called French-weed, is a native of tropical America. It came to the eastern coast of the United States a hundred years or so ago. It was carried, it is thought, in the sand ballast of cargo ships. A cargo vessel without a heavy load might carry sand to make it sail well, then dump the sand at the end of the trip to make room for new cargo. Of course, any seeds in the sand were dumped with it.

At first galinsoga grew along the coast only where sand had been dumped. But well before 1900 its parachutes had carried it far and wide. Gardeners in all parts of the continent know this little weed well.

Cotton seeds are often called flyaways. They are covered with so much down, or lint, that they are hidden by it. But this lint is so tangled, and often so sticky, that it does not make a good parachute. It does, however, frequently stick to an animal passing by. Cotton seeds really belong with the hitchhikers you will soon meet.

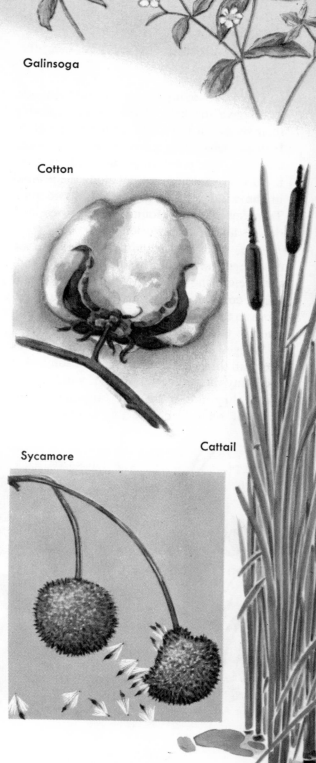

Galinsoga

Cotton

Sycamore

Cattail

Russian Thistle, a Tumbleweed

There are many kinds of tumbleweeds. They have the help of the air in scattering their seeds but the seeds are not borne aloft. Instead, when the seeds of a tumbleweed are ripe, the plant dries up and its stem breaks. Then it goes rolling along the ground in the wind, dropping its seeds as it goes. Tumbleweeds are found on prairies and deserts all over the world.

Some seeds and fruits fly through the air on wings rather than parachutes. The picture below shows a few. Winged seeds and fruits come mostly from trees. The wind close to the ground is not likely to be strong enough to lift them.

Winged seeds and fruits turn and twist as they fall through the air. They are somewhat like tiny helicopters. As the wind drives them they are more like airplanes. One kind of seed is called the airplane seed.

It comes from an East Indian vine. Its wings measure 6 inches from tip to tip.

Some seeds make long air journeys without the help of either wings or parachutes. They travel "by bird." Wading birds carry many seeds in mud on their feet. Birds may carry sticky seeds for a long way on their bills. When they clean their bills they scrape the seeds off. Mistletoe is one of the plants that have been scattered in this way. Birds may also carry small seeds in their feathers.

Riding on the feet or in the feathers or on the bill of a bird is like riding on the outside of an airplane. There is always danger of falling off. Sometimes seeds ride on the inside of their bird airplanes. Birds eat fruits. If the seeds are small, as they are in such a fruit as a blackberry, they swallow the fruit, seeds and all. The bird digests the soft part of the fruit, but it may not

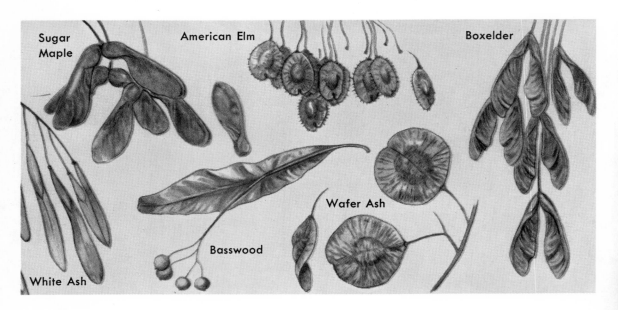

Sugar Maple

American Elm

Boxelder

White Ash

Basswood

Wafer Ash

344

digest the seeds. They may go through the bird's body and still be able to grow.

Birds are not the only animals that scatter seeds by carrying them inside their bodies. Box turtles scatter the seeds of wild strawberries in this way. Lizards, snails, freshwater fishes, and land crabs are seed carriers, too. The famous scientist Charles Darwin once found water lily seeds in the stomach of a fish that was in the stomach of a heron!

Animals usually carry seeds quite by accident. But sometimes they carry seeds to store them away as food. They may even plant them! Blue jays, for instance, often dig holes in the ground and put acorns in them. They may never come back to get the acorns they have buried; the acorns have a chance to grow. Squirrels plant nuts of different kinds in the same way.

The seeds that catch a ride on the feet, bills, and feathers of birds are well called hitchhikers. The seeds pictured at the right are hitchhikers, too. They are carried in the fur of mammals and in people's clothing. The sharp prickles on the hard cases that hold the seeds can catch in fur or clothing easily. They often cling so tight that the seeds are hard to pull off. Anyone who has

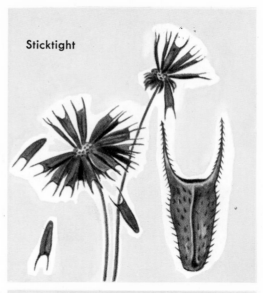

Sticktight

Burdock

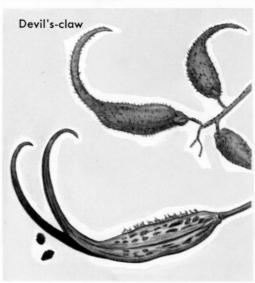

Devil's-claw

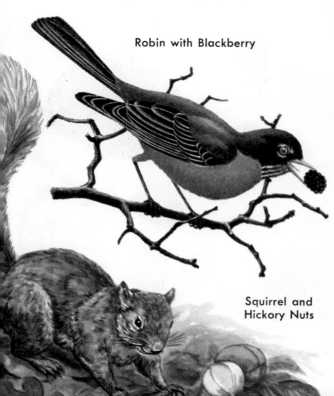

Robin with Blackberry

Squirrel and Hickory Nuts

Witch Hazel

walked through a patch of cockleburs knows how easy it is for cocklebur seeds to get a free ride.

The seedpods of some plants shoot out their seeds. Witch hazel pods pop open like tiny firecrackers when the seeds are ready to be scattered. The ripe pod of a touch-me-not plant shoots out its seeds if touched. Violet and pansy seedpods explode, too.

Another plant that shoots out its seeds is the sandbox tree that grows in the hot, wet lands of tropical America. Travelers have given this tree another name—the monkeys' dinner bell. Its ripe seedpods explode with so much force that the noise is like a pistol shot. There are monkeys in the forests where the tree grows. The explosions of the pods gave people the idea that the tree calls the monkeys to dinner.

Wings not only help seeds travel by air; they also help them travel by water. Seeds cannot stand being in water long, but with wings to help them, they may float on the surface of a pond or stream until they reach a bank. They may float for several miles. The coconut's fibrous shell keeps it afloat. Snug in its outside husk this seed can safely island-hop if the trip by sea is not too long.

Touch-me-not

Violet

Pansy

Sandbox Tree

American Lotus

The American lotus has an unusual way of sending its seeds on journeys by water. The seed holder it produces serves as a boat. It can float for a long way. The seeds are held firmly inside it until the "boat" breaks or rots away.

Such seeds as walnuts may roll quite a distance. The water that runs off after a heavy rain often washes seeds along the ground. Seeds in pods may go coasting over ice and crusty snow. A flat pod like those of the locusts makes a good sled. A few seeds can actually crawl a little way. Some grass seeds, for instance, do so by means of stiff hairs that move when they get wet.

Some seeds have gluey seed coats. They may stick to dead leaves and be carried away as the leaves are whirled along.

Seeds can endure long periods of bad weather. They make it possible for seed plants to hold their own in many places where other plants cannot. And, as you have seen, seed plants have any number of ways of getting their seeds scattered. Is it any wonder that, after seed plants once appeared, they spread over most of the earth?

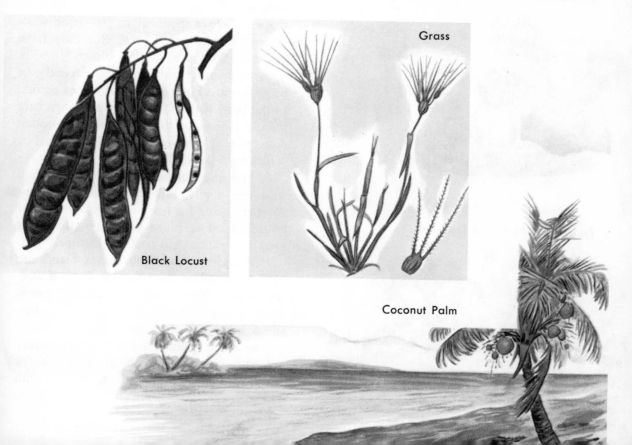

Black Locust

Grass

Coconut Palm

Wandering Jew

African Violet

Cacti and Hen
and Chickens

Peperomia, Aloe, and Jade Plant

House Plants

Even in cold winter weather, when the trees are bare and our gardens show nothing but dead stalks, we can have growing plants around us. For many different kinds of plants can be raised indoors. Florist shops are full of plants for indoor gardens. Some of these plants are liked for their flowers, others for their leaves. These pictures show a few of the plants that can be grown indoors successfully.

Wandering Jew is a trailing plant. It was a favorite with our great-grandmothers because of its pretty leaves. Now other trailing plants have crowded it aside somewhat. English ivy, grape ivy, and philodendron are three of them. Philodendron is often seen growing without soil. It will do well if it is simply planted in water.

African violets are very popular partly because they bloom so well when properly taken care of. Many varieties will bloom almost the year round.

Cactus plants make an interesting indoor garden. Different kinds have different shapes, some of them rather grotesque. Cactus plants have no leaves. But they have beautiful flowers when they bloom.

Some cactus plants are tiny. Several can be grown in a bowl only a few inches across. In the bowl with the two cacti in the picture there is a hen and chickens plant. This plant does not yet have any small plants, or "chickens," around it.

A hen and chickens bears flowers on a stalk but it is raised chiefly for its leaves. Another name for hen and chickens is roof houseleek. The plant is a common sight growing on thatched roofs in Europe.

Hen and chickens and cactus plants are *succulents,* plants with special ways of storing water. The word "succulent" means "full of juice." Cacti store water in their stems, a hen and chickens in its thick leaves.

The three plants in the bottom picture are also succulents with thick leaves for storing water. The jade plant, the one with

Geranium

the small leaves, grows into interesting shapes and throws pretty shadows when the sun shines on it. It is a cousin of hen and chickens. Aloe belongs to the lily family. Peperomia, the plant with the heart-shaped leaves, is in the pepper family—the family that includes not the green pepper but the plant black pepper comes from.

In early summer, geraniums are planted by the millions in gardens, parks, and window boxes. They make good indoor plants for the winter, too. There are more than 650 varieties to choose from. The varieties differ chiefly in the color of their blossoms. There are pink, deep-red, and white blossoms as well as scarlet ones.

349

Poinsettia

The secret of being a successful indoor gardener is knowing that not all plants that will grow indoors should be treated the same way. They do not all thrive with the same amount of light. Some do best in a sunny south window, others in a north window. They do not all need the same amount of water. Some must be protected from drafts. Some can stand higher or lower temperatures than others. Some need well-drained soil, while others will grow in pots that have no drainage.

A good rule is to try to give plants as nearly as possible the conditions they would thrive in outdoors. Cacti, for instance, are desert plants. They live in regions where there are occasional heavy showers. A cactus plant, therefore, should be watered thoroughly. Then it should not be given any more water until the soil is quite dry. If the soil around it is kept wet all the time, a cactus is likely to rot. As another example, primroses grow outdoors in cool regions. If a primrose is to last long indoors, it should not be kept in a warm room.

At Christmastime and other special times potted plants by the thousands are sent as gifts. Some of them do not last any longer than a bouquet of cut flowers would last. A poinsettia that has lost all its leaves is, for instance, a common sight a day or two after Christmas. Many florists now send a card with every potted plant telling how the plant should be cared for. The directions should be followed.

An aquarium is too often thought of only as a home for fish. But if it is planted care-

Aquarium

Terrarium

fully, it can be made into an attractive underwater garden.

A little glassed-in garden, or terrarium, is fun to plan and plant. The one in the picture above has four kinds of plants in it: twinberry—the plant with the red berries—moss, a small fern, and a lichen of the kind called British soldiers because of its red caps. (The British of Revolutionary War days wore red uniforms.)

To have an attractive garden indoors it is not necessary to buy plants from a florist. A sweet potato vine, which is as pretty as a philodendron, can be raised from any sweet potato that has not been oven-dried to keep it from rotting. The sweet potato needs only to be stood on end in a jar of water. Grapefruit seeds planted in a pot of dirt grow into plants with shiny dark-green leaves. If the top third of a carrot is stood in a shallow bowl of water and held in place with pebbles, it will send up dainty feathery leaves. Slips taken from such plants as begonias and geraniums may be started in moist sand, then planted in pots with every hope of their growing well. Interesting plants for a terrarium can be gathered in almost any woods.

The paper-white narcissus is among the most successful blooming plants that can be raised indoors. Paper-white narcissus bulbs can be planted in water and pebbles, and need little care. On a cold, dark morning in winter a bowl of blooming narcissus does a great deal to make one forget the weather.

Primrose

Paper-white Narcissus

New Plants from Old

Almost all the plants we raise in our fields and orchards and gardens are seed plants. The commonest way of raising them is to plant their seeds. The story of a great many of our crop plants is much like the pumpkin life history pictured here.

Planting a seed means putting it in a situation that will allow the small plant inside the seed to break its way out through the seed coat and keep on growing. Warmth and moisture and air must be provided. Many people who plant seeds do not understand that seeds need air. It is possible to drown the tiny plants in seeds by pouring on so much water that it shuts air out.

The depth at which a seed is planted is important. In every seed some food is stored for the baby plant. If the seedling is to keep

on growing, this food must last until the plant is above the surface of the ground and can make food for itself.

A pumpkin seed has enough food stored in it to let the young plant grow a few inches. It can be planted some two inches deep without any danger that the seedling will run out of food. There is an advantage in planting a large seed rather deep. If it is planted close to the surface, a heavy rain is likely to wash away the soil from around it. If, on the other hand, a tiny petunia seed is planted deep in the ground, the seedling will run out of food and never reach the sunshine.

Rhizome

Cuttings

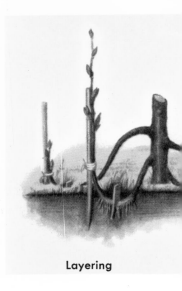

Layering

In some cases there are other ways of raising new seed plants that are better than planting seeds. Many kinds of flowers are commonly raised from *bulbs*. Almost no one, for instance, plants tulip seeds except flowergrowers who are trying to produce new varieties of tulips.

Bulbs furnish an easy way of growing sturdy plants. A bulb is made up mostly of thick leaves that overlap one another. A great deal of food is stored in them. There is ever and ever so much more food in a tulip bulb than there is in a tulip seed. A strong, vigorous plant can grow from a bulb and come into bloom much more quickly than from a seed.

A *corm* is very much like a bulb. Crocuses and gladioli are commonly raised from corms rather than from seeds.

Some plants can be raised from *roots*. The dahlia has fleshy roots in which a large amount of food is stored.

As you know, a potato is a thick underground stem of the kind called a *tuber*. A gardener, to plant potatoes, cuts potatoes into pieces, each piece with an eye, or bud. There is enough food in the pieces to let their buds grow.

A *rhizome* is another kind of thick underground stem. Iris plants are usually raised from rhizomes. Tubers, rhizomes, corms, and fleshy roots have the same advantage over seeds that bulbs have.

The branches of some plants send out roots wherever they touch the ground. New plants can be started by bending a branch down to the ground, fastening it in place until it sends roots down and a shoot up,

Fleshy Root

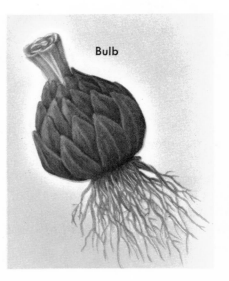

Bulb

Corm

Golden Delicious Apple

Geranium Slip

and then cutting the branch so that it is no longer joined to the parent plant. This plan of starting new plants is called *layering*. Many new blackberry and raspberry bushes are started by layering.

Geraniums are usually raised from *cuttings* often called slips. A cutting is a piece —in many cases a branch—cut from a plant. Geranium slips, as you know, will send out roots when put in moist sand. A cutting may include both a young branch and a part of the stem it grew from.

Such woody plants as apple trees are often raised from cuttings fastened in certain ways, or *grafted,* to other similar woody plants so that the different plants grow together. A cutting of Apple A, for instance, could be grafted on to a hardy crab apple tree. The whole top of the crab apple tree would be cut off with only the cutting of Apple A grafted in its place left to grow. Soon the tree would look like the parent Apple A tree. No one would know by looking at it that it had crab apple roots. It would bear apples like those on Apple A.

It has been said that there is really only one Golden Delicious tree in the world. This saying is true in the sense that every Golden Delicious tree except the first one

came from a cutting that was grafted on to the roots of some other kind of tree. The same thing could be said of countless other varieties of woody plants. For many of the fruit trees, rosebushes, grapevines, and ornamental shrubs and trees nurseries sell are grafted. Grafting is an important help in multiplying plants of new varieties that are developed.

In some cases it is not possible to raise a seed plant from its seeds. Suppose a new kind of apple—let us call it Apple X—has been produced by crossing two kinds of apples. Suppose, too, that Apple X proves to be one of the many kinds of apples that do not produce seeds unless pollen has been brought to their flowers from apple trees of a different variety. The trees that grow from Apple X seeds are not, then, Apple X trees. The reason they are not is that they have two parents—the Apple X tree and the tree that furnished the pollen. They are crosses between Apple X and the variety the pollen came from.

Of course, seed plants that rarely or never produce seeds, such as pineapple and navel oranges, must be raised in some other way than by seeds. It is lucky that such plants have other ways of multiplying.

Hen and Chickens

Thimble Cactus

Plant Adaptations

Many plants, like many animals, are specially fitted for living where they do. They may be so well fitted for living in certain kinds of places that they cannot live anywhere else. A seaweed and a morning glory could not change habitats any more successfully than could a swallow and a cod.

A desert is one of the kinds of places that present many problems to plants. The deserts of our own Southwest, for instance, are likely to be very hot in the daytime and cold at night. The air as well as the soil is usually dry. When rain does fall, it frequently comes down in torrents. Much of the water runs off instead of sinking in.

The plants called succulents have solved the problems of living in such deserts. Most cacti have no leaves at all except when they are very young. Their stems do the work leaves do for such plants as elms and daffodils. Cactus stems are thick and pulpy. As you already know, they make good water storage tanks.

It would do a cactus plant no good to have a storage tank if it had no way of filling the tank. Its roots spread out near the surface of the ground. They are ready to soak up fast any water that reaches them.

Having no leaves helps a cactus save the water it has stored. Many gallons of water may evaporate from a maple tree on a hot summer day, because there is an enormous amount of surface from which evaporation can take place. In the case of a cactus there is little surface exposed to the air.

Juicy cactus plants would not have much of a chance to escape being eaten by thirsty desert animals if it were not for their spines. Spines, then, are another desert adaptation.

The thick leaves of hen and chickens—its water reservoirs—form a rosette close to the ground. Not much surface is exposed.

Welwitschia grows in the deserts of southwestern Africa. In its whole life of perhaps more than a hundred years it has only two leaves. They grow from the broad top of the plant's thick root-trunk. The wind tears the leaves into narrow ribbons, and pieces break off the ends, but the leaves keep growing at the base. The root-trunk

Welwitschia

Torch

Saguaro

Cacti

Hedgehog

Englemann's Pear

Purple Tinge Pear

Barrel

Pincushion

Beavertail

Joshua Tree

stores water as well as food. Welwitschia is a living fossil. It has no close relatives.

The Joshua tree of our Southwest is a yucca. It may grow to be 30 or 40 feet tall. In contrast, many yuccas, like the candle of God pictured on page 114, are stemless or nearly stemless plants with swordlike leaves growing in a rosette. The Joshua tree and the candle of God are both water-thrifty desert plants. Water does not evaporate fast from their tough, stiff leaves.

Venus's-flytrap

Sundew

Pitcher Plant

from these drops of liquid, which look like dew. But this dew does not go away when the sun shines.

The dew is sticky. A little insect that alights or crawls up on a leaf gets stuck in the dew. The hairs it touches bend over to the center of the leaf. The other hairs bend down, too. They hold the insect tight. The dew helps turn the soft part of the insect into a liquid, which is absorbed by the leaf. When the sundew has finished digesting the insect, the hairs open out again. The hard parts of the insect blow away and the leaf is ready for another meal.

The ends of the leaves of a Venus's-flytrap are its traps. They catch insects by folding together. On each half of the trap at the end of a leaf there are some stiff hairs that stand up. These are the triggers that make the trap work. When an insect touches one of them the trap closes. Stiff hairs around the edges keep the insect from escaping. The trap stays closed until the insect is digested. Then it opens again.

Pitcher plants trap insects in pitcher-shaped leaves that usually are partly full of

A bog is very different as a habitat from a desert. Here there is always a great deal of water. But there may be a shortage of another important material—nitrogen. Plants as a rule get all their nitrogen from the soil or water in which they grow. But a bog plant may get some nitrogen just as many animals do—by "eating" meat.

The pictures on this page show four plants well fitted for living in bogs because they are meat-eaters. They eat insects.

The hairy leaves of the tiny sundew are insect traps. At the end of each hair there is a drop of liquid. The plant gets its name

Bladderwort

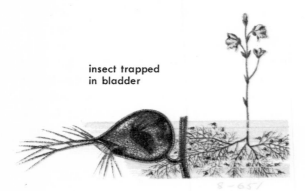

insect trapped
in bladder

water. Inside are downward-pointing hairs. Insects can crawl down into a pitcher but not back up again. They drown in the water and are then digested.

Little hollow balls with one-way doors grow on the stems of bladderwort, a water plant. Insects that swim in cannot escape.

The water hyacinth, duckweed, and water lily are also water plants. Cattails grow in marshes and other very wet areas. None of these plants, however, depend on insects for food. They live where they can get all the materials they need for making food.

The water hyacinth floats about in many of the streams and ponds of our south-eastern states. Often it is a serious nuisance. No plant is better fitted for floating. The stalk of each leaf is an air-filled balloon. Each leaf thus has its own life preserver.

The common duckweed floats, too. This tiny plant without stems or leaves is very light. A close relative called watermeal is the smallest of all flowering plants.

The roots of a water lily are in the mud at the bottom of the water, but its leaves usually float on the surface. These leaves differ from most aerial leaves in an important way—the stomata, or air openings, are on the upper side of the leaf. Otherwise they could not take in from the air the carbon dioxide needed for food-making.

Water Hyacinth

Duckweed (greatly enlarged)

Water Lily

Cattail

Air Pine

In warm, rainy forests plants have to struggle to get the light they need. Some put themselves in the sunshine by perching on the branches of trees. Such pickaback plants are called *epiphytes*. Perching high on a tree makes it hard for a plant to get water. Different epiphytes solve the problem in different ways. Some, like air pine, have stiff leaves cupped at the base that form a rain barrel. Many small animals, from tree frogs to mosquitoes, use the rain barrels of these epiphytes as nurseries.

Long moss, a common epiphyte on trees in the South and a close relative of air pine, has a different way of getting water. This plant has many fine stems and leaves covered with hair scales. The hair scales let water in when it rains, then "shut the door" when the rains are over.

Many orchids are epiphytes. These epiphytes have aerial roots that quickly soak up water from rains.

The primrose shows how a low-growing plant may be fitted for getting enough light. Its leaves spread out in an open rosette.

The strangler fig has a strange way of establishing itself in a crowded forest. A seed lights in a crevice or fork somewhere on another kind of tree—often a palm. It starts growing and sending roots down the

Strangler Fig

Bristlecone Pine

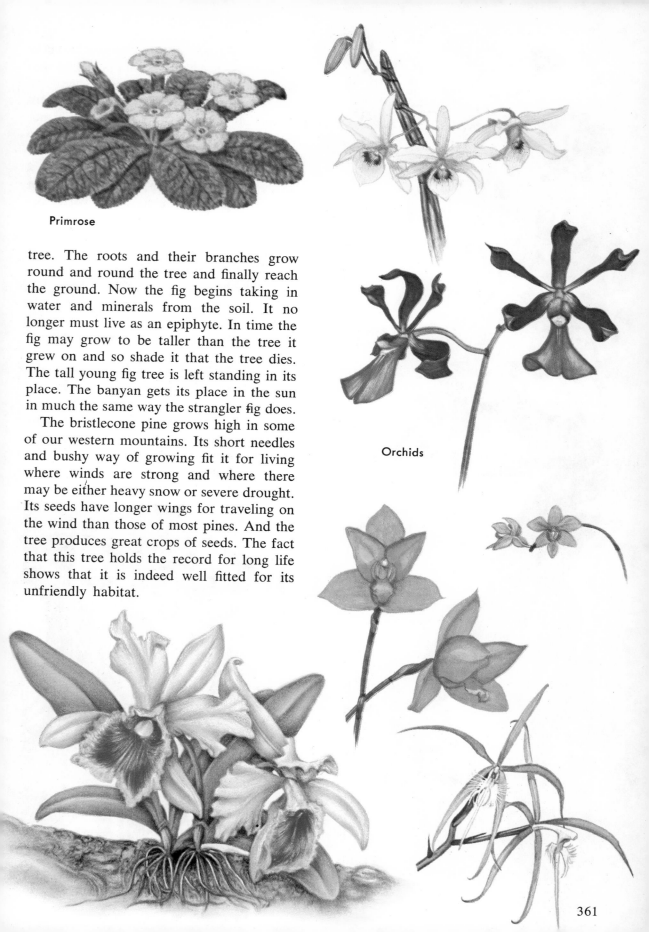

Primrose

Orchids

tree. The roots and their branches grow round and round the tree and finally reach the ground. Now the fig begins taking in water and minerals from the soil. It no longer must live as an epiphyte. In time the fig may grow to be taller than the tree it grew on and so shade it that the tree dies. The tall young fig tree is left standing in its place. The banyan gets its place in the sun in much the same way the strangler fig does.

The bristlecone pine grows high in some of our western mountains. Its short needles and bushy way of growing fit it for living where winds are strong and where there may be either heavy snow or severe drought. Its seeds have longer wings for traveling on the wind than those of most pines. And the tree produces great crops of seeds. The fact that this tree holds the record for long life shows that it is indeed well fitted for its unfriendly habitat.

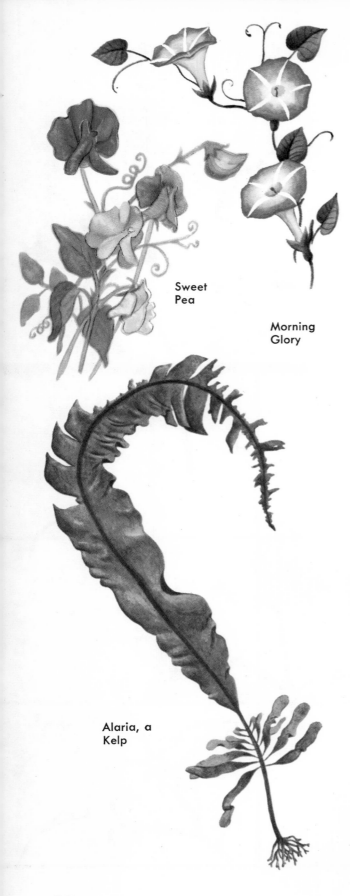

Sweet
Pea

Morning
Glory

Alaria, a
Kelp

These pictures show a few of the many other ways in which various plants fit into their surroundings. The sweet pea and morning glory have tendrils which help them climb. Climbing devices are especially important in tropical forests where there is a constant fight for sunlight.

The kelp has a holdfast which anchors it securely to rock along the shore. It can stand the buffeting of the waves partly because of this good anchor.

The trunk of the kapok tree of tropical America flares out at the base into giant folds that are like the flying buttresses of Gothic cathedrals. They help keep this tall, heavily branched tree from being uprooted easily in windstorms.

The dense covering of hairs on mullein leaves, the arrangement of prickly-lettuce leaves so that they always face the sun, and the stilt roots of the mangrove tree are still other plant adaptations. The list is almost endless. Any species of plant that is alive and thriving today is, you may be sure, fitted in many ways for living where it does. Survival depends on adaptation.

Kapok Tree

Charts

The charts that begin on this page will summarize for you some of what you have now found out about the history of the earth and about the world of living things. They will also add a great deal of new information. These are the charts:

NORTH AMERICA'S DIARY

		EVENTS	LIFE
PRE-CRUSTAL TIME 2 billion years or more		Earth "born." Mantle and core of earth separated. Earliest rocks formed.	No life.
EARLY PRECAMBRIAN	1 billion years	Great volcanic activity. Parts of North America covered with shallow seas. Mountains pushed up and worn away. First sedimentary rocks formed.	Very simple one-celled plants and animals probably present. At least blue-green algae by end of era.
LATE PRECAMBRIAN	1 billion years	Many sedimentary rocks formed. Earliest known glaciers. Great mountains pushed up in Great Lakes and Grand Canyon regions and then worn away. Vast lava flows in Lake Superior region.	Sponges and many other invertebrates probably common. Many seaweeds.

	EVENTS	LIFE

PALEOZOIC ERA

CAMBRIAN — 105 million years

Events: Climate mild.

Large areas of North America covered with shallow arms of sea.

Life: All life still in sea.
Seaweeds and invertebrates very abundant.
Trilobites the leading animals.

ORDOVICIAN — 70 million years

Events: Nearly two-thirds of North America covered by shallow seas.

Life: First vertebrates—armored fishes.

Invertebrates still the dominant animals.

SILURIAN — 25 million years

Events: Much of continent still covered with shallow seas.

Some land areas very dry.

Life: First known land plants—liverworts.
First known land animals—scorpions.
Many reefs formed by corals.

DEVONIAN — 55 million years

Events: Large areas under water till very late in period.

Some volcanic activity.

Thick layers of shale, sandstone, and limestone formed in shallow seas.

Life: First ferns, horsetails, and club mosses. First forest
First backboned animals on land—amphibians.
Fishes the dominant animals of the lakes and seas.

MISSISSIPPIAN — 35 million years

Events: By middle of period much of continent under water.

Climate warm.

Life: Amphibians numerous.

Insects becoming prominent.

Sea lilies (crinoids) very common.

Many sharks in seas.

PENNSYLVANIAN — 30 million years

Events: Much rising and sinking of land in relation to sea level.
Vast swamps.
Great deposits of coal formed.

Life: Great forests of tree horset
club mosses, and early
plants.

Insects large and numerous

First reptiles.

PERMIAN — 50 million years

Events: Land uplifted.
Appalachians formed.

Great aridity.

Glaciers in small areas.

Life: First conifers.

Reptiles common.

Numbers of plants and animals greatly reduced.

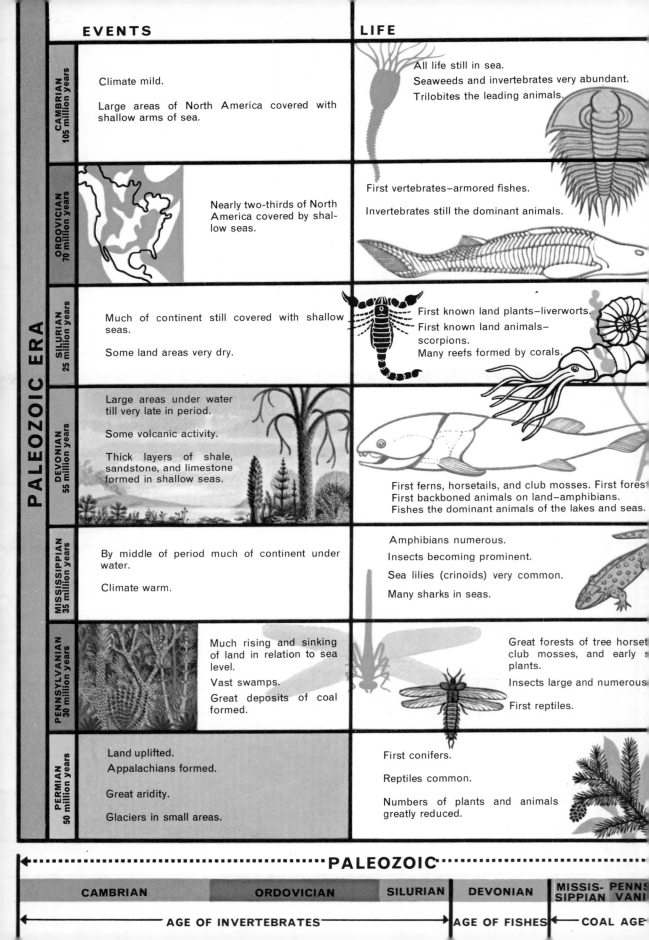

PALEOZOIC

CAMBRIAN	ORDOVICIAN	SILURIAN	DEVONIAN	MISSIS-SIPPIAN	PENNS VANI

←————— AGE OF INVERTEBRATES —————→ | AGE OF FISHES | ← COAL AGE

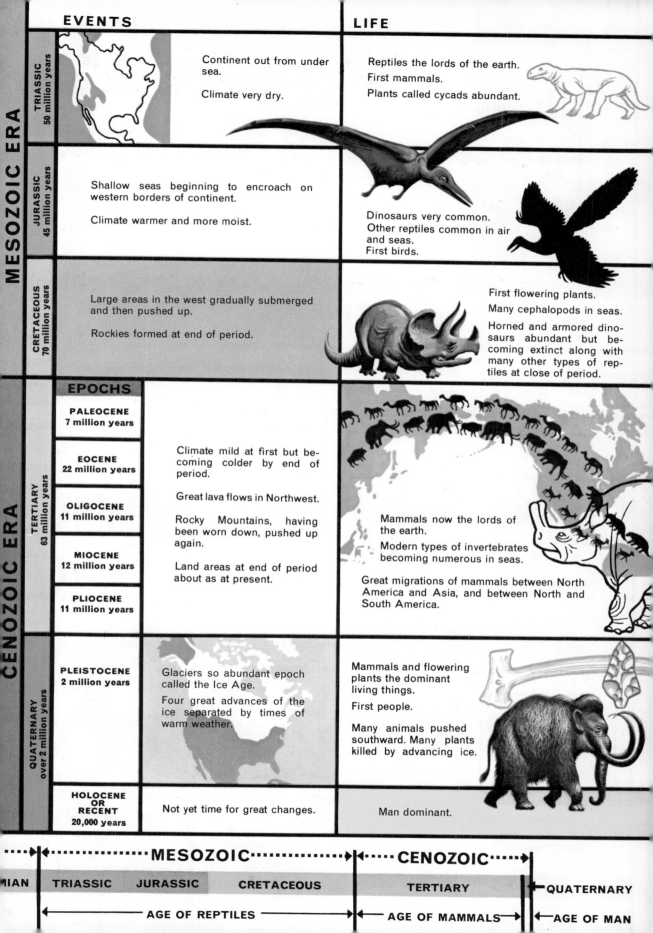

	EVENTS	LIFE

MESOZOIC ERA

TRIASSIC — 50 million years

Events:
Continent out from under sea.

Climate very dry.

Life:
Reptiles the lords of the earth.
First mammals.
Plants called cycads abundant.

JURASSIC — 45 million years

Events:
Shallow seas beginning to encroach on western borders of continent.

Climate warmer and more moist.

Life:
Dinosaurs very common.
Other reptiles common in air and seas.
First birds.

CRETACEOUS — 70 million years

Events:
Large areas in the west gradually submerged and then pushed up.

Rockies formed at end of period.

Life:
First flowering plants.
Many cephalopods in seas.

Horned and armored dinosaurs abundant but becoming extinct along with many other types of reptiles at close of period.

CENOZOIC ERA

TERTIARY — 63 million years

EPOCHS

PALEOCENE	7 million years
EOCENE	22 million years
OLIGOCENE	11 million years
MIOCENE	12 million years
PLIOCENE	11 million years

Events:
Climate mild at first but becoming colder by end of period.

Great lava flows in Northwest.

Rocky Mountains, having been worn down, pushed up again.

Land areas at end of period about as at present.

Life:
Mammals now the lords of the earth.
Modern types of invertebrates becoming numerous in seas.

Great migrations of mammals between North America and Asia, and between North and South America.

QUATERNARY — over 2 million years

PLEISTOCENE — 2 million years

Events:
Glaciers so abundant epoch called the Ice Age.
Four great advances of the ice separated by times of warm weather.

Life:
Mammals and flowering plants the dominant living things.
First people.
Many animals pushed southward. Many plants killed by advancing ice.

HOLOCENE OR RECENT — 20,000 years

Events:
Not yet time for great changes.

Life:
Man dominant.

← ··········· MESOZOIC ··········· → ← ·········· CENOZOIC ·········· →

| ...MIAN | TRIASSIC | JURASSIC | CRETACEOUS | TERTIARY | QUATERNARY |

← ————— AGE OF REPTILES ————— → ← ——— AGE OF MAMMALS ——— → ← AGE OF MAN →

CLASSIFICATION OF LIVING THINGS

HOW THIS ANIMAL IS CLASSIFIED

In classifying plants and animals, scientists group the plants and animals that are very much alike into species. Species that are much alike are grouped into genera (the plural of genus). Genera are put together to form families, families make up orders, orders make up classes, and classes make up phyla. For an even more exact classification, classes may be grouped into subphyla and the subphyla into phyla. There may also be suborders, subgenera, and so on. Subspecies are often called varieties.

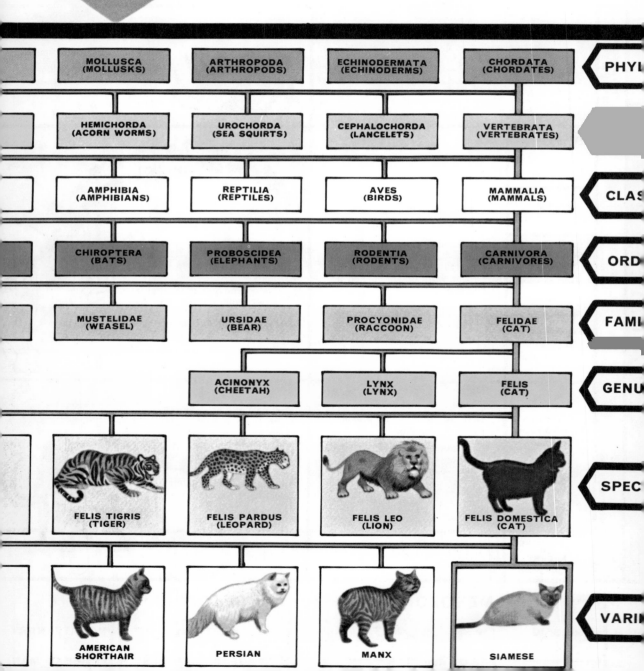

PHYL				
MOLLUSCA (MOLLUSKS)	ARTHROPODA (ARTHROPODS)	ECHINODERMATA (ECHINODERMS)	CHORDATA (CHORDATES)	
HEMICHORDA (ACORN WORMS)	UROCHORDA (SEA SQUIRTS)	CEPHALOCHORDA (LANCELETS)	VERTEBRATA (VERTEBRATES)	
AMPHIBIA (AMPHIBIANS)	REPTILIA (REPTILES)	AVES (BIRDS)	MAMMALIA (MAMMALS)	CLAS
CHIROPTERA (BATS)	PROBOSCIDEA (ELEPHANTS)	RODENTIA (RODENTS)	CARNIVORA (CARNIVORES)	ORD
MUSTELIDAE (WEASEL)	URSIDAE (BEAR)	PROCYONIDAE (RACCOON)	FELIDAE (CAT)	FAMI
	ACINONYX (CHEETAH)	LYNX (LYNX)	FELIS (CAT)	GENU
FELIS TIGRIS (TIGER)	FELIS PARDUS (LEOPARD)	FELIS LEO (LION)	FELIS DOMESTICA (CAT)	SPEC
AMERICAN SHORTHAIR	PERSIAN	MANX	SIAMESE	VARI

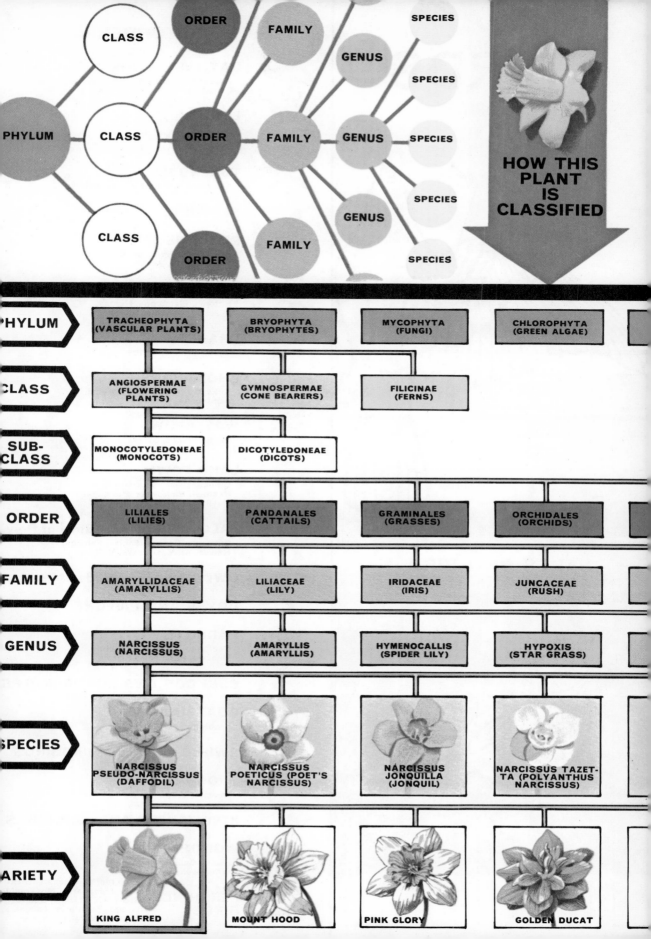

HOW THIS PLANT IS CLASSIFIED

PHYLUM	TRACHEOPHYTA (VASCULAR PLANTS)	BRYOPHYTA (BRYOPHYTES)	MYCOPHYTA (FUNGI)	CHLOROPHYTA (GREEN ALGAE)
CLASS	ANGIOSPERMAE (FLOWERING PLANTS)	GYMNOSPERMAE (CONE BEARERS)	FILICINAE (FERNS)	
SUB-CLASS	MONOCOTYLEDONEAE (MONOCOTS)	DICOTYLEDONEAE (DICOTS)		
ORDER	LILIALES (LILIES)	PANDANALES (CATTAILS)	GRAMINALES (GRASSES)	ORCHIDALES (ORCHIDS)
FAMILY	AMARYLLIDACEAE (AMARYLLIS)	LILIACEAE (LILY)	IRIDACEAE (IRIS)	JUNCACEAE (RUSH)
GENUS	NARCISSUS (NARCISSUS)	AMARYLLIS (AMARYLLIS)	HYMENOCALLIS (SPIDER LILY)	HYPOXIS (STAR GRASS)
SPECIES	NARCISSUS PSEUDO-NARCISSUS (DAFFODIL)	NARCISSUS POETICUS (POET'S NARCISSUS)	NARCISSUS JONQUILLA (JONQUIL)	NARCISSUS TAZETTA (POLYANTHUS NARCISSUS)
VARIETY	KING ALFRED	MOUNT HOOD	PINK GLORY	GOLDEN DUCAT

BIRDS

FEATHERS

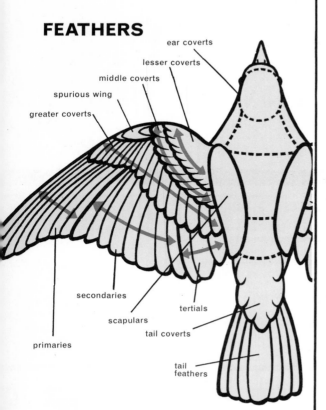

- ear coverts
- lesser coverts
- middle coverts
- spurious wing
- greater coverts
- secondaries
- scapulars
- tertials
- tail coverts
- primaries
- tail feathers

PARTS OF A BIRD

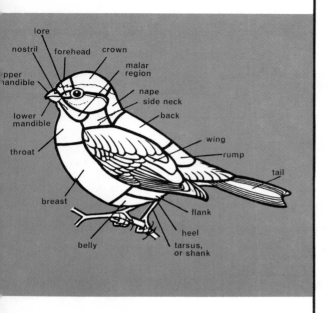

- lore
- nostril
- forehead
- crown
- malar region
- upper mandible
- nape
- side neck
- back
- lower mandible
- throat
- wing
- rump
- tail
- breast
- flank
- heel
- belly
- tarsus, or shank

BIRD ORDERS

RATITES (5 orders)
Cassowaries and Emus, Kiwis, Ostriches, Rheas, Tinamous

LOONS

GREBES

TUBENOSES
Albatrosses, Petrels, Shearwaters

PENGUINS

PELICANS
Boobies, Cormorants, Gannets, Frigate Birds, Pelicans

STORKS
Bitterns, Flamingos, Herons, Ibises, Spoonbills, Storks

CRANES
Coots, Cranes, Gallinules, Rails

SHOREBIRDS
Auks, Gulls, Jacanas, Plovers, Sandpipers, Terns

WATERFOWL
Ducks, Geese, Swans

LAND FOWL
Chickens, Grouse, Partridges, Peafowl, Pheasants, Ptarmigans, Quail, Turkeys

FALCONS (Daytime Birds of Prey)
Buzzards, Condor, Eagles, Falcons, Hawks, Kites, Ospreys, Vultures

OWLS (Nighttime Birds of Prey)

DOVES AND PIGEONS

PARROTS
Cockatoos. Lories, Lovebirds, Macaws, Parakeets, Parrots

CUCKOOS AND ROADRUNNERS

GOATSUCKERS
Nighthawk, Whipporwill

SWIFTS AND HUMMINGBIRDS

TROGONS
Quetzal, Trogons

KINGFISHERS AND HORNBILLS

WOODPECKERS
Honey Guides, Toucans, Woodpeckers

PERCHING BIRDS
Blackbirds, Flycatchers, Grosbeaks, Jays, Larks, Mockingbirds, Nuthatches, Shrikes, Sparrows, Starlings, Swallows, Tanagers, Thrushes, Warblers, Wrens

MAMMAL ORDERS

MONOTREMES
Platypus, Spiny Anteater

EDENTATES
Anteaters, Armadillos,
Sloths

AARDVARK

MARSUPIALS
Bandicoots, Kangaroos,
Koala, Opossums,
Phalangers, Tasmanian
Devil, Wombats

PANGOLINS

ELEPHANTS

INSECTIVORES
Hedgehogs, Moles,
Shrews, Tenrecs

RODENTS
Beavers, Chinchillas,
Chipmunks, Dormice,
Guinea Pigs, Hamsters,
Mice, Muskrats, Porcu-
pines, Prairie Dogs, Rats,
Squirrels, Woodchucks

HYRAXES

FLYING LEMURS

LAGOMORPHS
Hares, Pikas, Rabbits

SEA COWS
Dugong, Manatees

BATS

CETACEANS
Dolphins, Porpoises,
Whales

**ODD-TOED
UNGULATES**
Asses, Horses, Rhinoc-
eroses, Tapirs, Zebras

PRIMATES
Apes, Aye-aye, Lemurs,
Lorises, Man, Marmosets,
Monkeys, Tarsiers

CARNIVORES
Bears, Cats, Civets,
Dogs, Foxes, Hyenas,
Otters, Pandas, Rac-
coons, Sea Lions, Seals,
Skunks, Walruses,
Weasels, Wolves

**EVEN-TOED
UNGULATES**
Alpacas, Antelopes,
Camels, Cattle, Deer,
Giraffes, Goats, Hippo-
potamuses, Llamas, Pigs,
Pronghorn, Sheep, Yak

INSECT ORDERS

THYSANURA
Bristletails

PLECOPTERA
Stoneflies

NEUROPTERA
Ant Lions, Dobsonflies,
Lacewings

ORTHOPTERA
Crickets, Grasshoppers,
Katydids, Locusts, Mantids,
Roaches, Walking Sticks

ODONATA
Damselflies, Dragonflies

TRICHOPTERA
Caddisflies

DERMAPTERA
Earwigs

ANOPLURA
Lice

COLEOPTERA
Beetles

ISOPTERA
Termites

SIPHONAPTERA
Fleas

LEPIDOPTERA
Butterflies, Moths

THYSANOPTERA
Thrips

HEMIPTERA
True Bugs

DIPTERA
Flies, Gnats,
Mosquitoes

EPHEMEROPTERA
Mayflies

HOMOPTERA
Aphids, Cicadas,
Scales, Treehoppers

HYMENOPTERA
Ants, Bees, Wasps

MAMMAL FAMILIES

The several thousand kinds of mammals living today are grouped into 18 orders. These orders are divided into more than 100 families. This chart names eleven of the well-known mammal families and pictures some of the animals that belong in each.

BEAR (Ursidae)

SUN BEAR

SPECTACLED BEAR

SLOTH BEAR

POLAR BEAR

GRIZZLY BEAR

BLACK BEAR (CINNAMON)

CAT (Felidae)

DOMESTIC CAT

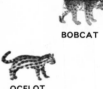

BOBCAT

OCELOT

LYNX

LEOPARD

CHEETAH

COUGAR, OR PUMA, OR MOUNTAIN LION

JAGUAR

DEER (Cervidae)

VIRGINIA DEER

MOOSE

CARIBOU, OR REINDEER

ELK, OR WAPITI

WEASEL (Mustelidae)

WEASEL

MINK

FERRET

MARTEN

FISHER

RIVER OTTER

SEA OTTER

CATTLE (Bovidae)

DAIRY COW

WATER BUFFALO

ZEBU

MOUNTAIN SHEEP

BISON

CHAMOIS

MOUNTAIN GOAT

DOMESTIC GOAT

GNU

MUSKOX

YAK

DOMESTIC SHEEP

MOUSE (Cricetidae)

EER MOUSE

MEADOW MOUSE,
OR VOLE

LEMMING

HAMSTER

MUSKRAT

PACK RAT

SQUIRREL (Sciuridae)

RED SQUIRREL

GRAY SQUIRREL

FOX SQUIRREL

FLYING
SQUIRREL

CHIPMUNK

PRAIRIE DOG

GOPHER

WOODCHUCK

HOARY
MARMOT

DOG (Canidae)

TIGER

LION

DOMESTIC DOG

COYOTE

FOX

WOLF

CAMEL (Camelidae)

ARABIAN CAMEL

VICUÑA

LLAMA

SKUNK

BADGER

WOLVERINE

ALPACA

BACTRIAN CAMEL

GUANACO

APE (Pongidae, or Simiidae)

GIBBON

CHIMPANZEE

ORANGUTAN

GORILLA

HORSE (Equidae)

ZEBRA

MULE

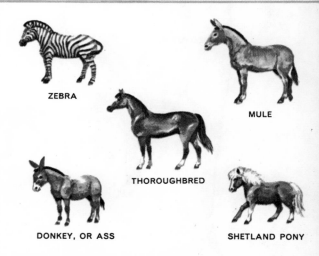
THOROUGHBRED

DONKEY, OR ASS

SHETLAND PONY

SOME FAMILIES OF FLOWERING PLANTS

After flowering plants first appeared some 130 million years ago, they rapidly "took the earth." Now there are more kinds of flowering plants than of all other plants put together. There are perhaps as many as 250,000 species. They belong in several hundred plant families. In some families there are hundreds of species; in others there are only a few.

Scientists study chiefly the flowers of a flowering plant to find out to what other flowering plants it is closely related. Without a study of their flowers it is hard to see why, for example, the wild rose and the apple belong in the same family or why the onion and the Easter lily are cousins. This chart names some of the many families of flowering plants and shows a few of the plants that belong in those families.

MALLOW (Malvacea) 1,000 species

COTTON

HOLLYHO

BUTTERPRINT

ROSE OF SHARON

HIBISCUS   OKRA

PALM (Palmaceae) 1,200-1,500 species

PALMETTO

COCONUT PALM

ROYAL PALM

DATE PALM

MADDER (Rubiaceae) 5,000 species

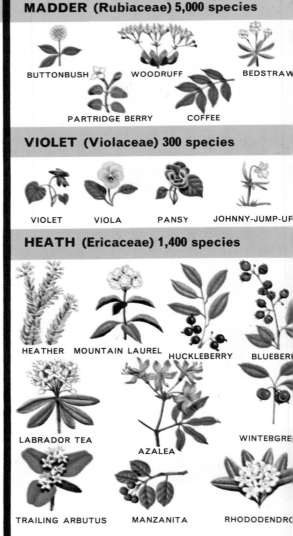

BUTTONBUSH   WOODRUFF   BEDSTRAW

PARTRIDGE BERRY   COFFEE

VIOLET (Violaceae) 300 species

VIOLET   VIOLA   PANSY   JOHNNY-JUMP-UP

HEATH (Ericaceae) 1,400 species

HEATHER   MOUNTAIN LAUREL   HUCKLEBERRY   BLUEBER

LABRADOR TEA   AZALEA   WINTERGRE

TRAILING ARBUTUS   MANZANITA   RHODODENDRO

SE (Rosaceae) 2,500 species

ROSE BLACKBERRY RASPBERRY CINQUEFOIL MOUNTAIN ASH

PPLE CHERRY PEAR PLUM PEACH APRICOT

B APPLE ALMOND QUINCE HAWTHORN STRAWBERRY

MORNING GLORY (Con-volvulaceae) 1,000 species

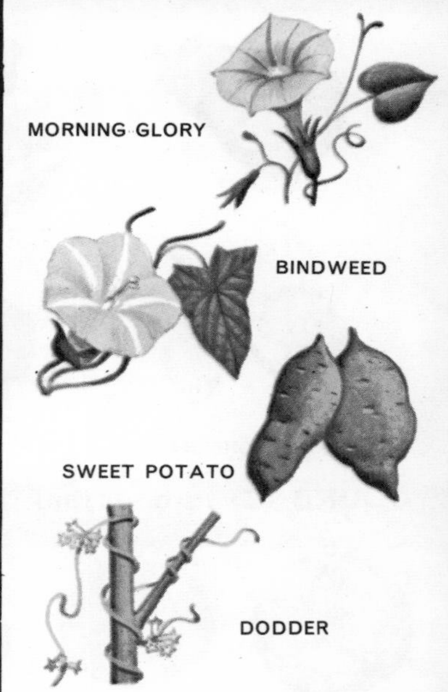

MORNING GLORY

BINDWEED

SWEET POTATO

DODDER

UE (Rutaceae) 900 species

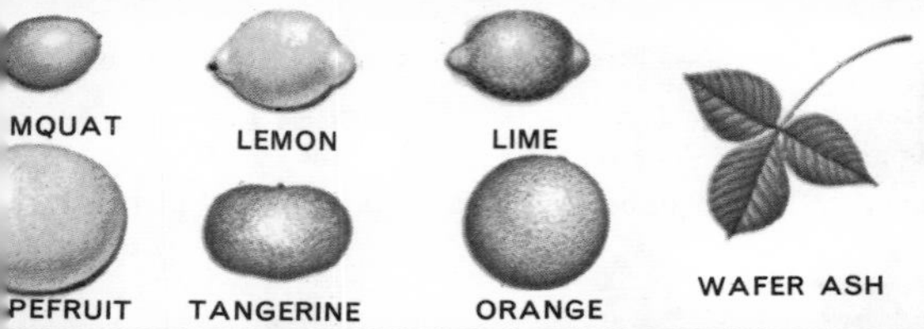

MQUAT LEMON LIME WAFER ASH

PEFRUIT TANGERINE ORANGE

A (Theaceae) More than 200 species

TEA FRANKLINIA TREE CAMELLIA

RASS (Poaceae) 7,000 species

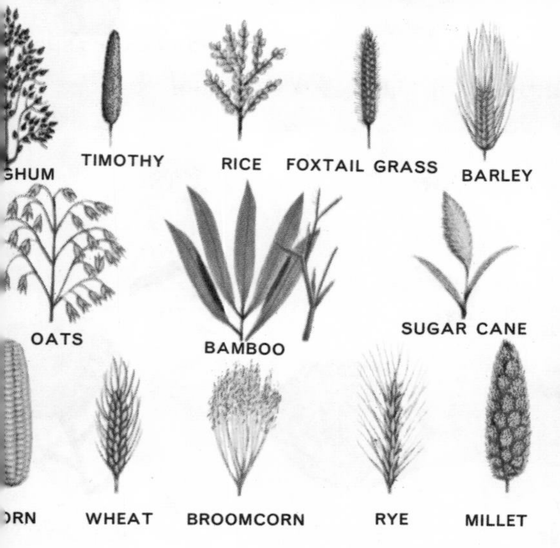

SHUM TIMOTHY RICE FOXTAIL GRASS BARLEY

OATS BAMBOO SUGAR CANE

ORN WHEAT BROOMCORN RYE MILLET

PEA (Leguminosae) 12,000 species

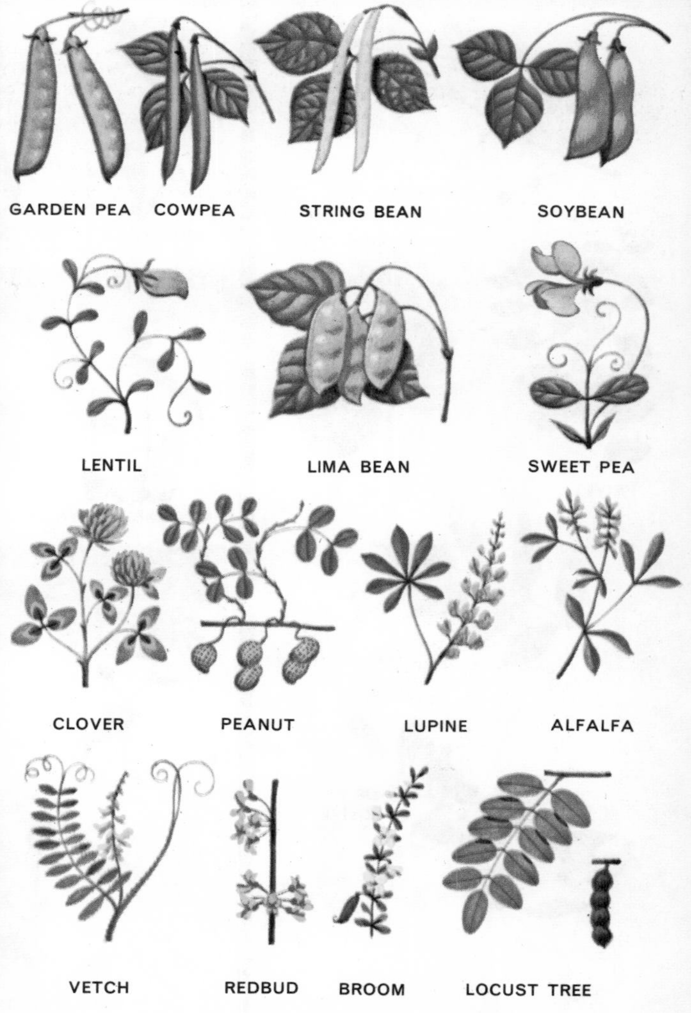

GARDEN PEA COWPEA STRING BEAN SOYBEAN

LENTIL LIMA BEAN SWEET PEA

CLOVER PEANUT LUPINE ALFALFA

VETCH REDBUD BROOM LOCUST TREE

NIGHTSHADE (Solanaceae) 1,700 species

EGGPLANT

BITTERSWEET

PETUNIA

NIGHTSHADE

PEPPER

GROUND CHERRY

TOMATO

JERUSALEM CHERRY

POTATO

TOBACCO

GOURD (Cucurbitaceae) 700 species

CANTALOUPE   HONEYDEW MELON   SQUASH   WATERMELON   GOURD   CUCUMBER   PUMPKIN

OLIVE (Oleaceae) 500 species

FORSYTHIA

PRIVET

LILAC

ASH TREE

OLIVE

BUTTERCUP (Ranunculaceae) 1,200 species

PASQUEFLOWER   CLEMATIS   PEONY   COLUMBINE   BUTTERCUP

MONKSHOOD   LARKSPUR   BANEBERRY   HEPATICA   MEADOW R

ORCHID (Orchidaceae) 5,000-10,000 species

MOCCASIN FLOWER   ORCHID   SHOWY LADY'S-SLIPPER

COMPOSITE (Compositae) 13,000-20,000 species

ASTER   DAISY   SUNFLOWER

CANADA THISTLE   LETTUCE   MARIGOLD

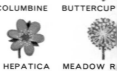

MUSTARD (Cruciferae) 2,000 species

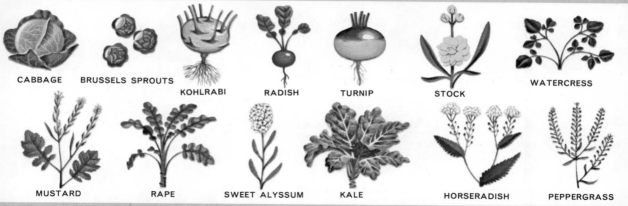

CABBAGE BRUSSELS SPROUTS KOHLRABI RADISH TURNIP STOCK WATERCRESS

MUSTARD RAPE SWEET ALYSSUM KALE HORSERADISH PEPPERGRASS

PARSLEY (Umbelliferae) 2,500 species

RROT PARSNIP CELERY CARAWAY QUEEN ANNE'S LACE POISON HEMLOCK PARSLEY

LILY (Liliaceae) 12,500 species

ARLIC ONION LILY OF THE VALLEY TULIP TRILLIUM HYACINTH

R LILY DOG'S-TOOTH VIOLET EASTER LILY DAY LILY YUCCA ASPARAGUS

MINT (Labiatae) 3,000 species

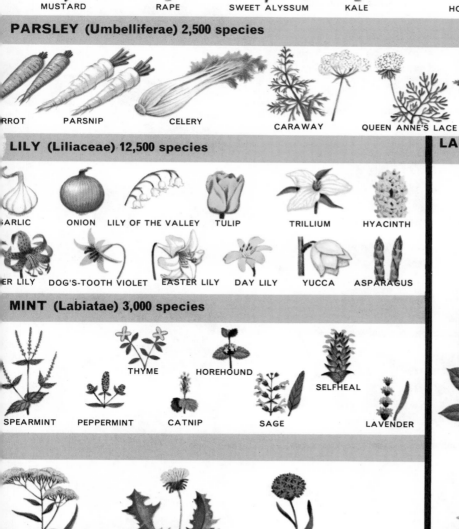

THYME HOREHOUND SELFHEAL

SPEARMINT PEPPERMINT CATNIP SAGE LAVENDER

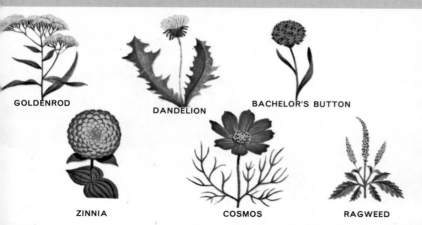

GOLDENROD DANDELION BACHELOR'S BUTTON

ZINNIA COSMOS RAGWEED

LAUREL (Lauraceae) 1,100 species

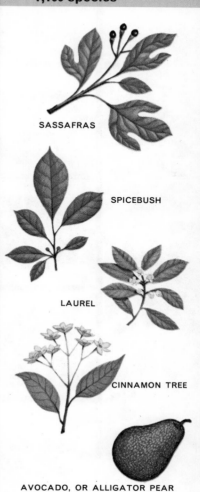

SASSAFRAS

SPICEBUSH

LAUREL

CINNAMON TREE

AVOCADO, OR ALLIGATOR PEAR

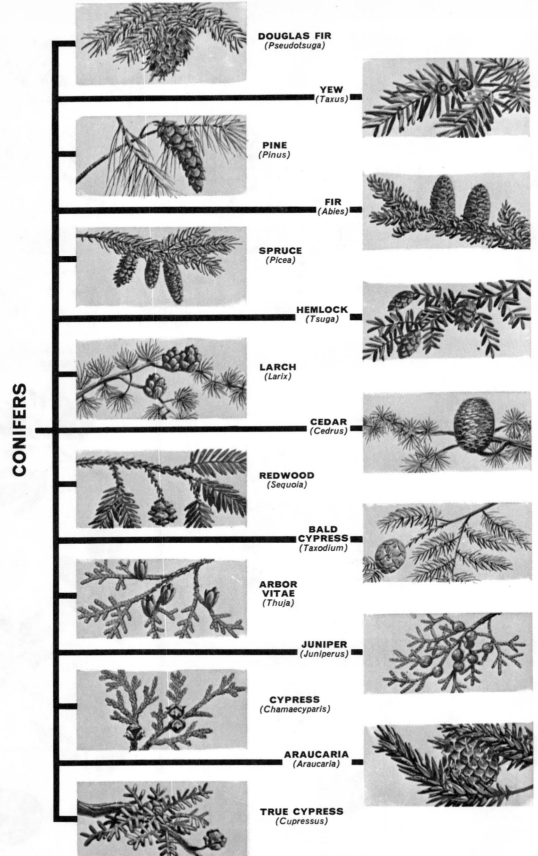

CONIFERS

DOUGLAS FIR
(Pseudotsuga)

YEW
(Taxus)

PINE
(Pinus)

FIR
(Abies)

SPRUCE
(Picea)

HEMLOCK
(Tsuga)

LARCH
(Larix)

CEDAR
(Cedrus)

REDWOOD
(Sequoia)

BALD
CYPRESS
(Taxodium)

ARBOR
VITAE
(Thuja)

JUNIPER
(Juniperus)

CYPRESS
(Chamaecyparis)

ARAUCARIA
(Araucaria)

TRUE CYPRESS
(Cupressus)

Index

Heavy type indicates those pages on which illustrations of the subjects appear.